Marcus Dods

**The Gospel of St. John**

Marcus Dods

**The Gospel of St. John**

ISBN/EAN: 9783337282332

Printed in Europe, USA, Canada, Australia, Japan

Cover: Foto ©Thomas Meinert / pixelio.de

More available books at **www.hansebooks.com**

# THE GOSPEL OF ST. JOHN

BY

MARCUS DODS, D.D.

PROFESSOR OF EXEGETICAL THEOLOGY, NEW COLLEGE, EDINBURGH

IN TWO VOLUMES
*VOLUME TWO*

HODDER & STOUGHTON

NEW YORK

GEORGE H. DORAN COMPANY

# CONTENTS

### I.
THE ANOINTING OF JESUS . . . . . . . 3

### II.
THE ENTRY INTO JERUSALEM . . . . . . 19

### III.
THE CORN OF WHEAT . . . . . . . . 31

### IV.
THE ATTRACTIVE FORCE OF THE CROSS . . . . 47

### V.
RESULTS OF CHRIST'S MANIFESTATION . . . . 65

### VI.
THE FOOT-WASHING . . . . . . . . 75

### VII.
JUDAS . . . . . . . . . . . 91

### VIII.
JESUS ANNOUNCES HIS DEPARTURE . . . . . 109

### IX.
THE WAY, THE TRUTH, AND THE LIFE . . . . 123

### X.
THE FATHER SEEN IN CHRIST . . . . . . 137

### XI.
THE BEQUEST OF PEACE . . . . . . . 159

### XII.
THE VINE AND THE BRANCHES . . . . . . 175

## XIII.
NOT SERVANTS, BUT FRIENDS . . . . 193

## XIV.
THE SPIRIT CHRIST'S WITNESS . . . 205

## XV.
LAST WORDS . . . . . . . 220

## XVI.
CHRIST'S INTERCESSORY PRAYER . . . 247

## XVII.
THE ARREST . . . . . . . 263

## XVIII.
PETER'S DENIAL AND REPENTANCE . . . 281

## XIX.
JESUS BEFORE PILATE . . . . . . 299

## XX.
MARY AT THE CROSS . . . . . . 321

## XXI.
THE CRUCIFIXION . . . . . 335

## XXII.
THE RESURRECTION . . . . . 351

## XXIII.
THOMAS' TEST . . . . . . 365

## XXIV.
APPEARANCE AT SEA OF GALILEE . . . 383

## XXV.
RESTORATION OF PETER . . . . 399

## XXVI.
CONCLUSION . . . . . 413

# I.
## *THE ANOINTING OF JESUS.*

VOL. II.

"Jesus therefore six days before the Passover came to Bethany, where Lazarus was, whom Jesus raised from the dead. So they made Him a supper there: and Martha served; but Lazarus was one of them that sat at meat with Him. Mary therefore took a pound of ointment of spikenard, very precious, and anointed the feet of Jesus, and wiped His feet with her hair: and the house was filled with the odour of the ointment. But Judas Iscariot, one of His disciples, which should betray Him, saith, Why was not this ointment sold for three hundred pence, and given to the poor? Now this he said, not because he cared for the poor; but because he was a thief, and having the bag took away what was put therein. Jesus therefore said, Suffer her to keep it against the day of My burying. For the poor ye have always with you; but Me ye have not always. The common people therefore of the Jews learned that He was there: and they came, not for Jesus' sake only, but that they might see Lazarus also, whom He had raised from the dead. But the chief priests took counsel that they might put Lazarus also to death; because that by reason of him many of the Jews went away, and believed on Jesus."—JOHN xii. 1-11.

# I.

## *THE ANOINTING OF JESUS.*

THIS twelfth chapter is the watershed of the Gospel. The self-manifestation of Jesus to the world is now ended; and from this point onwards to the close we have to do with the results of that manifestation. He hides Himself from the unbelieving, and allows their unbelief full scope; while He makes further disclosures to the faithful few. The whole Gospel is a systematic and wonderfully artistic exhibition of the manner in which the deeds, words, and claims of Jesus produced,— on the one hand, a growing belief and enthusiasm; on the other, a steadily hardening unbelief and hostility. In this chapter the culmination of these processes is carefully illustrated by three incidents. In the first of these incidents evidence is given that there was an intimate circle of friends in whose love Jesus was embalmed, and His work and memory insured against decay; while the very deed which had riveted the faith and affection of this intimate circle is shown to have brought the antagonism of His enemies to a head. In the second incident the writer shows that on the whole popular mind Jesus had made a profound impression, and that the instincts of the Jewish people acknowledged Him as King. In the third incident the influence He was destined to have and was already to some extent exerting beyond the bounds of Judaism is illustrated by the request of the Greeks that they might see Jesus.

In this first incident, then, is disclosed a devotedness of faith which cannot be surpassed, an attachment which is absolute; but here also we see that the hostility of avowed enemies has penetrated even the inner circle of the personal followers of Jesus, and that one of the chosen Twelve has so little faith or love that he can see no beauty and find no pleasure in any tribute paid to his Master. In this hour there meet a ripeness of love which suddenly reveals the permanent place which Jesus has won for Himself in the hearts of men, and a maturity of alienation which forebodes that His end cannot be far distant. In this beautiful incident, therefore, we turn a page in the gospel and come suddenly into the presence of Christ's death. To this death He Himself freely alludes, because He sees that things are now ripe for it, that nothing short of His death will satisfy His enemies, while no further manifestation can give Him a more abiding place in the love of His friends. The chill, damp odour of the tomb first strikes upon the sense, mingling with and absorbed in the perfume of Mary's ointment. If Jesus dies, He cannot be forgotten. He is embalmed in the love of such disciples.

On His way to Jerusalem for the last time Jesus reached Bethany "six days before the Passover"—that is to say, in all probability[1] on the Friday evening previous to His death. It was natural that He should wish to spend His last Sabbath in the congenial and

---

[1] It is uncertain whether the "six days" are inclusive or exclusive of the day of arrival and of the first day of the Feast. It is also uncertain on what day of the week the Crucifixion happened.

strengthening society of a family whose welcome and whose affection He could rely upon. In the little town of Bethany He had become popular, and since the raising of Lazarus He was regarded with marked veneration. Accordingly they made Him a feast, which, as Mark informs us, was given in the house of Simon the leper. Any gathering of His friends in Bethany must have been incomplete without Lazarus and his sisters. Each is present, and each contributes an appropriate addition to the feast. Martha serves; Lazarus, mute as he is throughout the whole story, bears witness by his presence as a living guest to the worthiness of Jesus; while Mary makes the day memorable by a characteristic action. Coming in, apparently after the guests had reclined at table, she broke an alabaster of very costly spikenard[1] and anointed the feet of Jesus and wiped His feet with her hair.

This token of affection took the company by surprise. Lazarus and his sisters may have been in sufficiently good circumstances to admit of their making a substantial acknowledgment of their indebtedness to Jesus; and although this alabaster of ointment had cost as much as would keep a labouring man's family for a year, this could not seem an excessive return to make for service so valuable as Jesus had rendered. It was the manner of the acknowledgment which took the company by surprise. Jesus was a poor man, and His very appearance may have suggested that there were other things He needed more urgently than such

---

[1] In *The Classical Review* for July 1890 Mr. Bennett suggests that the difficult word πιστικῆς should be written πιστακῆς, and that it refers to the *Pistacia terebinthus*, which grows in Cyprus and Judæa, and yields a very fragrant and very costly unguent.

a gift as this. Had the family provided a home for Him or given Him the price of this ointment, no one would have uttered a remark. But this was the kind of demonstration reserved for princes or persons of great distinction; and when paid to One so conspicuously humble in His dress and habits, there seemed to the uninstructed eye something incongruous and bordering on the grotesque. When the fragrance of the ointment disclosed its value, there was therefore an instantaneous exclamation of surprise, and at any rate in one instance of blunt disapproval. Judas, instinctively putting a money value on this display of affection, roundly and with coarse indelicacy declared it had better have been sold and given to the poor.

Jesus viewed the act with very different feelings. The rulers were determining to put Him out of the way, as not only worthless but dangerous; the very man who objected to this present expenditure was making up his mind to sell Him for a small part of the sum; the people were scrutinising His conduct, criticising Him;—in the midst of all this hatred, suspicion, treachery, coldness, and hesitation comes this woman and puts aside all this would-be wisdom and caution, and for herself pronounces that no tribute is rich enough to pay to Him. It is the rarity of such action, not the rarity of the nard, that strikes Jesus. This, He says, is a noble deed she has done, far rarer, far more difficult to produce, far more penetrating and lasting in its fragrance than the richest perfume that man has compounded. Mary has the experience that all those have who for Christ's sake expose themselves to the misunderstanding and abuse of vulgar and unsympathetic minds; she receives from Himself more explicit assurance that her offering has given pleasure to Him and is gratefully accepted. We may sometimes find ourselves obliged to do what we perfectly well know will be misunderstood and censured; we may be compelled to adopt a line of conduct which seems to convict us of heedlessness and of the neglect of duties we owe to others; we may be driven to action which lays us open to the charge of being romantic and extravagant; but of one thing we may be perfectly sure—that however our motives are mis-read and condemned by those who first make their voices heard, He for whose sake we do these things will not disparage our action nor misunderstand our motives. The way to a fuller intimacy with Christ often lies through passages in life we must traverse alone.

But we are probably more likely to misunderstand than to be misunderstood. We are so limited in our sympathies, so scantily furnished with knowledge, and have so slack a hold upon great principles, that for the most part we can understand only those who are like ourselves. When a woman comes in with her effusiveness, we are put out and irritated; when a man whose mind is wholly uneducated utters his feelings by shouting hymns and dancing on the street, we think him a semi-lunatic; when a member of our family spends an hour or two a day in devotional exercises, we condemn it as waste of time which might be better spent on practical charities or household duties.

Most liable of all to this vice of misjudging the actions of others, and indeed of misapprehending generally wherein the real value of life consists, are those who, like Judas, measure all things by a utilitarian, if not a money, standard. Actions which have no immediate results are pronounced by such persons to be mere sentiment and waste, while in fact they redeem human nature and make life seem worth living. The charge of the Light Brigade at Balaclava served none of the immediate purposes of the battle, and was indeed a blunder and waste from that point of view; yet are not our annals enriched by it as they have been by few victories? On the Parthenon there were figures placed with their backs hard against the wall of the pediment; these backs were never seen and were not intended to be seen, but yet were carved with the same care as was spent upon the front of the figures. Was that care waste? There are thousands of persons in our own society who think it essential to teach their children arithmetic, but pernicious to instil into their minds a love of poetry or art. They judge of education by the test, Will it pay? can this attainment be turned into money? The other question Will it enrich the nature of the child and of the man? is not asked. They proceed as if they believed that the man is made for business, not business for the man; and thus it comes to pass that everywhere among us men are found sacrificed to business, stunted in their moral development, shut off from the deeper things of life. The pursuits which such persons condemn are the very things which lift life out of the low level of commonplace buying and selling, and invite us to remember that man liveth not by bread alone, but by high thoughts, by noble sacrifice, by devoted love and all that love dictates, by the powers of the unseen, mightier by far than all that we see.

In the face, then, of so much that runs counter to such demonstrations as Mary's and condemns them as extravagance, it is important to note the principles upon which our Lord proceeds in His justification of her action.

First, He says, this is an occasional, exceptional tribute. "The poor always ye have with you, but me ye have not always." Charity to the poor you may continue from day to day all your life long: whatever you spend on me is spent once for all. You need not think the poor defrauded by this expenditure. Within a few days I shall be beyond all such tokens of regard, and the poor will still claim your sympathy. This principle solves for us some social and domestic problems. Of many expenses common in society, and especially of expenses connected with scenes such as this festive gathering at Bethany, the question always arises, Is this expenditure justifiable? When present at an entertainment costing as much and doing as little material good as the spikenard whose perfume had died before the guests separated, we cannot but ask, Is not this, after all, mere waste? had it not been better to have given the value to the poor? The hunger-bitten faces, the poverty-stricken outcasts, we have seen during the day are suggested to us by the superabundance now before us. The effort to spend most where least is needed suggests to us, as to these guests at Bethany, gaunt, pinched, sickly faces, bare rooms, cold grates, feeble, dull-eyed children—in a word, starving families who might be kept for weeks together on what is here spent in a few minutes; and the question is inevitable, Is this right? Can it be right to spend a man's ransom on a mere good smell, while at the end of the street a widow is pining with hunger? Our Lord replies that so long as one is day by day considering the poor and relieving their necessities, he need not grudge an occasional outlay to manifest his regard for his friends. The poor of Bethany would probably appeal to Mary much more hopefully than to Judas, and they would appeal all the more successfully because her heart had been allowed to utter itself thus to Jesus. There is, of course, an expenditure for display under the guise of friendship. Such expenditure finds no justification here or anywhere else. But those who in a practical way acknowledge the perpetual presence of the poor are justified in the occasional outlay demanded by friendship.

2. But our Lord's defence of Mary is of wider range. "Let her alone," He says, "against the day of my burying hath she kept this." It was not only occasional, exceptional tribute she had paid Him; it was solitary, never to be repeated. Against my burial she has kept this unguent; for me ye have not always. Would you blame Mary for spending this, were I lying in my tomb? Would you call it too costly a tribute, were it the last? Well, it is the last.[1] Such is our Lord's justification of her action. Was Mary herself conscious that this was a parting tribute? It is possible that her love and womanly instinct had revealed to her the nearness of that death of which Jesus Himself so often spoke, but which the disciples refused to think of. She may have felt that this was the last time she would have an opportunity of expressing her devotion. Drawn to Him with unutterable tenderness, with admiration, gratitude, anxiety mingling in her heart, she hastens to spend upon Him her costliest. Passing away from *her* world she knows He is; buried so far as she was concerned she knew Him to be if He was to keep the Passover at Jerusalem in the midst of His enemies. Had the others felt with her, none could have grudged her the last consolation of this utterance of her love, or

---

[1] So Stier.

have grudged Him the consolation of receiving it. For this made Him strong to die, this among other motives—the knowledge that His love and sacrifice were not in vain, that He had won human hearts, and that in their affection He would survive. This is His true embalming. This it is that forbids that His flesh see corruption, that His earthly manifestation die out and be forgotten. To die before He had attached to Himself friends as passionate in their devotion as Mary would have been premature. The recollection of His work might have been lost. But when He had won men like John and women like Mary, He could die assured that His name would never be lost from earth. The breaking of the alabaster box, the pouring out of Mary's soul in adoration of her Lord—this was the signal that all was ripe for His departure, this the proof that His manifestation had done its work. The love of His own had come to maturity and burst thus into flower. Jesus therefore recognises in this act His true embalming.

And it is probably from this point of view that we may most readily see the appropriateness of that singular commendation and promise which our Lord, according to the other gospels, added: "Verily I say unto you, wherever this gospel shall be preached throughout the whole world, this also that she hath done shall be spoken for a memorial of her."

At first sight the encomium might seem as extravagant as the action. Was there, a Judas might ask, anything deserving of immortality in the sacrifice of a few pounds? But no such measurements are admissible here. The encomium was deserved because the act was the irrepressible utterance of all-absorbing love—of a love so full, so rich, so rare that even the ordinary disciples of Christ were at first not in perfect sympathy with it. The absolute devotedness of her love found a fit symbol in the alabaster box or vase which she had to break that the ointment might flow out. It was not a bottle out of which she might take the stopper and let a carefully measured quantity dribble out, reserving the rest for other and perhaps very different uses—fit symbol of our love to Christ; but it was a hermetically sealed casket or flask, out of which, if she let one drop fall, the whole must go. It had to be broken; it had to be devoted to one sole use. It could not be in part reserved or in part diverted to other uses. Where you have such love as this, have you not the highest thing humanity can produce? Where is it now to be had on earth, where are we to look for this all-devoting, unreserving love, which gathers up all its possessions and pours them out at Christ's feet, saying, "Take all, would it were more"?

The encomium, therefore, was deserved and appropriate. In her love the Lord would ever live: so long as she existed the remembrance of Him could not die. No death could touch her heart with his chilly hand and freeze the warmth of her devotion. Christ was immortal in her, and she was therefore immortal in Him. Her love was a bond that could not be broken, the truest spiritual union. In embalming Him, therefore, she unconsciously embalmed herself. Her love was the amber in which He was to be preserved, and she became inviolable as He. Her love was the marble on which His name and worth were engraven, on which His image was deeply sculptured, and they were to live and last together. Christ "prolongs His days" in the love of His people. In every generation there arise those who will not let His remembrance die out, and who to their own necessities call out the living energy of Christ. In so doing they unwittingly make themselves undying as He; their love of Him is the little spark of immortality in their soul. It is that which indissolubly and by the only genuine spiritual affinity links them to what is eternal. To all who thus love Him Christ cannot but say, "Because I live, ye shall live also."

Another point in our Lord's defence of Mary's conduct, though it is not explicitly asserted, plainly is, that tributes of affection paid directly to Himself are of value to Him. Judas might with some plausibility have quoted against our Lord His own teaching that an act of kindness done to the poor was kindness to Him. It might be said that, on our Lord's own showing, what He desires is, not homage paid to Himself personally, but loving and merciful conduct. And certainly any homage paid to Himself which is not accompanied by such conduct is of no value at all. But as love to Him is the spring and regulator of all right conduct, it is necessary that we should cultivate this love; and because He delights in our well-being and in ourselves, and does not look upon us merely as so much material in which He may exhibit His healing powers, He necessarily rejoices in every expression of true devotedness that is paid to Him by any of us.

And on our side wherever there is true and ardent love it must crave direct expression. "If ye love me," says our Lord, "keep my commandments"; and obedience certainly is the normal test and exhibition of love. But there is that in our nature which refuses to be satisfied with obedience, which craves fellowship with what we love, which carries us out of ourselves and compels us to express our feeling directly. And that soul is not fully developed whose pent-up gratitude, cherished admiration, and warm affection do not from time to time break away from all ordinary modes of expressing devotion and choose some such direct method as Mary chose, or some such straightforward utterance as Peter's: "Lord, Thou knowest all things, Thou knowest that I love Thee."

It may, indeed, occur to us, as we read of Mary's tribute to her Lord, that the very words in which He justified her action forbid our supposing that any so grateful tribute can be paid Him by us. "Me ye have not always" may seem to warn us against expecting that so direct and satisfying an intercourse can be maintained now, when we no longer have Him. And no doubt this is one of the standing difficulties of Christian experience. We can love those who live with us, whose eye we can meet, whose voice we know, whose expression of face we can read. We feel it easy to fix our affections on one and another of those who are alive contemporaneously with ourselves. But with Christ it is different: we miss those sensible impressions made upon us by the living bodily presence; we find it difficult to retain in the mind a settled idea of the feeling He has towards us. It is an effort to accomplish by faith what sight without any effort effectually accomplishes. We do not *see* that He loves us; the looks and tones that chiefly reveal human love are absent; we are not from hour to hour confronted, whether we will or no, with one evidence or other of love. Were the life of a Christian nowadays no more difficult than it was to Mary, were it brightened with Christ's presence as a household friend, were the whole sum and substance of it merely a giving way to the love He kindled by palpable favours and measurable friendship, then surely the Christian life would be a very simple, very easy, very happy course.

But the connection between ourselves and Christ is not of the body that passes, but of the spirit which endures. It is spiritual, and such a connection may be seriously perverted by the interference of sense and of bodily sensations. To measure the love of Christ by His expression of face and by His tone of voice is legitimate, but it is not the truest measurement: to be drawn to Him by the accidental kindnesses our present difficulties must provoke is to be drawn by something short of perfect spiritual affinity. And, on the whole, it is well that our spirit should be allowed to choose its eternal friendship and alliance by what is specially and exclusively its own, so that its choice cannot be mistaken, as the choice sometimes is when there is a mixture of physical and spiritual attractiveness. So much are we guided in youth and in the whole of our life by what is material, so freely do we allow our tastes to be determined and our character to be formed by our connection with what is material, that the whole man gets blunted in his *spiritual* perceptions and incapable of appreciating what is not seen. And the great part of our education in this life is to lift the spirit to its true place and to its appropriate company, to teach it to measure its gains apart from material prosperity, and to train it to love with ardour what cannot be seen.

Besides, it cannot be doubted that this incident itself very plainly teaches that Christ came into this world to win our love and to turn all duty into a personal acting towards Him; to make the *whole* of life like those parts of it which are now its bright exceptional holiday times; to make all of it a pleasure by making all of it and not merely parts of it the utterance of love. Even a little love in our life is the sunshine that quickens and warms and brightens the whole. There seems at length to be a reason and a satisfaction in life when love animates us. It is easy to act well to those whom we really love, and Christ has come for the express purpose of bringing our whole life within this charmed circle. He has come not to bring constraint and gloom into our lives, but to let us out into the full liberty and joy of the life that God Himself lives and judges to be the only life worthy of His bestowal upon us.

## II.
## *THE ENTRY INTO JERUSALEM.*

"On the morrow a great multitude that had come to the feast, when they heard that Jesus was coming to Jerusalem, took the branches of the palm trees, and went forth to meet Him, and cried out, Hosanna : Blessed is He that cometh in the name of the Lord, even the King of Israel. And Jesus, having found a young ass, sat thereon ; as it is written, Fear not, daughter of Zion : behold, thy King cometh, sitting on an ass's colt. These things understood not His disciples at the first : but when Jesus was glorified, then remembered they that these things were written of Him, and that they had done these things unto Him. The multitude therefore that was with Him when He called Lazarus out of the tomb, and raised him from the dead, bare witness. For this cause also the multitude went and met Him, for that they heard that He had done this sign. The Pharisees therefore said among themselves, Behold, how ye prevail nothing ; lo, the world is gone after Him."—JOHN xii. 12-19.

## II.

### THE ENTRY INTO JERUSALEM.

IF our Lord arrived in Bethany on Friday evening and spent the Sabbath with His friends there, "the next day" of ver. 12 is Sunday; and in the Church year this day is known as Palm Sunday, from the incident here related. It was also the day, four days before the Passover, on which the Jews were enjoined by the law to choose their paschal lamb. Some consciousness of this may have guided our Lord's action. Certainly He means finally to offer Himself to the people as the Messiah. Often as He had evaded them before, and often as He had forbidden His disciples to proclaim Him, He is now conscious that His hour has come, and by entering Jerusalem as King of peace He definitely proclaims Himself the promised Messiah. As plainly as the crowning of a new monarch and the flourish of trumpets and the kissing of his hand by the great officers of state proclaim him king, so unmistakably does our Lord by riding into Jerusalem on an ass and by accepting the hosannas of the people proclaim Himself the King promised to men through the Jews, as the King of peace who was to win men to His rule by love and sway them by a Divine Spirit.

The scene must have been one not easily forgotten. The Mount of Olives runs north and south parallel to the east wall of Jerusalem, and separated from it by a gully, through which flows the brook Kidron. The Mount is crossed by three paths. One of these is a steep footpath, which runs direct over the crest of the hill; the second runs round its northern shoulder; while the third crosses the southern slope. It was by this last route the pilgrim caravans were accustomed to enter the city. On the occasion of our Lord's entry the road was probably thronged with visitors making their way to the great annual feast. No fewer than three million persons are said to have been sometimes packed together in Jerusalem at the Passover; and all of them being on holiday, were ready for any kind of excitement. The idea of a festal procession was quite to their mind. And no sooner did the disciples appear with Jesus riding in their midst than the vast streams of people caught the infection of loyal enthusiasm, tore down branches of the palms and olives which were found in abundance by the roadside, and either waved them in the air or strewed them in the line of march. Others unwrapped their loose cloaks from their shoulders and spread them along the rough path to form a carpet as He approached—a custom which is still, it seems, observed in the East in royal processions, and which has indeed sometimes been imported into our own country on great occasions. Thus with every demonstration of loyalty, with ceaseless shoutings that were heard across the valley in the streets of Jerusalem itself, and waving the palm branches, they moved towards the city.

Those who have entered the city from Bethany by this road tell us that there are two striking points in it. The first is when at a turn of the broad and well-defined mountain track the southern portion of the city comes for an instant into view. This part of the city was called "the city of David," and the suggestion is not without probability that it may have been at this point the multitude burst out in words that linked Jesus with David. "Hosanna to the Son of David. Blessed is the King that cometh in the name of the Lord. Blessed is the kingdom of our father David. Hosanna, peace and glory in the highest." This became the watchword of the day, so that even the boys who had come out of the city to see the procession were heard afterwards, as they loitered in the streets, still shouting the same refrain.

After this the road again dips, and the glimpse of the city is lost behind the intervening ridge of Olivet; but shortly a rugged ascent is climbed and a ledge of bare rock is reached, and in an instant the whole city bursts into view. The prospect from this point must have been one of the grandest of its kind in the world, the fine natural position of Jerusalem not only showing to advantage, but the long line of city wall embracing, like the setting of a jewel, the marvellous structures of Herod, the polished marble and the gilded pinnacles glittering in the morning sun and dazzling the eye. It was in all probability at this point that our Lord was overcome with regret when He considered the sad fate of the beautiful city, and when in place of the smiling palaces and apparently impregnable walls His imagination filled His eye with smoke-blackened ruins, with pavements slippery with blood, with walls breached at all points and choked with rotting corpses.

Our Lord's choice of the ass was significant. The ass was commonly used for riding, and the well-cared-for ass of the rich man was a very fine animal, much larger and stronger than the little breed with which we are familiar. Its coat, too, is as glossy as a well-kept horse's —"shiny black, or satiny white, or sleek mouse colour." It was not chosen by our Lord at this time that He might show His humility, for it would have been still humbler to walk like His disciples. So far from being a token of humility, He chose a colt which apparently had never borne another rider. He rather meant by claiming the ass and by riding into Jerusalem upon it to assert His royalty; but He did not choose a horse, because that animal would have suggested royalty of quite another kind from His—royalty which was maintained by war and outward force; for the horse and the chariot had always been among the Hebrews symbolic of warlike force. The disciples themselves, strangely enough, did not see the significance of this action, although, when they had time to reflect upon it, they remembered that Zechariah had said: " Rejoice greatly, O daughter of Zion ; shout, O daughter of Jerusalem: behold, thy King cometh unto thee: He is just, and having salvation ; lowly, and riding upon an ass, and upon a colt the foal of an ass. And I will cut off the chariot from Ephraim, and the horse from Jerusalem, and the battle bow shall be cut off: and He shall speak peace unto the heathen."

When John says, "these things understood not His disciples at the first," he cannot mean that they did not understand that Jesus by this act claimed to be the Messiah, because even the mob perceived the significance of this entry into Jerusalem and hailed Him "Son of David." What they did not understand, probably, was why He chose this mode of identifying Himself with the Messiah. At any rate, their perplexity brings out very clearly that the conception was not suggested to Jesus. He was not induced by the disciples nor led on by the people to make a demonstration which He Himself scarcely approved or had not intended to make. On the contrary, from His first recorded act that morning He had taken command of the situation. Whatever was done was done with deliberation, at His own instance and as His own act.[1]

This then in the first place; it was His own deliberate act. He put Himself forward, knowing that He would receive the hosannas of the people, and intending that He should receive them. All His backwardness is gone; all shyness of becoming a public spectacle is gone. For this also is to be noted—that no place or occasion could have been more public than the Passover at Jerusalem. Whatever it was He meant to indicate by His action, it was to the largest possible public He meant to indicate it. No longer in the retirement of a Galilean village, nor in a fisherman's cottage, nor in dubious or ambiguous terms, but in the full blaze of the utmost publicity that could possibly be given to His proclamation, and in language that could not be forgotten or misinterpreted, He now declared Himself. He knew He must attract the attention of the authorities, and His entrance was a direct challenge to them.

What was it then that with such deliberation and such publicity He meant to proclaim? What was it that in these last critical hours of His life, when He knew He should have few more opportunities of speaking to the people, He sought to impress upon them? What was it that, when free from the solicitations of

---

[1] This is more distinctly brought out in the Synoptic Gospels than in St. John: cp. Mark xi. 1-10.

men and the pressure of circumstances, He sought to declare? It was that He was the Messiah. There might be those in the crowd who did not understand what was meant. There might be persons who did not know Him, or who were incompetent judges of character, and supposed He was a mere enthusiast carried away by dwelling too much on some one aspect of Old Testament prophecy. In every generation there are good men who become almost crazed upon some one topic, and sacrifice everything to the promotion of one favourite hope. But however He might be misjudged, there can be no question of His own idea of the significance of His action. He claims to be the Messiah.

Such a claim is the most stupendous that could be made. To be the Messiah is to be God's Viceroy and Representative on earth, able to represent God adequately to men, and to bring about that perfect condition which is named "the kingdom of God." The Messiah must be conscious of ability perfectly to accomplish the will of God with man, and to bring men into absolute harmony with God. This is claimed by Jesus. He stands in His sober senses and claims to be that universal Sovereign, that true King of men, whom the Jews had been encouraged to expect, and who when He came would reign over Gentiles as well as Jews. By this demonstration, to which His previous career had been naturally leading up, He claims to take command of earth, of this world in all its generations, not in the easier sense of laying down upon paper a political constitution fit for all races, but in the sense of being able to deliver mankind from the source of all their misery and to lift men to a true superiority. He has gone about on earth, not secluding Himself from the woes and ways of men, not delicately isolating Himself, but exposing Himself freely to the touch of the malignities, the vulgarities, the ignorance and wickedness of all; and He now claims to rule all this, and implies that earth can present no complication of distress or iniquity which he cannot by the Divine forces within Him transform into health and purity and hope.

This then is His deliberate claim. He quietly but distinctly proclaims that He fulfils all God's promise and purpose among men; is that promised King who was to rectify all things, to unite men to Himself, and to lead them on to their true destiny; to be practically God upon earth, accessible to men and identified with all human interests. Many have tested His claim and have proved its validity. By true allegiance to Him many have found that they have gained the mastery over the world. They have entered into peace, have felt eternal verities underneath their feet, and have attained a connection with God such as must be everlasting. They are filled with a new spirit towards men and see all things with purged eyes. Not abruptly and unintelligibly, by leaps and bounds, but gradually and in harmony with the nature of things, His kingdom is extending. Already His Spirit has done much: in time His Spirit will everywhere prevail. It is by Him and on the lines which He has laid down that humanity is advancing to its goal.

This was the claim He made; and this claim was enthusiastically admitted by the popular instinct.[1] The populace was not merely humouring in holiday mood a whimsical person for their own diversion. Many of them knew Lazarus and knew Jesus, and taking the

---

[1] According to the reading of the scene by St. John, the people needed no prompting.

matter seriously gave the tone to the rest. The people indeed did not, any more than the disciples, understand how different the kingdom of their expectation was from the kingdom Jesus meant to found. But while they entirely misapprehended the purpose for which He was sent, they believed that He was sent by God: His credentials were absolutely satisfactory, His work incomprehensible. But as yet they still thought He must be of the same mind as themselves regarding the work of the Messiah. To His claim, therefore, the response given by the people was loud and demonstrative. It was indeed a very brief reign they accorded to their King, but their prompt acknowledgment of Him was the instinctive and irrepressible expression of what they really felt to be His due. A popular demonstration is notoriously untrustworthy, always running to extremes, necessarily uttering itself with a loudness far in excess of individual conviction, and gathering to itself the loose and floating mass of people who have no convictions of their own, and are thankful to any one who leads them and gives them a cue, and helps them to feel that they have after all a place in the community. Who has not stood by as an onlooker at a public demonstration and smiled at the noise and glare that a mass of people will produce when their feelings are ever so little stirred, and marked how even against their own individual sentiments they are carried away by the mere tide of the day's circumstances, and for the mere sake of making a demonstration? This crowd which followed our Lord with shoutings very speedily repented and changed their shouts into a far blinder shriek of rage against Him who had been the occasion of their folly. And it must indeed have been a humbling experience for our Lord to have Himself ushered into Jerusalem by a crowd through whose hosannas He already heard the mutter of their curses. Such is the homage He has to content Himself with— such is the homage a perfect life has won.

For He knew what was in man; and while His disciples might be deceived by this popular response to His claim, He Himself was fully aware how little it could be built upon. Save in His own heart, there is no premonition of death. More than ever in His life before does His sky seem bright without a cloud. He Himself is in His early prime with life before Him; His followers are hopeful, the multitude jubilant; but through all this gay enthusiasm He sees the scowling hate of the priests and scribes; the shouting of the multitude does not drown in His ear the mutterings of a Judas and of the Sanhedrim. He knew that the throne He was now hailed to was the cross, that His coronation was the reception on His own brows of all the thorns and stings and burdens that man's sin had brought into the world. He did not fancy that the redemption of the world to God was an easy matter which could be accomplished by an afternoon's enthusiasm. He kept steadily before His mind the actual condition of the men who were by His spiritual influence to become the willing and devoted subjects of God's kingdom. He measured with accuracy the forces against Him, and understood that His warfare was not with the legions of Rome, against whom this Jewish patriotism and indomitable courage and easily roused enthusiasm might tell, but with principalities and powers a thousand-fold stronger, with the demons of hatred and jealousy, of lust and worldliness, of carnality and selfishness. Never for a moment did He forget His true mission and sell His spiritual throne, hard-earned as it was to be, for popular applause and the glories of the hour. Knowing that only by the utmost of human goodness and self-sacrifice, and by the utmost of trial and endurance, could any true and lasting rule of men be gained, He chose this path and the throne it led to. With the most comprehensive view of the kingdom He was to found, and with a spirit of profound seriousness strangely contrasting in its composed and self-possessed insight with the blind tumult around Him, He claimed the crown of the Messiah. His suffering was not formal and nominal, it was not a mere pageant; equally real was the claim He now made and which brought Him to that suffering.

# III.
## *THE CORN OF WHEAT.*

"Now there were certain Greeks among those that went up to worship at the feast : these therefore came to Philip, which was of Bethsaida of Galilee, and asked him, saying, Sir, we would see Jesus. Philip cometh and telleth Andrew : Andrew cometh, and Philip, and they tell Jesus. And Jesus answereth them, saying, The hour is come, that the Son of man should be glorified. Verily, verily, I say unto you, Except a grain of wheat fall into the earth and die, it abideth by itself alone ; but if it die, it beareth much fruit. He that loveth his life loseth it ; and he that hateth his life in this world shall keep it unto life eternal."—JOHN xii. 20-26.

## III.

### THE CORN OF WHEAT.

ST. JOHN now introduces a third incident to show that all is ripe for the death of Jesus. Already he has shown us that in the inmost circle of His friends He has now won for Himself a permanent place, a love which ensures that His memory will be had in everlasting remembrance. Next, he has lifted into prominence the scene in which the outer circle of the Jewish people were constrained, in an hour when their honest enthusiasm and instincts carried them away, to acknowledge Him as the Messiah who had come to fulfil all God's will upon earth. He now goes on to tell us how this agitation at the centre was found rippling in ever-widening circles till it broke with a gentle whisper on the shores of the isles of the Gentiles. This is the significance which St. John sees in the request of the Greeks that they might be introduced to Jesus.

These Greeks were "of those that came up to worship at the feast." They were proselytes, Greeks by birth, Jews by religion. They suggest the importance for Christianity of the leavening process which Judaism was accomplishing throughout the world. They may not have come from any remoter country than Galilee, but from traditions and customs separate as the poles from the Jewish customs and thoughts.

From their heathen surroundings they came to Jerusalem, possibly for the first time, with wondering anticipations of the blessedness of those who dwelt in God's house, and feeling their thirst for the living God burning within them as their eyes lighted on the pinnacles of the Temple, and as at last their feet stood within its precincts. But up through all these desires grew one that overshadowed them, and, through all the petitions which a year or many years of sin and difficulty had made familiar to their lips, this petition made its way: "Sir, we would see Jesus."

This petition they address to Philip, not only because he had a Greek name, and therefore presumably belonged to a family in which Greek was spoken and Greek connections cultivated, but because, as St. Jchn reminds us, he was "of Bethsaida of Galilee," and might be expected to understand and speak Greek, if, indeed, he was not already known to these strangers in Jerusalem. And by their request they obviously did not mean that Philip should set them in a place of vantage from which they might have a good view of Jesus as He passed by, for this they could well have accomplished without Philip's friendly intervention. But they wished to question and make Him out, to see for themselves whether there were in Jesus what even in Judaism they felt to be lacking—whether He at last might not satisfy the longings of their Divinely awakened spirits. Possibly they may even have wished to ascertain His purposes regarding the outlying nations, how the Messianic reign was to affect them. Possibly they may even have thought of offering Him an asylum where He might find shelter from the hostility of His own people.

Evidently Philip considered that this request was

critical. The Apostles had been charged not to enter into any Gentile city, and they might naturally suppose that Jesus would be reluctant to be interviewed by Greeks. But before dismissing the request, he lays it before Andrew his friend, who also bore a Greek name; and after deliberation the two make bold, if not to urge the request, at least to inform Jesus that it had been made. At once in this modestly urged petition He hears the whole Gentile world uttering its weary, long-disappointed sigh, "We would see." This is no mere Greek inquisitiveness; it is the craving of thoughtful men recognising their need of a Redeemer. To the eye of Jesus, therefore, this meeting opens a prospect which for the moment overcomes Him with the brightness of its glory. In this little knot of strangers He sees the firstfruits of the immeasurable harvest which was henceforth to be continuously reaped among the Gentiles. No more do we hear the heart-broken cry, "O Jerusalem, Jerusalem!" no longer the reproachful "Ye will not come to Me, that ye might have life," but the glad consummation of His utmost hope utters itself in the words, "The hour is come that the Son of man should be glorified."

But while promise was thus given of the glorification of the Messiah by His reception among all men, the path which led to this was never absent from the mind of our Lord. Second to the inspiriting thought of His recognition by the Gentile world came the thought of the painful means by which alone He could be truly glorified. He checks, therefore, the shout of exultation which He sees rising to the lips of His disciples with the sobering reflection: "Verily, verily, I say unto you, except a corn of wheat fall into the ground and die, it abideth alone; but if it die, it bringeth forth much fruit." As if He said, Do not fancy that I have nothing to do but to accept the sceptre which these men offer, to seat Myself on the world's throne. The world's throne is the Cross. These men will not know My power until I die. The manifestation of Divine presence in My life, has been distinct enough to win them to inquiry; they will be for ever won to Me by the Divine presence revealed in My death. Like the corn of wheat, I must die if I would be abundantly fruitful. It is through death My whole living power can be disengaged and can accomplish all possibilities.

Two points are here suggested: (I.) That the life, the living force that was in Christ, reached its proper value and influence through His death; and (II.) that the proper value of Christ's life is that it propagates similar lives.

I. The life of Christ acquired its proper value and received its fit development through His death. This truth He sets before us in the illuminating figure of the corn of wheat. "Except a corn of wheat fall into the ground and die, it abideth alone." There are three uses to which wheat may be put: it may be stored for sale, it may be ground and eaten, it may be sown. For our Lord's purposes these three uses may be considered as only two. Wheat may be eaten, or it may be sown. With a pickle of wheat or a grain of oats you may do one of two things: you may eat it and enjoy a momentary gratification and benefit; or you may put it in the ground, burying it out of sight and suffering it to pass through uncomely processes, and it will reappear multiplied a hundredfold, and so on in everlasting series. Year by year men sacrifice their choicest sample of grain, and are content to bury it in the earth instead of exposing it in the market, because they understand that except it die it abideth alone, but if it die it bringeth forth much fruit. The proper life of the grain is terminated when it is used for immediate gratification: it receives its fullest development and accomplishes its richest end when it is cast into the ground, buried out of sight, and apparently lost.

As with the grain, so is it with each human life. One of two things you can do with your life; both you cannot do, and no third thing is possible. You may consume your life for your own present gratification and profit, to satisfy your present cravings and tastes and to secure the largest amount of immediate enjoyment to yourself—you may eat your life; or you may be content to put aside present enjoyment and profits of a selfish kind and devote your life to the uses of God and men. In the one case you make an end of your life, you consume it as it goes; no good results, no enlarging influence, no deepening of character, no fuller life, follows from such an expenditure of life—spent on yourself and on the present, it terminates with yourself and with the present. But in the other case you find you have entered into a more abundant life; by living for others your interests are widened, your desire for life increased, the results and ends of life enriched. "He that loveth his life shall lose it; and he that hateth his life in this world shall keep it unto life eternal." It is a law we cannot evade. He that consumes his life now, spending it on himself—he who cannot bear to let his life out of his own hand, but cherishes and pampers it and gathers all good around it, and will have the fullest present enjoyment out of it,—this man is losing his life; it comes to an end as certainly as the seed that is eaten. But he who devotes his life to other uses than his own gratification, who does not so prize self that everything must minister to its comfort and advancement, but who can truly yield himself to God and put himself at God's disposal for the general good,—this man, though he may often seem to lose his life, and often does lose it so far as present advantage goes, keeps it to life everlasting.

The law of the seed is the law of human life. Use your life for present and selfish gratification and to satisfy your present cravings, and you lose it for ever. Renounce self, yield yourself to God, spend your life for the common good, irrespective of recognition or the lack of it, personal pleasure or the absence of it, and although your life may thus seem to be lost, it is finding its best and highest development and passes into life eternal. Your life is a seed now, not a developed plant, and it can become a developed plant only by your taking heart to cast it from you and sow it in the fertile soil of other men's needs. This will seem, indeed, to disintegrate it and fritter it away, and leave it a contemptible, obscure, forgotten thing; but it does, in fact, set free the vital forces that are in it, and give it its fit career and maturity.

Looking at the thing itself, apart from figure, it is apparent that "he that loveth his life shall lose it; and he that hateth his life in this world shall keep it unto life eternal." The man who most freely uses his life for others, keeping least to himself and living solely for the common interests of mankind, has the most enduring influence. He sets in motion forces which propagate fresh results eternally. And not only so. He who freely sows his life has it eternally, not only in so far as he has set in motion an endless series of beneficent influences, but inasmuch as he himself enters into life eternal. An immortality of influence is one thing and a very great thing; but an immortality of personal life is another, and this also is promised by our Lord when He says (ver. 26), " Where I am, there shall also My servant be."

This, then, being the law of human life, Christ, being man, must not only enounce but observe it. He speaks of Himself even more directly than of us when He says, "He that loveth his life shall lose it." His disciples thought they had never seen such promise in His life as at this hour: seedtime seemed to them to be past, and the harvest at hand. Their Master seemed to be fairly launched on the tide that was to carry Him to the highest pinnacle of human glory. And so He was, but not, as they thought, by simply yielding Himself to be set as King and to receive adoration from Jew and Gentile. He saw with different eyes, and that it was a different exaltation which would win for Him lasting sovereignty: " I, if I be lifted up, will draw all men unto Me." He knew the law which governed the development of human life. He knew that a total and absolute surrender of self to the uses and needs of others was the one path to permanent life, and that in His case this absolute surrender involved death.

A comparison of the good done by the life of Christ with that done by His death shows how truly He judged when He declared that it was by His death He should effectually gather all men to Him. His death, like the dissolution of the seed, seemed to terminate His work, but really was its germination. So long as He lived, it was but His single strength that was used; He abode alone. There was great virtue in His life—great power for the healing, the instruction, the elevation of mankind. In His brief public career He suggested much to the influential men of His time, set all men who knew Him a-thinking, aided many to reform their lives, and removed a large amount of distress and disease. He communicated to the world a mass of new truth, so that those who have lived after Him have stood at quite a different level of knowledge from that of those who lived before Him. And yet how little of the proper results of Christ's influence, how little understanding of Christianity, do you find even in His nearest friends until He died. By the visible appearance and the external benefits and the false expectations His greatness created, the minds of men were detained from penetrating to the spirit and mind of Christ. It was expedient for them that He should go away, for until He went they depended on His visible power, and His spirit could not be wholly received by them. They were looking at the husk of the seed, and its life could not reach them. They were looking for help from Him instead of themselves becoming like Him.

And therefore He chose at an early age to cease from all that was marvellous and beneficent in His life among men. He might, as these Greeks suggested, have visited other lands and have continued His healing and teaching there. He might have done more in His own time than He did, and His time might have been indefinitely prolonged; but He chose to cease from all this and voluntarily gave Himself to die, judging that thereby He could do much more good than by His life. He was straitened till this was accomplished; He felt as a man imprisoned and whose powers are held in check. It was winter and not spring-time with Him. There was a change to pass upon Him which should disengage the vital forces that were in Him and cause their full power to be felt—a change which should thaw the springs of life in Him and let them flow forth to all.

To use His own figure, He was as a seed unsown so long as He lived, valuable only in His own proper person; but by dying His life obtained the value of seed sown, propagating its kind in everlasting increase.

II. The second point suggested is, that the proper value of Christ's life consists in this—that it propagates similar lives. As seed produces grain of its own kind, so Christ produces men like Christ. He ceasing to do good in this world as a living man, a multitude of others by this very cessation are raised in His likeness. By His death we receive both inclination and ability to become with Him sons of God. "The love of Christ constraineth us, because we thus judge that if one died for all, then all died; and that He died for all, that they which live should not henceforth live unto themselves, but unto Him that died for them." By His death He has effected an entrance for this law of self-surrender into human life, has exhibited it in a perfect form, and has won others to live as He lived. So that, using the figure He used, we may say that the company of Christians now on earth are Christ in a new form, His body indeed. "That which thou sowest, thou sowest not that body which shall be, but bare grain: but God giveth it a body as it hath pleased Him, and to every seed his own body." Christ having been sown, lives now in His people. They are the body in which He dwells. And this will be seen. For standing and looking at a head of barley waving on its stalk, no amount of telling would persuade you that that had sprung from a seed of wheat; and looking at any life which is characterised by selfish ambition and eagerness for advancement and little regard for the wants of other men, no persuasion can make it credible that that life springs from the self-sacrificing life of Christ.

What Christ here shows us, then, is that the principle which regulates the development of seed regulates the growth, continuance, and fruitfulness of human life; that whatever is of the nature of seed gets to its full life only through death; that our Lord, knowing this law, submitted to it, or rather by His native love was attracted to the life and death which revealed this law to Him. He gave His life away for the good of men, and therefore prolongs His days and sees His seed eternally. There is not one way for Him and another for us. The same law applies to all. It is not peculiar to Christ. The work He did was peculiar to Him, as each individual has his own place and work; but the principle on which all right lives are led is one and the same universally. What Christ did He did because He was living a human life on right principles. We need not die on the cross as He did, but we must as truly yield ourselves as living sacrifices to the interests of men. If we have not done so, we have yet to go back to the very beginning of all lasting life and progress; and we are but deceiving ourselves by attainments and successes which are not only hollow, but are slowly cramping and killing all that is in us. Whoever will choose the same destiny as Christ must take the same road to it that He took. He took the one right way for men to go, and said, "If any man follow Me, where I am there will he be also." If we do not follow Him, we really walk in darkness and know not whither we go. We cannot live for selfish purposes and then enjoy the common happiness and glory of the race. Self-seeking is self-destroying.

And it is needful to remark that this self-renunciation

must be real. The law of sacrifice is the law not for a year or two in order to gain some higher selfish good—which is not self-sacrifice, but deeper self-seeking; it is the law of all human life, not a short test of our fidelity to Christ, but the only law on which life can ever proceed. It is not a barter of self I make, giving it up for a little that I may have an enriched self to eternity; but it is a real foregoing and abandonment of self for ever, a change of desire and nature, so that instead of finding my joy in what concerns myself only I find my joy in what is serviceable to others.

Thus only can we enter into permanent happiness. Goodness and happiness are one—one in the long-run, if not one in every step of the way. We are not asked to live for others without any heart to do so. We are not asked to choose as our eternal life what will be a constant pain and can only be reluctantly done. The very heathen would not offer in sacrifice the animal that struggled as it was led to the altar. All sacrifice must be willingly made; it must be the sacrifice which is prompted by love. God and this world demand our best work, and only what we do with pleasure can be our best work. Sacrifice of self and labour for others are not like Christ's sacrifice and labour unless they spring from love. Forced, reluctant, constrained sacrifice or service—service which is no joy to ourselves through the love we bear to those for whom we do it—is not the service that is required of us. Service into which we can throw our whole strength, because we are convinced it will be of use to others, and because we long to see them enjoying it—this is the service required. Love, in short, is the solution of all. Find your happiness in the happiness of many rather than in the happiness of one, and life becomes simple and inspiring.

Nor are we to suppose that this is an impracticable, high-pitched counsel of perfection with which plain men need not trouble themselves. *Every* human life is under this law. There is no path to goodness or to happiness save this one. Nature herself teaches us as much. When a man is truly attracted by another, and when genuine affection possesses his heart, his whole being is enlarged, and he finds it his best pleasure to serve that person. The father who sees his children enjoying the fruit of his toil feels himself a far richer man than if he were spending all on himself. But this family affection, this domestic solution of the problem of happy self-sacrifice, is intended to encourage and show us the way to a wider extension of our love, and thereby of our use and happiness. The more love we have, the happier we are. Self-sacrifice looks miserable, and we shrink from it as from death and destitution, because we look at it in separation from the love it springs from. Self-sacrifice without love *is* death; we abandon our own life and do not find it again in any other. It is a seed ground under the heel, not a seed lightly thrown into prepared soil. It is in love that goodness and happiness have their common root. And it is this love which is required of us and promised to us. So that as often as we shudder at the dissolution of our own personal interests, the scattering of our own selfish hopes and plans, the surrender of our life to the service of others, we are to remember that this, which looks so very like death, and which often throws around our prospects the chilling atmosphere of the tomb, is not really the termination, but the beginning of the true and eternal life of the spirit. Let us keep our heart in the fellowship of the sacrifice of Christ, let us feel our way into the meanings and uses of that sacrifice, and learn its reality, its utility, its grace, and at length it will lay hold of our whole nature, and we shall find that it impels us to regard other men with interest and to find our **true joy and life in serving them.**

## IV.
## THE ATTRACTIVE FORCE OF THE CROSS.

"Now is my soul troubled ; and what shall I say? Father, save Me from this hour. But for this cause came I unto this hour. Father, glorify Thy name. There came therefore a voice out of heaven, saying, I have both glorified it, and will glorify it again. The multitude therefore, that stood by, and heard it, said that it had thundered: others said, An angel hath spoken to Him. Jesus answered and said, This voice hath not come for My sake, but for your sakes. Now is the judgment of this world: now shall the prince of this world be cast out. And I, if I be lifted up from the earth, will draw all men unto Myself. But this He said, signifying by what manner of death He should die. The multitude therefore answered Him, We have heard out of the law that the Christ abideth for ever : and how sayest thou, The Son of man must be lifted up? who is this Son of man? Jesus therefore said unto them, Yet a little while is the light among you. Walk while ye have the light, that darkness overtake you not : and he that walketh in the darkness knoweth not whither he goeth. While ye have the light, believe on the light, that ye may become sons of light."—JOHN xii. 27-36.

## IV.

### THE ATTRACTIVE FORCE OF THE CROSS.

THE presence of the Greeks had stirred in the soul of Jesus conflicting emotions. Glory by humiliation, life through death, the secured happiness of mankind through His own anguish and abandonment, —well might the prospect disturb Him. So masterly is His self-command, so steadfast and constant His habitual temper, that one almost inevitably underrates the severity of the conflict. The occasional withdrawal of the veil permits us reverently to observe some symptoms of the turmoil within—symptoms which it is probably best to speak of in His own words: "Now is My soul troubled; and what shall I say? Shall I say, 'Father, save Me from this hour'? But for this cause came I unto this hour. Father, glorify Thy name." This Evangelist does not describe the agony in the Garden of Gethsemane. It was needless after this indication of the same conflict. Here is the same shrinking from a public and shameful death conquered by His resolution to deliver men from a still darker and more shameful death. Here is the same foretaste of the bitterness of the cup as it now actually touches His lips, the same clear reckoning of all it meant to drain that cup to the dregs, together with the deliberate assent to all that the will of the Father might require Him to endure.

In response to this act of submission, expressed in the words, "Father, glorify Thy name," there came a voice from heaven, saying, "I have both glorified it, and will glorify it again." The meaning of this assurance was, that as in all the past manifestation of Christ the Father had become better known to men, so in all that was now impending, however painful and disturbed, however filled with human passions and to all appearance the mere result of them, the Father would still be glorified. Some thought the voice was thunder; others seemed almost to catch articulate sounds, and said, "An angel spake to Him." But Jesus explained that it was not "to Him" the voice was specially addressed, but rather for the sake of those who stood by. And it was indeed of immense importance that the disciples should understand that the events which were about to happen were overruled by God that He might be glorified in Christ. It is easy for us to see that nothing so glorifies the Father's name as these hours of suffering; but how hard for the onlookers to believe that this sudden transformation of the Messianic throne into the criminal's cross was no defeat of God's purpose, but its final fulfilment. He leads them, therefore, to consider that in His judgment the whole world is judged, and to perceive in His arrest and trial and condemnation not merely the misguided and wanton outrage of a few men in power, but the critical hour of the world's history.

This world has commonly presented itself to thoughtful minds as a battle-field in which the powers of good and evil wage ceaseless war. In the words He now utters the Lord declares Himself to be standing at the very crisis of the battle, and with the deepest assurance He announces that the opposing power is broken and that victory remains with Him. "Now is the prince of this world cast out; and I will draw all men unto Me." The prince of this world, that which actually rules and leads men in opposition to God, was judged, condemned, and overthrown in the death of Christ. By His meek acceptance of God's will in the face of all that could make it difficult and dreadful to accept it, He won for the race deliverance from the thraldom of sin. At length a human life had been lived without submission at any point to the prince of this world. As man and in the name of all men Jesus resisted the last and most violent assault that could be made upon His faith in God and fellowship with Him, and so perfected His obedience and overcame the prince of this world,—overcame him not in one act alone— many had done that—but in a completed human life, in a life which had been freely exposed to the complete array of temptations that can be directed against men in this world.

In order more clearly to apprehend the promise of victory contained in our Lord's words, we may consider (I.) the object He had in view—to "draw all men" to Him; and (II.) the condition of His attaining this object—namely, His death.

I. The object of Christ was to draw all men to Him. The opposition in which He here sets Himself to the prince of this world shows us that by "drawing" He means attracting *as a king attracts*, to His name, His claims, His standard, His person. Our life consists in our pursuance of one object or another, and our devotion is continually competed for. When two claimants contest a kingdom, the country is divided between them, part cleaving to the one and part to the other. The individual determines to which side he shall cleave,—by his prejudices or by his justice, as it may be; by his knowledge of the comparative capacity of the claimants, or by his ignorant predilection. He is taken in by sounding titles, or he penetrates through all bombast and promises and douceurs to the real merit or demerit of the man himself. One person will judge by the personal manners of the respective claimants; another by their published manifesto, and professed object and style of rule; another by their known character and probable conduct. And while men thus range themselves on this side or on that, they really pass judgment on themselves, betraying as they do what it is that chiefly draws them, and taking their places on the side of good or evil. It is thus that we all judge ourselves by following this or that claimant to our faith, regard, and devotion, to ourself and our life. What we spend ourselves on, what we aim at and pursue, what we make our object, that judges us and that rules us and that determines our destiny.

Christ came into the world to be our King, to lead us to worthy achievements. He came that we might have a worthy object of choice and of the devotion of our life. He serves the same purpose as a king: He embodies in His own person, and thereby makes visible and attractive, the will of God and the cause of righteousness. Persons who could only with great difficulty apprehend His objects and plans can appreciate His person and trust Him. Persons to whom there would seem little attraction in a cause or in an undefined "progress of humanity" can kindle with enthusiasm towards Him personally, and unconsciously promote His cause and the cause of humanity. And therefore, while some are attracted by His person, others by the legitimacy of His claims, others by His programme of government, others by His benefactions, we must beware of denying loyalty to any of these. Expressions of love to His person may be lacking in the man who yet most intelligently enters into Christ's views for the race, and sacrifices his means and his life to forward these views. Those who gather to His standard are various in temperament, are drawn by various attractions, and must be various in their forms of showing allegiance. And this, which is the strength of His camp, can only become its weakness when men begin to think there is no way but their own; and that allegiance which is strenuous in labour but not fluent in devout expression, or loyalty which shouts and throws its cap in the air but lacks intelligence, is displeasing to the King. The King, who has great ends in view, will not inquire what it is precisely which forms the bond between Him and His subjects so long as they truly sympathise with Him and second His efforts. The one question is, Is He their actual leader?

Of the kingdom of Christ, though a full description cannot be given, one or two of the essential characteristics may be mentioned.

1. It is *a kingdom*, a community of men under one head. When Christ proposed to attract men to Himself, it was for the good of the race He did so. It could achieve its destiny only if He led it, only if it yielded itself to His mind and ways. And those who are attracted to Him, and see reason to believe that the hope of the world lies in the universal adoption of His mind and ways, are formed into one solid body or community. They labour for the same ends, are governed by the same laws, and whether they know one another or not they have the most real sympathy and live for one cause. Being drawn to Christ, we enter into

abiding fellowship with all the good who have laboured or are labouring in the cause of humanity. We take our places in the everlasting kingdom, in the community of those who shall see and take part in the great future of mankind and the growing enlargement of its destiny. We are hereby entered among the living, and are joined to that body of mankind which is to go on and which holds the future—not to an extinct party which may have memories, but has no hopes. In sin, in selfishness, in worldliness, individualism reigns, and all profound or abiding unity is impossible. Sinners have common interests only for a time, only as a temporary guise of selfish interests. Every man out of Christ is really an isolated individual. But passing into Christ's kingdom we are no longer isolated, abandoned wretches stranded by the stream of time, but members of the undying commonwealth of men in which our life, our work, our rights, our future, our association with all good, are assured.

2. It is a *universal* kingdom. "I will draw *all* men unto Me." The one rational hope of forming men into one kingdom shines through these words. The idea of a universal monarchy has visited the great minds of our race. They have cherished their various dreams of a time when all men should live under one law and possibly speak one language, and have interests so truly in common that war should be impossible. But an effectual instrument for accomplishing this grand design has ever been wanting. Christ turns this grandest dream of humanity into a rational hope. He appeals to what is universally present in human nature. There is that in Him which every man needs,—a door to the Father; a visible image of the unseen God; a gracious, wise, and holy Friend. He does not appeal

exclusively to one generation, to educated or to uneducated, to Orientals or to Europeans alone, but to man, to that which we have in common with the lowest and the highest, the most primitive and most highly developed of the species. The attractive influence He exerts upon men is not conditioned by their historical insight, by their ability to sift evidence, by this or that which distinguishes man from man, but by their innate consciousness that some higher power than themselves exists, by their ability, if not to recognise goodness when they see it, at least to recognise love when it is spent upon them.

But while our Lord affirms that there is that in Him which all men can recognise and learn to love and serve, He does not say that His kingdom will therefore be quickly formed. He does not say that this greatest work of God will take a shorter time than the common works of God which prolong one day of our hasty methods into a thousand years of solidly growing purpose. If it has taken a million ages for the rocks to knit and form for us a standing-ground and dwelling-place, we must not expect that this kingdom, which is to be the one enduring result of this world's history, and which can be built up only of thoroughly convinced men and of generations slowly weeded of traditional prejudices and customs, can be completed in a few years. No doubt interests are at stake in human destiny and losses are made by human waste which had no place in the physical creation of the world; still, God's methods are, as we judge, slow, and we must not think that He who "works hitherto" is doing nothing because the swift processes of jugglery or the hasty methods of human workmanship find no place in the extension of Christ's kingdom. This kingdom has a firm hold of the world and must grow. If there is one thing certain about the future of the world, it is that righteousness and truth will prevail. The world is bound to come to the feet of Christ.

3. Christ's kingdom being universal, it is also and necessarily *inward*. What is common to all men lies deepest in each. Christ was conscious that He held the key to human nature. He knew what was in man. With the penetrating insight of absolute purity He had gone about among men, freely mixing with rich and with poor, with the sick and the healthy, with the religious and the irreligious. He was as much at home with the condemned criminal as with the blameless Pharisee; saw through Pilate and Caiaphas alike; knew all that the keenest dramatist could tell Him of the meannesses, the depravities, the cruelties, the blind passions, the obstructed goodness, of men; but knew also that He could sway all that was in man and exhibit that to men which should cause the sinner to abhor his sin and seek the face of God. This He would do by a simple moral process, without violent demonstration or disturbance or assertion of authority. He would "draw" men. It is by inward conviction, not by outward compulsion, men are to become His subjects. It is by the free and rational working of the human mind that Jesus builds up His kingdom. His hope lies in a fuller and fuller light, in a clearer and clearer recognition of facts. Attachment to Christ must be the act of the soul's self; everything, therefore, which strengthens the will or enlightens the mind or enlarges the man brings him nearer to the kingdom of Christ, and makes it more likely he will yield to His drawing.

And because Christ's rule is inward it is therefore of

universal application. The inmost choice of the man being governed by Christ, and his character being thus touched at its inmost spring, all his conduct will be governed by Christ and be a carrying out of the will of Christ. It is not the frame of society Christ seeks to alter, but the spirit of it. It is not the occupations and institutions of human life which the subject of Christ finds to be incompatible with Christ's rule, so much as the aim and principles on which they are conducted. The kingdom of Christ claims all human life as its own, and the spirit of Christ finds nothing that is essentially human alien from it. If the statesman is a Christian, it will be seen in his policy; if the poet is a Christian, his song will betray it; if a thinker be a Christian, his readers soon find it out. Christianity does not mean religious services, churches, creeds, Bibles, books, equipment of any kind; it means the Spirit of Christ. It is the most portable and flexible of all religions, and therefore the most pervasive and dominant in the life of its adherent. It needs but the Spirit of God and the spirit of man, and Christ mediating between them.

II. Such being Christ's object, what is the condition of His attaining it? "I, *if I be lifted up*, will draw all men unto Me." The elevation requisite for becoming a visible object to men of all generations was the elevation of the Cross. His death would accomplish what His life could not accomplish. The words betray a distinct consciousness that there was in His death a more potent spell, a more certain and real influence for good among men than in His teaching or in His miracles or in His purity of life.

What is it, then, in the death of Christ which so far surpasses His life in its power of attraction? The life was equally unselfish and devoted ; it was more prolonged ; it was more directly useful,—why, then, would it have been comparatively ineffective without the death ? It may, in the first place, be answered, Because His death presents in a dramatic and compact form that very devotedness which is diffused through every part of His life. Between the life and the death there is the same difference as between sheet lightning and forked lightning, between the diffused heat of the sun and the same heat focussed upon a point through a lens. It discloses what was actually but latently there. The life and the death of Christ are one and mutually explain each other. From the life we learn that no motive can have prompted Christ to die but the one motive which ruled Him always—the desire to do all God willed in men's behalf. We cannot interpret the death as anything else than a consistent part of a deliberate work undertaken for men's good. It was not an accident; it was not an external necessity : it was, as the whole life was, a willing acceptance of the uttermost that was required to set men on a higher level and unite them to God. But as the life throws this light upon the death of Christ, how that light is gathered up and thrown abroad in world-wide reflection from the death of Christ ! For here His self-sacrifice shines completed and perfect ; here it is exhibited in that tragic and supreme form which in all cases arrests attention and commands respect. Even when a man of wasted life sacrifices himself at last, and in one heroic act saves another by his death, his past life is forgotten or seems to be redeemed by his death, and at all events we own the beauty and the pathos of the deed. A martyr to the faith may have been but a poor creature, narrow, harsh and overbearing, vain and vulgar in spirit; but all the past is blotted out, and our attention is arrested on the blazing pile or the bloody scaffold. So the death of Christ, though but a part of the self-sacrificing life, yet stands by itself as the culmination and seal of that life; it catches the eye and strikes the mind, and conveys at one view the main impression made by the whole life and character of Him who gave Himself upon the cross.

But Christ is no mere hero or teacher sealing his truth with his blood; nor is it enough to say that His death renders, in a conspicuous form, the perfect self-sacrifice with which He devoted Himself to our good. It is conceivable that in a long-past age some other man should have lived and died for his fellows, and yet we at once recognise that, though the history of such a person came into our hands, we should not be so affected and drawn by it as to choose him as our king and rest upon him the hope of uniting us to one another and to God. Wherein, then, lies the difference? The difference lies in this—that Christ was the representative of God. This He Himself uniformly claimed to be. He knew He was unique, different from all others; but He advanced no claim to esteem that did not pass to the Father who sent Him. Always he explained His powers as being the proper equipment of God's representative. " The words that I speak unto you, I speak not of Myself." His whole life was the message of God to man, the Word made flesh. His death was but the last syllable of this great utterance—the utterance of God's love for man, the final evidence that nothing is grudged us by God. Greater love hath no man than this, that he lay down his life for his friends. His death draws us because there is in it more than human heroism and self-sacrifice. It draws us because in it the very heart of God is laid bare to us. It softens, it breaks us down, by the irresistible tenderness it discloses in the mighty and ever-blessed God. Every man feels it has a message for him, because in it the God and Father of us all speaks to us.

It is this which is special to the death of Christ, and which separates it from all other deaths and heroic sacrifices. It has a universal bearing—a bearing upon every man, because it is a Divine act, the act of that One who is the God and Father of all men. In the same century as our Lord many men died in a manner which strongly excites our admiration. Nothing could well be more noble, nothing more pathetic, than the fearless and loving spirit in which Roman after Roman met his death. But beyond respectful admiration these heroic deeds win from us no further sentiment. They are the deeds of men who have no connection with us. The well-worn words, "What's Hecuba *to me* or I to Hecuba?" rise to our lips when we try to fancy any deep connection. But the death of Christ concerns all men without exception, because it is the greatest declarative act of the God of all men. It is the manifesto all men are concerned to read. It is the act of One with whom all men are already connected in the closest way. And the result of our contemplation of it is, not that we admire, but that we are drawn, are attracted, into new relations with Him whom that death reveals. This death moves and draws us as no other can, because here we get to the very heart of that which most deeply concerns us. Here we learn what our God is and where we stand eternally. He who is nearest us of all, and in whom our life is bound up, reveals Himself; and seeing Him here full of ungrudging and most reliable love, of tenderest and utterly self-sacrificing devotedness to us, we cannot but give way to this central attraction, and with all other willing creatures be drawn into fullest intimacy and firmest relations to the God of all.

The death of Christ, then, draws men chiefly because God here shows men His sympathy, His love, His trustworthiness. What the sun is in the solar system, Christ's death is in the moral world. The sun by its physical attraction binds the several planets together and holds them within range of its light and heat. God, the central intelligence and original moral Being, draws to Himself and holds within reach of His life-giving radiance all who are susceptible of moral influences; and He does so through the death of Christ. This is His supreme revelation. Here, if we may say so with reverence, God is seen at His best—not that at any time or in any action He is different, but here He is *seen* to be the God of love He ever is. Nothing is better than self-sacrifice: that is the highest point a moral nature can touch. And God, by the sacrifice which is rendered visible on the cross, gives to the moral world a real, actual, immovable centre, round which moral natures will more and more gather, and which will hold them together in self-effacing unity.

To complete the idea of the attractiveness of the Cross, it must further be kept in view that this particular form of the manifestation of the Divine love was adapted to the needs of those to whom it was made. To sinners the love of God manifested itself in providing a sacrifice for sin. The death on the cross was not an irrelevant display, but was an act required for the removal of the most insuperable obstacles that lay in man's path. The sinner, believing that in the death of Christ his sins are atoned for, conceives hope in God and claims the Divine compassion in his own behalf. To the penitent the Cross is attractive as an open door to the prisoner, or the harbour-heads to the storm-tossed ship.

Let us not suppose, then, that we are not welcome to Christ. He desires to draw us to Himself and to form a connection with us. He understands our hesitations, our doubts of our own capacity for any steady and enthusiastic loyalty; but He knows also the power of truth and love, the power of His own person and of His own death to draw and fix the hesitating and wavering soul. And we shall find that as we strive to serve Christ in our daily life it is still His death that holds and draws us. It is His death which gives us compunction in our times of frivolity, or selfishness, or carnality, or rebellion, or unbelief. It is there Christ appears in His own most touching attitude and with His own most irresistible appeal. We cannot further wound One already so wounded in His desire to win us from evil. To strike One already thus nailed to the tree in helplessness and anguish, is more than the hardest heart can do. Our sin, our infidelity, our unmoved contemplation of His love, our blind indifference to His purpose—these things wound Him more than the spear and the scourge. To rid us of these things was His purpose in dying, and to see that His work is in vain and His sufferings unregarded and unfruitful is the deepest injury of all. It is not to the mere sentiment of pity He appeals: rather He says, " Weep not for Me; weep for yourselves." It is to our power to recognise perfect goodness and to appreciate perfect love. He appeals to our power to see below the surface of things, and through the outer shell of this world's life to the Spirit of good that is at the root of all and that manifests itself in Him. Here is the true stay of the human soul : " Come unto Me, all ye that labour and are heavy laden " ; " I am come a light into the world : walk in the light."

# V.
## *RESULTS OF CHRIST'S MANIFESTATION.*

"But though He had done so many signs before them, yet they believed not on Him: that the word of Isaiah the prophet might be fulfilled, which he spake, Lord, who hath believed our report? and to whom hath the arm of the Lord been revealed? For this cause they could not believe, for that Isaiah said again, He hath blinded their eyes, and He hardened their heart; lest they should see with their eyes, and perceive with their heart, and should turn, and I should heal them. These things said Isaiah, because he saw His glory; and he spake of Him. Nevertheless even of the rulers many believed on Him; but because of the Pharisees they did not confess it, lest they should be put out of the synagogue: for they loved the glory of men more than the glory of God. And Jesus cried and said, He that believeth on Me, believeth not on Me, but on Him that sent Me. And he that beholdeth Me beholdeth Him that sent Me. I am come a light into the world, that whosoever believeth on Me may not abide in the darkness. And if any man hear My sayings, and keep them not, I judge him not: for I came not to judge the world, but to save the world. He that rejecteth Me, and receiveth not My sayings, hath One that judgeth him: the word that I spake, the same shall judge him in the last day. For I spake not from Myself; but the Father which sent Me, He hath given Me a commandment, what I should say, and what I should speak. And I know that His commandment is life eternal: the things therefore which I speak, even as the Father hath said unto Me, so I speak."— JOHN xii. 37-50.

## V.

### RESULTS OF CHRIST'S MANIFESTATION.

IN this Gospel the death of Christ is viewed as the first step in His glorification. When He speaks of being "lifted up," there is a double reference in the expression, a local and an ethical reference.[1] He is lifted up on the cross, but lifted up on it as His true throne and as the necessary step towards His supremacy at God's right hand. It was, John tells us, with direct reference to the cross that Jesus now used the words: "I, if I be lifted up, will draw all men unto Me." The Jews, who heard the words, perceived that, whatever else was contained in them, intimation of His removal from earth was given. But, according to the current Messianic expectation, the Christ "abideth for ever," or at any rate for four hundred or a thousand years. How then could this Person, who announced His immediate departure, be the Christ? The Old Testament gave them ground for supposing that the Messianic reign would be lasting; but had they listened to our Lord's teaching they would have learned that this reign was spiritual, and not in the form of an earthly kingdom with a visible sovereign.

Accordingly, although they had recognised Jesus as

---

[1] See iii. 14.

the Messiah, they are again stumbled by this fresh declaration of His. They begin to fancy that perhaps after all by calling Himself "the Son of man" He has not meant exactly what they mean by the Messiah. From the form of their question it would seem that Jesus had used the designation "the Son of man" in intimating His departure; for they say, "How sayest thou, The Son of man must be lifted up?" Up to this time, therefore, they had taken it for granted that by calling Himself the Son of man He claimed to be the Christ, but now they begin to doubt whether there may not be two persons signified by those titles.

Jesus furnishes them with no direct solution of their difficulty. He never betrays any interest in these external identifications. The time for discussing the relation of the Son of man to the Messiah is past. His manifestation is closed. Enough light has been given. Conscience has been appealed to and discussion is no longer admissible. "Ye have light: walk in the light." The way to come to a settlement of all their doubts and hesitations is to follow Him. There is still time for that. "Yet a little while is the light among you." But the time is short; there is none to waste on idle questionings, none to spend on sophisticating conscience—time only for deciding as conscience bids.

By thus believing in the light they will themselves become "children of light." The "children of light" are those who live in it as their element,—as "the children of this world" are those who wholly belong to this world and find in it what is congenial; as "the son of perdition" is he who is identified with perdition. The children of light have accepted the revelation that is in Christ, and live in the "day" that the Lord has made. Christ contains the truth for them—the truth which penetrates to their inmost thought and illuminates the darkest problems of life. In Christ they have seen that which determines their relation to God; and that being determined, all else that is of prime importance finds a settlement. To know God and ourselves; to know God's nature and purpose, and our own capabilities and relation to God,—these constitute the light we need for living by; and this light Christ gives. It was in a dim, uncertain twilight, with feebly shining lanterns, the wisest and best of men sought to make out the nature of God and His purposes regarding man; but in Christ God has made noonday around us.

They, therefore, that stood, or that stand, in His presence, and yet recognise no light, must be asleep, or must turn away from an excess of light that is disagreeable or inconvenient. If we are not the fuller of life and joy the more truth we know, if we shrink from admitting the consciousness of a present and holy God, and do not feel it to be the very sunshine of life in which alone we thrive, we must be spiritually asleep or spiritually dead. And this cry of Christ is but another form of the cry that His Church has prolonged: "Awake, thou that sleepest, and arise from the dead, and Christ shall give thee light."

The "little while" of their enjoyment of the light was short indeed, for no sooner had He made an end of these sayings than He "departed, and did hide Himself from them." He probably found retirement from the feverish, inconstant, questioning crowd with His friends in Bethany. At any rate this removal of the light, while it meant darkness to those who had not received Him and who did not keep His words, could bring no darkness to His own, who had received Him and the light in Him. Perhaps the best comment on this is the memorable passage from *Comus*:

> "Virtue could see to do what virtue would
> By her own radiant light, though sun and moon
> Were in the great sea sunk.
> He that has light within his own clear breast
> May sit i' the centre and enjoy bright day;
> But he that hides a dark soul and foul thoughts
> Benighted walks under the midday sun,
> Himself is his own dungeon."

And now the writer of this Gospel, before entering upon the closing scenes, pauses and presents a summary of the results of all that has been hitherto related. First, he accounts for the unbelief of the Jews. It could not fail to strike his readers as remarkable that, "though He had done so many miracles before the people, yet they believed not in Him." In this John sees nothing inexplicable, however sad and significant it may be. At first sight it is an astounding fact that the very people who had been prepared to recognise and receive the Messiah should not have believed in Him. Might not this to some minds be convincing evidence that Jesus was not the Messiah? If the same God who sent Him forth had for centuries specially prepared a people to recognise and receive Him when He came, was it possible that this people should repudiate Him? Was it likely that such a result should be produced or should be allowed? But John turns the point of this argument by showing that a precisely similar phenomenon had often appeared in the history of Israel. The old prophets had the very same complaint to make: "Who hath believed our report? and to whom hath the arm of the Lord been revealed?" The people had habitually, as a people with individual exceptions, refused to listen to God's voice or to acknowledge His presence in prophet and providence.

Besides, might it not very well be that the blindness and callousness of the Jews in rejecting Jesus was the inevitable issue of a long process of hardening? If, in former periods of their history, they had proved themselves unworthy of God's training and irresponsive to it, what else could be expected than that they should reject the Messiah when He came? This hardening and blinding process was the inevitable, natural result of their past conduct. But what nature does, God does; and therefore the Evangelist says "they could not believe, because that Esaias said again, He hath blinded their eyes, and hardened their heart; that they should not see with their eyes, nor understand with their heart." The organ for perceiving spiritual truth was blinded, and their susceptibility to religious and moral impressions had become callous and hardened and impervious.

And while this was no doubt true of the people as a whole, still there were not a few individuals who eagerly responded to this last message from God. In the most unlikely quarters, and in circumstances calculated to counteract the influence of spiritual forces, some were convinced. "Even among the chief rulers many believed on Him." This belief, however, did not tell upon the mass, because, through fear of excommunication, those who were convinced dared not utter their conviction. "They loved the praise of men more than the praise of God." They allowed their relations to men to determine their relation to God. Men were more real to them than God. The praise of men came home to their hearts with a sensible relish that the praise of God could not rival. They reaped what they had sown; they had sought the esteem of men, and now they were unable to find their strength in God's approval. The glory which consisted in following the lowly and outcast Jesus, the glory of fellowship with God, was quite eclipsed by the glory of living in the eye of the people as wise and estimable persons.

In the last paragraph of the chapter John gives a summary of the claims and message of Jesus. He has told us (ver. 36) that Jesus had departed from public view and had hidden Himself, and he mentions no return to publicity. It is therefore probable that in these remaining verses, and before he turns to a somewhat different aspect of Christ's ministry, he gives in rapid and brief retrospect the sum of what Jesus had advanced as His claim. He introduces this paragraph, indeed, with the words, "Jesus cried and said"; but as neither time nor place is mentioned, it is quite likely that no special time or place is supposed; and in point of fact each detail adduced in these verses can be paralleled from some previously recorded utterance of Jesus.

First, then, as everywhere in the Gospel, so here, He claims to be the representative of God in so close and perfect a manner that "he that believeth on Me, believeth not on Me, but on Him that sent Me. And he that seeth Me, seeth Him that sent Me." No belief terminates in Christ Himself: to believe in Him is to believe in God, because all that He is and does proceeds from God and leads to God. The whole purpose of Christ's manifestation was to reveal God. He did not wish to arrest thought upon Himself, but through Himself to guide thought to Him whom He revealed. He was sustained by the Father, and all He said and did was of the Father's inspiration. Whoever, therefore, "saw" or understood Him "saw" the Father; and whoever believed in Him believed in the Father.

Second, as regards men, He is "come a light into the world." Naturally there is in the world no sufficient light. Men feel that they are in darkness. They feel the darkness all the more appalling and depressing the more developed their own human nature is. "More light" has been the cry from the beginning. What are we? where are we? whence are we? whither are we going? what is there above and beyond this world? These questions are echoed back from an unanswering void, until Christ comes and gives the answer. Since He came men have felt that they did not any longer walk in darkness. They see where they are going, and they see why they should go

And if it be asked, as among the Jews it certainly must have been asked, why, if Jesus is the Messiah, does He not punish men for rejecting Him? the answer is, "I came not to judge the world, but to save the world." Judgment, indeed, necessarily results from His coming. Men are divided by His coming. "The words that I have spoken, the same shall judge men in the last day." The offer of God, the offer of righteousness, is that which judges men. Why are they still dead, when life has been offered? This is the condemnation. "The commandment of the Father is life everlasting." This is the sum of the message of God to men in Christ; this is "the commandment" which the Father has given Me; this is Christ's commission: to bring God in the fulness of His grace and love and life-giving power within men's reach. It is to give life eternal to men that God has come to them in Christ To refuse that life is their condemnation.

# VI.
## THE FOOT-WASHING.

"Now before the feast of the Passover, Jesus knowing that His hour was come that He should depart out of this world unto the Father, having loved His own which were in the world, He loved them unto the end. And during supper, the devil having already put into the heart of Judas Iscariot, Simon's son, to betray Him. Jesus, knowing that the Father had given all things into His hands, and that He came forth from God, and goeth unto God, riseth from supper, and layeth aside His garments; and He took a towel, and girded Himself. Then He poureth water into the basin, and began to wash the disciples' feet, and to wipe them with the towel wherewith He was girded. So He cometh to Simon Peter. He saith unto Him, Lord, dost Thou wash my feet? Jesus answered and said unto him, What I do thou knowest not now; but thou shalt understand hereafter Peter saith unto Him, Thou shalt never wash my feet. Jesus answered him, If I wash thee not, thou hast no part with Me. Simon Peter saith unto Him, Lord, not my feet only, but also my hands and my head. Jesus saith to him, He that is bathed needeth not save to wash his feet, but is clean every whit: and ye are clean, but not all. For He knew him that should betray Him; therefore said He, Ye are not all clean. So when He had washed their feet, and taken His garments, and sat down again, He said unto them, Know ye what I have done to you? Ye call Me, Master, and, Lord: and ye say well; for so I am. If I then, the Lord and the Master, have washed your feet, ye also ought to wash one another's feet. For I have given you an example, that ye also should do as I have done to you. Verily, verily, I say unto you, A servant is not greater than his lord; neither one that is sent greater than he that sent him. If ye know these things, blessed are ye if ye do them."—JOHN xiii. 1-17.

# VI.

## *THE FOOT-WASHING.*

ST. JOHN, having finished his account of the public manifestation of Jesus, proceeds now to narrate the closing scenes, in which the disclosures He made to "His own" form a chief part. That the transition may be observed, attention is drawn to it. At earlier stages of our Lord's ministry He has given as His reason for refraining from proposed lines of action that His hour was not come: now He "knew that His hour was come, that He should depart out of this world unto the Father." This indeed was the last evening of His life. Within twenty-four hours He was to be in the tomb. Yet according to this writer it was not the paschal supper which our Lord now partook of with His disciples; it was "before the feast of the Passover." Jesus being Himself the Paschal Lamb was sacrificed on the day on which the Passover was eaten, and in this and the following chapters we have an account of the preceding evening.

In order to account for what follows, the precise time is defined in the words "supper being served"[1] or "supper-time having arrived"; not, as in the Authorised Version, "supper being ended," which

---

[1] Compare Mark vi. 2, γενομένου σαββάτου; and the Latin "posita mensa."

plainly was not the case;[1] nor, as in the Revised Version, "during supper." The difficulty about washing the feet could not have arisen after or during supper, but only as the guests entered and reclined at table. In Palestine, as in other countries of the same latitude, shoes were not universally worn, and were not worn at all within doors; and where some protection to the foot was worn, it was commonly a mere sandal, a sole tied on with a thong. The upper part of the foot was thus left exposed, and necessarily became heated and dirty with the fine and scorching dust of the roads. Much discomfort was thus produced, and the first duty of a host was to provide for its removal. A slave was ordered to remove the sandals and wash the feet.[2] And in order that this might be done, the guest either sat on the couch appointed for him at table, or reclined with his feet protruding beyond the end of it, that the slave, coming round with the pitcher and basin,[3] might pour cool water gently over them. So necessary to comfort was this attention that our Lord reproached the Pharisee who had invited Him to dinner with a breach of courtesy because he had omitted it.

On ordinary occasions it is probable that the disciples would perform this humble office by turns, where there was no slave to discharge it for all. But this evening, when they gathered for the last supper, all took their places at the table with a studied ignorance of the necessity, a feigned unconsciousness that any such attention was required. As a matter of course, the pitcher of cool water, the basin, and the towel had been set as part of the requisite furnishing of the supper chamber; but no one among the disciples betrayed the

---

[1] See ver. 2.    [2] ὑπολύετε, παῖδες, καὶ ἀπονίζετε.
[3] The "tûsht" and "ibrîek" of modern Palestine.

slightest consciousness that he understood that any such custom existed. Why was this? Because, as Luke tells us (xxii. 24), "there had arisen among them a contention, which of them is accounted to be the greatest." Beginning, perhaps, by discussing the prospects of their Master's kingdom, they had passed on to compare the importance of this or that faculty for forwarding the interests of the kingdom, and had ended by easily recognised personal allusions and even the direct pitting of man against man. The assumption of superiority on the part of the sons of Zebedee and others was called in question, and it suddenly appeared how this assumption had galled the rest and rankled in their minds. That such a discussion should arise may be disappointing, but it was natural. All men are jealous of their reputation, and crave that credit be given them for their natural talent, their acquired skill, their professional standing, their influence, or at any rate for their humility.

Heated, then, and angry and full of resentment these men hustle into the supper-room and seat themselves like so many sulky schoolboys. They streamed into the room and doggedly took their places; and then came a pause. For any one to wash the feet of the rest was to declare himself the servant of all; and that was precisely what each one was resolved he, for his part, would not do. No one of them had humour enough to see the absurdity of the situation. No one of them was sensitive enough to be ashamed of showing such a temper in Christ's presence. There they sat, looking at the table, looking at the ceiling, arranging their dress, each resolved upon this—that he would not be the man to own himself servant of all.

But this unhealthy heat quite unfits them to listen to

what their Lord has to say to them that last evening. Occupied as they are, not with anxiety about Him nor with absorbing desire for the prosperity of His kingdom, but with selfish ambitions that separate them alike from Him and from one another, how can they receive what He has to say? But how is He to bring them into a state of mind in which they can listen wholly and devotedly to Him? How is He to quench their heated passions and stir within them humility and love? "He riseth from the supper-table, and laid aside His garments, and took a towel, and girded Himself. After that He poureth water into the basin, and began to wash the disciples' feet, and to wipe them with the towel wherewith He was girded." Each separate action is a fresh astonishment and a deeper shame to the bewildered and conscience-stricken disciples. "Who is not able to picture the scene,—the faces of John and James and Peter; the intense silence, in which each movement of Jesus was painfully audible; the furtive watching of Him, as He rose, to see what He would do; the sudden pang of self-reproach as they perceived what it meant; the bitter humiliation and the burning shame?"

But not only is the time noted, in order that we may perceive the relevancy of the foot-washing, but the Evangelist steps aside from his usual custom and describes the mood of Jesus that we may more deeply penetrate into the significance of the action. Around this scene in the supper-chamber St. John sets lights which permit us to see its various beauty and grace. And first of all he would have us notice what seems chiefly to have struck himself as from time to time he reflected on this last evening—that Jesus, even in these last hours, was wholly possessed and governed by love.

Although He knew "that His hour had come, that He should depart out of this world unto the Father, yet having loved His own which were in the world He loved them unto the end." Already the deep darkness of the coming night was touching the spirit of Jesus with its shadow. Already the pain of the betrayal, the lonely desolation of desertion by His friends, the defenceless exposure to fierce, unjust, ruthless men, the untried misery of death and dissolution, the critical trial of His cause and of all the labour of His life, these and many anxieties that cannot be imagined, were pouring in upon His spirit, wave upon wave. If ever man might have been excused for absorption in His own affairs Jesus was then that man. On the edge of what He knew to be the critical passage in the world's history, what had He to do attending to the comfort and adjusting the silly differences of a few unworthy men? With the weight of a world on His arm, was He to have His hands free for such a trifling attention as this? With His whole soul pressed with the heaviest burden ever laid on man, was it to be expected He should turn aside at such a call?

But His love made it seem no turning aside at all. His love had made Him wholly theirs, and though standing on the brink of death He was disengaged to do them the slightest service. His love was love, devoted, enduring, constant. He had loved them, and He loved them still. It was their condition which had brought Him into the world, and His love for them was that which would carry Him through all that was before Him. The very fact that they showed themselves still so jealous and childish, so unfit to cope with the world, drew out His affection towards them. He was departing from the world and they were remaining in it, exposed to all its opposition and destined to bear the brunt of hostility directed against Him—how then can He but pity and strengthen them? Nothing is more touching on a death-bed than to see the sufferer hiding and making light of his own pain, and turning the attention of those around him away from him to themselves, and making arrangements, not for his own relief, but for the future comfort of others. This which has often dimmed with tears the eyes of the bystanders struck John when he saw his Master ministering to the wants of His disciples, although He knew that His own hour had come.

Another side-light which serves to bring out the full significance of this action is Jesus' consciousness of His own dignity. "Jesus, knowing that the Father had given all things into His hands, and that He came forth from God, and goeth unto God," riseth from supper, and took a towel and girded Himself. It was not in forgetfulness of His Divine origin, but in full consciousness of it, He discharged this menial function. As He had divested Himself of the "form of God" at the first, stripping Himself of the outward glory attendant on recognised Divinity, and had taken upon Him the form of a servant, so now He "laid aside His garments and girded Himself," assuming the guise of a household slave. For a fisherman to pour water over a fisherman's feet was no great condescension; but that He, in whose hands are all human affairs and whose nearest relation is the Father, should thus condescend is of unparalleled significance. It is this kind of action that is suitable to One whose consciousness is Divine. Not only does the dignity of Jesus vastly augment the beauty of the action, but it sheds new light on the Divine character.

Still another circumstance which seemed to John to accentuate the grace of the foot-washing was this—that Judas was among the guests, and that "the devil had now put into the heart of Judas Iscariot, Simon's son, to betray him." The idea had at last formed itself in Judas' mind that the best use he could make of Jesus was to sell Him to His enemies. His hopes of gain in the Messianic kingdom were finally blighted, but he might still make something out of Jesus and save himself from all implication in a movement frowned upon by the authorities. He clearly apprehended that all hopes of a temporal kingdom were gone. He had probably not strength of mind enough to say candidly that he had joined the company of disciples on a false understanding, and meant now quietly to return to his trading at Kerioth. If he could break up the whole movement, he would be justified in his dissatisfaction, and would also be held to be a useful servant of the nation. So he turns traitor. And John does not whitewash him, but plainly brands him as a traitor. Now, much may be forgiven a man; but treachery—what is to be done with it; with the man who uses the knowledge only a friend can have, to betray you to your enemies? Suppose Jesus had unmasked him to Peter and the rest, would he ever have left that room alive? Instead of unmasking him, Jesus makes no difference between him and the others, kneels by his couch, takes his feet in His hands, washes and gently dries them. However difficult it is to understand why Jesus chose Judas at the first, there can be no question that throughout His acquaintance with him He had done all that was possible to win him. The kind of treatment Judas had received throughout may be inferred from the treatment he received now. Jesus knew him to be a man of a low type and impenitent, He knew him to be at that very time out of harmony with the little company, false, plotting, meaning to save himself by bringing ruin on the rest. Yet Jesus will not denounce him to the others. His sole weapon is love. Conquests which He cannot achieve with this He will not achieve at all. In the person of Judas the utmost of malignity the world can show is present to Him, and He meets it with kindness. Well may Astié exclaim: "Jesus at the feet of the traitor—what a picture! what lessons for us!"

Shame and astonishment shut the mouths of the disciples, and not a sound broke the stillness of the room but the tinkle and plash of the water in the basin as Jesus went from couch to couch. But the silence was broken when He came to Peter. The deep reverence which the disciples had contracted for Jesus betrays itself in Peter's inability to suffer Him to touch his feet. Peter could not endure that the places of master and servant should thus be reversed. He feels that shrinking and revulsion which we feel when a delicate person or one much above us in station proceeds to do some service from which we ourselves would shrink as beneath us. That Peter should have drawn up his feet, started up on the couch, and exclaimed, "Lord, do you actually propose to wash my feet!" is to his credit, and just what we should have expected of a man who never lacked generous impulses. Our Lord therefore assures him that his scruples will be removed, and that what he could not understand would be shortly explained to him. He treats Peter's scruples very much as He treated the Baptist's when John hesitated about baptizing Him. Let Me, says Jesus, do it now, and I will explain My reason when

I have finished the washing of you all. But this does not satisfy Peter. Out he comes with one of his blunt and hasty speeches: " Lord, Thou shalt never wash my feet!" He knew better than Jesus, that is to say, what should be done. Jesus was mistaken in supposing that any explanation could be given of it. Hasty, self-confident, knowing better than anybody else, Peter once again ran himself into grave fault. The first requirement in a disciple is entire self-surrender. The others had meekly allowed Jesus to wash their feet, cut to the heart with shame as they were, and scarcely able to let their feet lie in His hands; but Peter must show himself of a different mind. His first refusal was readily forgiven as a generous impulse; the second is an obstinate, proud, self-righteous utterance, and was forthwith met by the swift rebuke of Jesus: "If I wash thee not, thou hast no part with Me."

Superficially, these words might have been understood as intimating to Peter that, if he wished to partake of the feast prepared, he must allow Jesus to wash his feet. Unless he was prepared to leave the room and reckon himself an outcast from that company, he must submit to the feet-washing which his friends and fellow-guests had submitted to. There was that in the tone of our Lord which awakened Peter to see how great and painful a rupture this would be. He almost hears in the words a sentence of expulsion pronounced on himself; and as rapidly as he had withdrawn from the touch of Christ, so rapidly does he now run to the opposite extreme and offer his whole body to be washed —"not my feet only, but my hands and my head." If this washing means that we are Thy friends and partners, let me be all washed, for every bit of me is Thine. Here again Peter was swayed by blind impulse, and here again he erred. If he could only have been quiet! If he could only have held his tongue! If only he could have allowed his Lord to manage without his interference and suggestion at every point! But this was precisely what Peter had as yet not learned to do. In after-years he was to learn meekness; he was to learn to submit while others bound him and carried him whither they would; but as yet that was impossible to him. His Lord's plan is never good enough for him; Jesus is never exactly right. What He proposes must always be eked out by Peter's superior wisdom. What gusts of shame must have stormed through Peter's soul when he looked back on this scene! Yet it concerns us rather to admire than to condemn Peter's fervour. How welcome to our Lord as He passed from the cold and treacherous heart of Judas must this burst of enthusiastic devotion have been! "Lord, if washing be any symbol of my being Thine, wash hands and head as well as feet."

Jesus throws a new light upon His action in His reply: "He that is washed, needeth not save to wash his feet, but is clean every whit: and ye are clean, but not all." The words would have more readily disclosed Christ's meaning had they been literally rendered: He that has bathed needeth not save to wash his feet. The daily use of the bath rendered it needless to wash more than the feet, which were soiled with walking from the bath to the supper-chamber. But that Christ had in view as He washed the disciples' feet something more than the mere bodily cleansing and comfort is plain from His remark that they were not all clean. All had enjoyed the feet-washing, but all were not clean. The feet of Judas were as clean as the feet of John or Peter, but his heart was foul. And what

Christ intended when He girt Himself with the towel and took up the pitcher was not merely to wash the soil from their feet, but to wash from their hearts the hard and proud feelings which were so uncongenial to that night of communion and so threatening to His cause. Far more needful to their happiness at the feast than the comfort of cool and clean feet was their restored affection and esteem for one another, and that humility that takes the lowest place. Jesus could very well have eaten with men who were unwashed; but He could not eat with men hating one another, glaring fiercely across the table, declining to answer or to pass what they were asked for, showing in every way malice and bitterness of spirit. He knew that at bottom they were good men; He knew that with one exception they loved Him and one another; He knew that as a whole they were clean, and that this vicious temper in which they at present entered the room was but the soil contracted for the hour. But none the less must it be washed off. *And He did effectually wash it off by washing their feet.* For was there a man among them who, when he saw his Lord and Master stooping at his couch-foot, would not most gladly have changed places with Him? Was there one of them who was not softened and broken down by the action of the Lord? Is it not certain that shame must have cast out pride from every heart; that the feet would be very little thought of, but that the change of feeling would be marked and obvious? From a group of angry, proud, insolent, implacable, resentful men, they were in five minutes changed into a company of humbled, meek, loving disciples of the Lord, each thinking hardly of himself and esteeming others better. They were effectually cleansed from the stain they had contracted, and could enter on the enjoyment of the Last Supper with pure conscience, with restored and increased affection for one another, and with deepened adoration for the marvellous wisdom and all-accomplishing grace of their Master.

Jesus, then, does not mistake present defilement for habitual impurity, nor partial stain for total uncleanness. He knows whom He has chosen. He understands the difference between deep-seated alienation of spirit and the passing mood which for the hour disturbs friendship. He discriminates between Judas and Peter: between the man who has not been in the bath, and the man whose feet are soiled in walking from it; between him who is at heart unmoved and unimpressed by His love, and him who has for a space fallen from the consciousness of it. He does not suppose that because we have sinned this morning we have no real root of grace in us. He knows the heart we bear Him; and if just at present unworthy feelings prevail, He does not misunderstand as men may, and straightway dismiss us from His company. He recognises that our feet need washing, that our present stain must be removed, but not on this account does He think we need to be all washed and have never been right in heart towards Him.

These present stains, then, Christ seeks to remove, that our fellowship with Him may be unembarrassed; and that our heart, restored to humility and tenderness, may be in a state to receive the blessing He would bestow. It is not enough to be once forgiven, to begin the day "clean every whit." No sooner do we take a step in the life of the day than our footfall raises a little puff of dust which does not settle without sullying us. Our temper is ruffled, and words fall from our lips that injure and exasperate. In one way or other stain attaches to our conscience, and we are moved away from cordial and open fellowship with Christ. All this happens to those who are at heart as truly Christ's friends as those first disciples. But we must have these stains washed away even as they had. Humbly we must own them, and humbly accept their forgiveness and rejoice in their removal. As these men had with shame to lay their feet in Christ's hands, so must we. As His hands had to come in contact with the soiled feet of the disciples, so has His moral nature to come in contact with the sins from which He cleanses us. His heart is purer than were His hands, and He shrinks more from contact with moral than with physical pollution; and yet without ceasing we bring Him into contact with such pollution. When we consider what those stains actually are from which we must ask Christ to wash us, we feel tempted to exclaim with Peter, "Lord, Thou shalt never wash my feet!" As these men must have shivered with shame through all their nature, so do we when we see Christ stoop before us to wash away once again the defilement we have contracted; when we lay our feet soiled with the miry and dusty ways of life in His sacred hands; when we see the uncomplaining, unreproachful grace with which He performs for us this lowly and painful office. But only thus are we prepared for communion with Him and with one another. Only by admitting that we need cleansing, and by humbly allowing Him to cleanse us, are we brought into true fellowship with Him. With the humble and contrite spirit which has thrown down all barriers of pride and freely admits His love and rejoices in His holiness does He abide. Whoso sits down at Christ's table must sit down clean; he may not have come clean, even as those first guests were not clean, but he must allow Christ to cleanse him, must honestly suffer Christ to remove from his heart, from his desire and purpose, all that He counts defiling.

But our Lord was not content to let His action speak for itself; He expressly explains (vv. 12-17) the meaning of what He had now done. He meant that they should learn to wash one another's feet, to be humble and ready to be of service to one another even when to serve seemed to compromise their dignity.[1] No disciple of Christ need go far to find feet that need washing, feet that are stained or bleeding with the hard ways that have been trodden. To recover men from the difficulties into which sin or misfortune has brought them—to wipe off some of the soil from men's lives—to make them purer, sweeter, readier to listen to Christ, even unostentatiously to do the small services which each hour calls for—is to follow Him who girt Himself with the slave's apron. As often as we thus condescend we become like Christ. By putting Himself in the servant's place, our Lord has consecrated all service. The disciple who next washed the feet of the rest would feel that he was representing Christ, and would suggest to the minds of the others the action of their Lord; and as often as we lay aside the conventional dignity in which we are clad, and gird ourselves to do what others despise, we feel that we are doing what Christ would do, and are truly representing Him.

---

[1] For the formal Foot-washing by the Lord High Almoner, the Pope, or other officials, see Augustine's *Letters* LV.; Herzog art. *Fusswaschung;* Smith's *Dict. of Christian Antiq.* art. *Maundy Thursday.*

# VII.
*JUDAS.*

"I speak not of you all : I know whom I have chosen : but that the Scripture may be fulfilled, He that eateth My bread lifted up his heel against Me. From henceforth I tell you before it come to pass, that, when it is come to pass, ye may believe that I am He. Verily, verily, I say unto you, He that receiveth whomsoever I send receiveth Me ; and he that receiveth Me receiveth Him that sent Me. When Jesus had thus said, He was troubled in the spirit, and testified, and said, Verily, verily, I say unto you, that one of you shall betray Me. The disciples looked one on another, doubting of whom He spake. There was at the table reclining in Jesus' bosom one of His disciples, whom Jesus loved. Simon Peter therefore beckoneth to him, and saith unto him, Tell us who it is of whom He speaketh. He leaning back, as he was, on Jesus' breast saith unto Him, Lord, who is it ? Jesus therefore answereth, He it is, for whom I shall dip the sop, and give it to him. So when He had dipped the sop, He taketh and giveth it to Judas, the son of Simon Iscariot. And after the sop, then entered Satan into him. Jesus therefore saith unto him, That thou doest, do quickly. Now no man at the table knew for what intent He spake this unto him. For some thought, because Judas had the bag, that Jesus said unto him, Buy what things we have need of for the feast ; or, that he should give something to the poor. He then having received the sop went out straightway ; and it was night."—JOHN xiii. 18-30.

## VII.

### *JUDAS.*

WHEN Jesus had washed the disciples' feet, apparently in dead silence save for the interruption of Peter, He resumed those parts of His dress He had laid aside, and reclined at the table already spread for the supper. As the meal began, and while He was explaining the meaning of His act and the lesson He desired them to draw from it, John, who lay next Him at table, saw that His face did not wear the expression of festal joy, nor even of untroubled composure, but was clouded with deep concern and grief. The reason of this was immediately apparent: already, while washing Peter's feet, He had awakened the attention and excited the consciences of the disciples by hinting that on some one of them at least, if not on more, uncleansed guilt still lay, even though all partook in the symbolic washing. And now in His explanation of the foot-washing He repeats this limitation and warning, and also points at the precise nature of the guilt, though not yet singling out the guilty person. "I speak not of you all; I know whom I have chosen; I have not been deceived: but it was necessary that this part of God's purpose be fulfilled, and that this Scripture, 'He that eateth bread with Me, hath lifted up his heel against Me,' receive accomplishment in Me."

It was impossible that Jesus should undisturbedly eat out of the same dish with the man whom He knew to have already sold Him to the priests; it were unfair to the other disciples and a violence to His own feelings to allow such a man any longer to remain in their company. But our Lord does not name the traitor and denounce him; he singles him out and sends him from the table on his hateful mission by a process that left every man at the table unaware on what errand he was despatched. In this process there were three steps. First of all, our Lord indicated that among the disciples there was a traitor. With dismay these true-hearted men hear the firmly pronounced statement "one of *you* shall betray Me" (ver. 21). All of them, as another Evangelist informs us, were exceeding sorrowful, and looked on one another in bewilderment; and unable to detect the conscious look of guilt in the face of any of their companions, or to recall any circumstance which might fix even suspicion on any of them, each, conscious of the deep, unfathomed capacity for evil in his own heart, can but frankly ask of the Master, "Lord, is it I?" It is a question that at once proves their consciousness of actual innocence and possible guilt. It was a kindness in the Lord to give these genuine men, who were so shortly to go through trial for His sake, an opportunity of discovering how much they loved Him and how closely knit their hearts had really become to Him. This question of theirs expressed the deep pain and shame that the very thought of the possibility of their being false to Him gave them. They must at all hazards be cleared of this charge. And from this shock of the very idea of being untrue their hearts recoiled towards Him with an enthusiastic tenderness that made this moment possibly as moving a passage as any that occurred that eventful night. But there was one of them that did not join in the question "Lord, is it I?"—else must not our Lord have broken silence? The Twelve are still left in doubt, none noticing in the eagerness of questioning who has not asked, each only glad to know he himself is not charged.

The second step in the process is recorded in the 26th chapter of Matthew, where we read that, when the disciples asked "Lord, is it I?" Jesus answered, "He that dippeth his hand with Me in the dish, the same shall betray Me." It was a large company, and there were necessarily several dishes on the table, so that probably there were three others using the same dish as our Lord: John we know was next Him; Peter was near enough to John to make signs and whisper to him; Judas was also close to Jesus, a position which he either always occupied as treasurer and purveyor of the company, or into which he thrust himself this evening with the purpose of more effectually screening himself from suspicion. The circle of suspicion is thus narrowed to the one or two who were not only so intimate as to be eating at the same table, but as to be dipping in the same dish.

The third step in the process of discovery went on almost simultaneously with this. The impatient Peter, who had himself so often unwittingly given offence to his Master, is resolved to find out definitely who is pointed at, and yet dare not say to Christ "Who is it?" He beckons therefore to John to ask Jesus privately, as he lay next to Jesus. John leans a little back towards Jesus and puts in a whisper the definite question "Who is it?" and Jesus in the ear of the beloved disciple whispers the reply, "He it is to whom

I shall give a sop when I have dipped it." And when He had dipped the sop, He gave it to Judas Iscariot. This reveals to John, but to no one else, who the traitor was, for the giving of the sop was no more at that table than the handing of a plate or the offer of any article of food is at any table. John alone knew the significance of it. But Judas had already taken alarm at the narrowing of the circle of suspicion, and had possibly for the moment ceased dipping in the same dish with Jesus, lest he should be identified with the traitor. Jesus therefore dips for him and offers him the sop which he will not himself take, and the look that accompanies the act, as well as the act itself, shows Judas that his treachery is discovered. He therefore mechanically takes up in a somewhat colder form the question of the rest, and says, " Master, is it I ? " His fear subdues his voice to a whisper, heard only by John and the Lord; and the answer, " Thou hast said. That thou doest, do quickly," is equally unobserved by the rest. Judas need fear no violence at their hands; John alone knows the meaning of his abrupt rising and hurrying from the room, and John sees that Jesus wishes him to go unobserved. The rest, therefore, thought only that Judas was going out to make some final purchases that had been forgotten, or to care for the poor in this season of festivity. But John saw differently. "The traitor," he says, "went immediately out; and it was night." As his ill-omened, stealthy figure glided from the chamber, the sudden night of the Eastern twilightless sunset had fallen on the company; sadness, silence, and gloom fell upon John's spirit; the hour of darkness had at length fallen in the very midst of this quiet feast.

This sin of Judas presents us with one of the most

perplexed problems of life and character that the strange circumstances of this world have ever produced. Let us first of all look at the connection of this betrayal with the life of Christ, and then consider the phase of character exhibited in Judas. In connection with the life of Christ the difficulty is to understand why the death of Christ was to be brought about in this particular way of treachery among His own followers. It may be said that it came to pass " that Scripture might be fulfilled," that this special prediction in the 41st Psalm might be fulfilled. But why was such a prediction made? It was of course the event which determined the prediction, not the prediction which determined the event. Was it, then, an accident that Jesus should be handed over to the authorities in this particular way? Or was there any significance in it, that justifies its being made so prominent in the narrative? Certainly if our Lord was to be brought into contact with the most painful form of sin, He must have experience of treachery. He had known the sorrow that death brings to the survivors; He had known the pain and disappointment of being resisted by stupid, obstinate, bad-hearted men; but if He was to know the utmost of misery which man can inflict upon man, He must be brought into contact with one who could accept His love, eat His bread, press His hand with assurance of fidelity, and then sell Him.

When we endeavour to set before our minds a clear idea of the character of Judas, and to understand how such a character could be developed, we have to acknowledge that we could desire a few more facts in order to certify us of what we can now only conjecture. Obviously we must start from the idea that with extraordinary capacity for wickedness Judas had also more than ordinary leanings to what was good. He was an Apostle, and had, we must suppose, been called to that office by Christ under the impression that he possessed gifts which would make him very serviceable to the Christian community. He was himself so impressed with Christ as to follow Him: making those pecuniary sacrifices of which Peter boastfully spoke, and which must have been specially sore to Judas. It is possible, indeed, that he may have followed Jesus as a speculation, hoping to receive wealth and honour in the new kingdom; but this motive mingled with the attachment to Christ's person which all the Apostles had, and mingles in a different form with the discipleship of all Christians. With this motive, therefore, there probably mingled in the mind of Judas a desire to be with One who could shield him from evil influences; he judged that with Jesus he would find continual aid against his weaker nature. Possibly he wished by one bold abandonment of the world to get rid for ever of his covetousness. That Judas was trusted by the other Apostles is manifest from the fact that to him they committed their common fund,—not to John, whose dreamy and abstracted nature ill fitted him for minute practical affairs; not to Peter, whose impulsive nature might often have landed the little company in difficulties; not even to Matthew, accustomed as he was to accounts; but to Judas, who had the economical habits, the aptitude for finance, the love of bargaining, which regularly go hand in hand with the love of money. This practical faculty for finance and for affairs generally might, if rightly guided, have become a most serviceable element in the Apostolate, and might have enabled Judas more successfully than any other of the Apostles to mediate between the Church and the world. That Judas in all other respects conducted himself circumspectly is proved by the fact that, though other Apostles incurred the displeasure of Christ and were rebuked by Him, Judas committed no glaring fault till this last week. Even to the end he was unsuspected by his fellow-Apostles; and to the end he had an active conscience. His last act, were it not so awful, would inspire us with something like respect for him: he is overwhelmed with remorse and shame; his sense of guilt is stronger even than the love of money that had hitherto been his strongest passion: he judges himself fairly, sees what he has become, and goes to his own place; recognises as not every man does recognise what is his fit habitation, and goes to it.

But this man, with his good impulses, his resolute will, his enlightened conscience, his favouring circumstances, his frequent feelings of affection towards Christ and desire to serve Him, committed a crime so unparalleled in wickedness that men practically make very little attempt to estimate it or measure it with sins of their own. Commonly we think of it as a special, exceptional wickedness—not so much the natural product of a heart like our own and what may be reproduced by ourselves, as the work of Satan using a man as his scarcely responsible tool to effect a purpose which needs never again to be effected.

If we ask what precisely it was in the crime of Judas that makes us so abhor it, manifestly its most hateful ingredient was its treachery. "It was not an enemy that reproached me; then I could have borne it; but it was thou, a man mine equal, my guide, and mine acquaintance." Cæsar defended himself till the dagger of a friend pierced him; then in indignant grief he covered his head with his mantle and accepted his fate. You can forgive the open blow of a declared enemy against whom you are on your guard; but the man that lives with you on terms of the greatest intimacy for years, so that he learns your ways and habits, the state of your affairs and your past history—the man whom you so confide in and like that you communicate to him freely much that you keep hidden from others, and who, while still professing friendship, uses the information he has gained to blacken your character and ruin your peace, to injure your family or damage your business,—this man, you know, has much to repent of. So one can forgive the Pharisees who knew not what they did, and were throughout the declared opponents of Christ; but Judas attached himself to Christ, knew that His life was one of unmixed benevolence, was conscious that Christ would have given up anything to serve him, felt moved and proud from time to time by the fact that Christ loved him, and yet at the last used all these privileges of friendship against his Friend.

And Judas did not scruple to use this power that only the love of Jesus could have given him, to betray Him to men whom he knew to be unscrupulous and resolved to destroy Him. The garden where the Lord prayed for His enemies was not sacred to Judas; the cheek that a seraph would blush to kiss, and to salute which was the beginning of joy eternal to the devout disciple, was mere common clay to this man into whom Satan had entered. The crime of Judas is invested with a horror altogether its own by the fact that this Person whom he betrayed was the Son of God and the Saviour of the world, the Best-beloved of God and every man's Friend. The greatest blessing that God had ever given to earth Judas was forward to reject: not altogether unaware of the majesty of Christ, Judas presumed to use Him in a little money-making scheme of his own.

The best use that Judas could think of putting Jesus to, the best use he could make of *Him* whom all angels worship, was to sell Him for £5.[1] He could get nothing more out of Christ than that. After three years' acquaintanceship and observation of the various ways in which Christ could bless people, this was all he could get from Him. And there are still such men: men for whom there is nothing in Christ; men who can find nothing in Him that they sincerely care for; men who, though calling themselves His followers, would, if truth were told, be better content and feel they had more substantial profit if they could turn Him into money.

So difficult is it to comprehend how any man who had lived as the friend of Jesus could find it in his heart to betray Him, should resist the touching expressions of love that were shown him, and brave the awful warning uttered at the supper-table—so difficult is it to suppose that any man, however infatuated, would so deliberately sell his soul for £5, that a theory has been started to explain the crime by mitigating its guilt. It has been supposed that when he delivered up his Master into the hands of the chief priests he expected that our Lord would save Himself by a miracle. He knew that Jesus meant to proclaim a kingdom; he had been waiting for three years now, eagerly expecting that this proclamation and its accompanying gains would arrive. Yet he feared the opportunity was once more passing: Jesus had been brought into the city in triumph, but seemed indisposed to make use of this

---

[1] More exactly, £3 10 8, the legal value of a slave.

popular excitement for any temporal advantage. Judas was weary of this inactivity: might he not himself bring matters to a crisis by giving Jesus into the hands of His enemies, and thus forcing Him to reveal His real power and assert by miracle His kingship? In corroboration of this theory, it is said that it is certain that Judas did not expect Jesus to be condemned; for when he saw that he was condemned he repented of his act.

This seems a shallow view to take of Judas' remorse, and a feeble ground on which to build such a theory. A crime seems one thing before, another after, its commission. The murderer expects and wishes to kill his victim, but how often is he seized with an agony of remorse as soon as the blow is struck? Before we sin, it is the gain we see; after we sin, the guilt. It is impossible to construe the act of Judas into a mistaken act of friendship or impatience; the terms in which he is spoken of in Scripture forbid this idea; and one cannot suppose that a keen-sighted man like Judas could expect that, even supposing he did force our Lord to proclaim Himself, his own share in the business would be rewarded. He could not suppose this after the terrible denunciation and explicit statement that still rang in his ears when he hanged himself: "The Son of man goeth as it is written of Him: but woe unto that man by whom the Son of man is betrayed! it had been good for that man if he had not been born."

We must then abide by the more commonplace view of this crime. The only mitigating circumstance that can be admitted is, that possibly among the many perplexed thoughts entertained by Judas he may have supposed that Jesus would be acquitted, or would at least not be punished with death. Still, this being admitted, the fact remains that he cared so little for the love of Christ, and regarded so little the good He was doing, and had so little common honour in him, that he sold his Master to His deadly enemies. And this monstrous wickedness is to be accounted for mainly by his love of money. Naturally covetous, he fed his evil disposition during those years he carried the bag for the disciples: while the rest are taken up with more spiritual matters, he gives more of his thought than is needful to the matter of collecting as much as possible; he counts it his special province to protect himself and the others against all "the probable emergencies and changes of life." This he does, regardless of the frequent admonitions he hears from the Lord addressed to others; and as he finds excuses for his own avarice in the face of these admonitions, and hardens himself against the better impulses that are stirred within him by the words and presence of Christ, his covetousness roots itself deeper and deeper in his soul. Add to this, that now he was a disappointed man: the other disciples, finding that the kingdom of Christ was to be spiritual, were pure and high-minded enough to see that their disappointment was their great gain. The love of Christ had transformed them, and to be like Him was enough for them; but Judas still clung to the idea of earthly grandeur and wealth, and finding Christ was not to give him these he was soured and embittered. He saw that now, since that scene at Bethany the week before, his covetousness and earthliness would be resisted and would also betray him. He felt that he could no longer endure this poverty-stricken life, and had some rage at himself and at Christ that he had been inveigled into it by what he might be pleased to say to himself were false pretences. His self-restraint, he felt, was breaking down; his covetousness was getting the better of him; he felt that he must break with Christ and His followers; but in doing so he would at once win what he had lost during these years of poverty, and also revenge himself on those who had kept him poor, and finally would justify his own conduct in deserting this society by exploding it and causing it to cease from among men.

The sin of Judas, then, first of all teaches us the great power and danger of the love of money. The mere thirty pieces of silver would not have been enough to tempt Judas to commit so dastardly and black a crime; but he was now an embittered and desperate man, and he had become so by allowing money to be all in all to him for these last years of his life. For the danger of this passion consists very much in this—that it infallibly eats out of the soul every generous emotion and high aim: it is the failing of a sordid nature—a little, mean, earthly nature—a failing which, like all others, may be extirpated through God's grace, but which is notoriously difficult to extirpate, and which notoriously is accompanied by or produces other features of character which are among the most repulsive one meets. The love of money is also dangerous, because it can be so easily gratified; all that we do in the world day by day is in the case of most of us connected with money, so that we have continual and not only occasional opportunity of sinning if we be inclined to the sin. Other passions are appealed to only now and again, but our employments touch this passion at all points. It leaves no long intervals, as other passions do, for repentance and amendment; but steadily, constantly, little by little, increases in force. Judas had his fingers in the bag all day; it was under his pillow and he dreamt upon it all night; and it was this that accelerated his ruin. And by this constant appeal it is sure to succeed at one time or other, if we be open to it. Judas could not suppose that his quiet self-aggrandisement by pilfering little coins from the bag could ever bring him to commit such a crime against his Lord: so may every covetous person fancy that his sin is one that is his own business, and will not damage his religious profession and ruin his soul as some wild lust or reckless infidelity would do. But Judas and those who sin with him in making continually little gains to which they have no right are wrong in supposing their sin is less dangerous; and for this reason—that covetousness is more a sin of the *will* than sins of the flesh or of a passionate nature; there is more choice in it; it is more the sin of the whole man unresisting; and therefore it, above all others, is called idolatry—it, above all others, proves that the man is in his heart choosing the world and not God. Therefore it is that even our Lord Himself spoke almost despairingly, certainly quite differently, of covetous men in comparison with other sinners.

Disappointment in Christ is not an unknown thing among ourselves. Men still profess to be Christians who are so only in the degree in which Judas was. They expect *some* good from Christ, but not all. They attach themselves to Christ in a loose, conventional way, expecting that, though they are Christians, they need not lose anything by their Christianity, nor make any great efforts or sacrifices. They retain command of their own life, and are prepared to go with Christ only so far as they find it agreeable or inviting. The eye of an observer may not be able to distinguish them from Christ's true followers; but the distinction is present and is radical. They are seeking to use Christ, and are not willing to be used by Him. They are not wholly and heartily His, but merely seek to derive some influences from Him. The result is that they one day find that, through all their religious profession and apparent Christian life, their characteristic sin has actually been gaining strength. And finding this, they turn upon Christ with disappointment and rage in their hearts, because they become aware that they have lost both this world and the next—have lost many pleasures and gains they might have enjoyed, and yet have gained no spiritual attainment. They find that the reward of double-mindedness is the most absolute perdition, that both Christ and the world, to be made anything of, require the whole man, and that he who tries to get the good of both gets the good of neither. And when a man awakes to see that this is the result of his Christian profession, there is no deadliness of hatred to which the bitter disappointment of his soul will not carry him. He has himself been a dupe, and he calls Christ an impostor. He know himself to be damned, and he says there is no salvation in Christ.

But to this disastrous issue *any* cherished sin may also in its own way lead; for the more comprehensive lesson which this sin of Judas brings with it is the rapidity of sin's growth and the enormous proportions it attains when the sinner is sinning against light, when he is in circumstances conducive to holiness and still sins. To discover the wickedest of men, to see the utmost of human guilt, we must look, not among the heathen, but among those who know God; not among the profligate, dissolute, abandoned classes of society, but among the Apostles. The good that was in Judas led him to join Christ, and kept him associated with Christ for some years; but the devil of covetousness that was cast out for a while returned and brought with him seven devils worse than himself. There was everything in his position to win him to unworldliness: the men he lived with cared not one whit for comforts or anything that money could buy; but instead of catching their spirit he took advantage of their carelessness. He was in a public position, liable to detection; but this, instead of making him honest perforce, made him only the more crafty and studiedly hypocritical. The solemn warnings of Christ, so far from intimidating him, only made him more skilful in evading all good influence, and made the road to hell easier. The position he enjoyed, and by which he might have been for ever enrolled among the foremost of mankind, one of the twelve foundations of the eternal city, he so skilfully misused that the greatest sinner feels glad that he has yet not been left to commit the sin of Judas. Had Judas not followed Christ he could never have attained the pinnacle of infamy on which he now for ever stands. In all probability he would have passed his days as a small trader with false weights in the little town of Kerioth, or, at the worst, might have developed into an extortionous publican, and have passed into oblivion with the thousands of unjust men who have died and been at last forced to let go the money that should long ago have belonged to others. Or had Judas followed Christ truly, then there lay before him the noblest of all lives, the most blessed of destinies. But he followed Christ and yet took his sin with him: and thence his ruin.

# VIII.
## JESUS ANNOUNCES HIS DEPARTURE.

"When therefore he was gone out, Jesus saith, Now is the Son of man glorified, and God is glorified in Him; and God shall glorify Him in Himself, and straightway shall He glorify Him. Little children, yet a little while I am with you. Ye shall seek Me: and as I said unto the Jews, Whither I go, ye cannot come; so now I say unto you. A new commandment I give unto you, that ye love one another; even as I have loved you, that ye also love one another. By this shall all men know that ye are My disciples, if ye have love one to another. Simon Peter saith unto Him, Lord, whither goest Thou? Jesus answered, Whither I go, thou canst not follow Me now; but thou shalt follow afterwards. Peter saith unto Him, Lord, why cannot I follow Thee even now? I will lay down my life for Thee. Jesus answereth, Wilt thou lay down thy life for Me? Verily, verily, I say unto thee, The cock shall not crow, till thou hast denied Me thrice. Let not your heart be troubled: ye believe in God, believe also in Me. In My Father's house are many mansions; if it were not so, I would have told you; for I go to prepare a place for you. And if I go and prepare a place for you, I come again, and will receive you unto Myself; that where I am, there ye may be also. And whither I go, ye know the way."—JOHN xiii. 31—xiv. 4.

# VIII.

## JESUS ANNOUNCES HIS DEPARTURE.

WHEN Judas glided out of the supper-room on his terrible mission, a weight seemed to be lifted from the spirit of Jesus. The words which fell from Him, however, indicated that He not only felt the relief of being rid of a disturbing element in the company, but that He recognised that a crisis in His own career had been reached and successfully passed through. "Now is the Son of man glorified, and God is glorified in Him." In sending Judas forth He had in point of fact delivered Himself to death. He had taken the step which cannot be withdrawn, and He is conscious of taking it in fulfilment of the will of the Father. The conflict in His own mind is revealed only by the decision of the victory. No man in soundness of body and of mind can voluntarily give himself to die without seeing clearly other possibilities, and without feeling it to be a hard and painful thing to relinquish life. Jesus had made up His mind. His death is the beginning of His glorification. In choosing the cross He chooses the crown. "The Son of man is glorified" in His perfect self-sacrifice that wins all men to Him; and God is glorified in Him because this sacrifice is a tribute at once to the justice and the love of God. The Cross reveals God as nothing else does.

Not only has this decision glorified the Son of man and God through Him and in Him, but as a consequence "God will glorify" the Son of man "in Himself." He will lift Him to participation in the Divine glory. It was well that the disciples should know that this would "straightway" result from all that their Master was now to pass through; that the perfect sympathy with the Father's will which He was now showing would be rewarded by permanent participation in the authority of God. It must be through such an one as their Lord, who is absolutely at one with God, that God fulfils His purpose towards men. By this life and death of perfect obedience, of absolute devotedness to God and man, Christ necessarily wins dominion over human affairs and exercises a determining influence on all that is to be. In all that Christ did upon earth God was glorified; His holiness, His fatherly love were manifested to men: in all that God now does upon earth Christ will be glorified; the uniqueness and power of His life will become more manifest, the supremacy of His Spirit be more and more apparent.

This glorification was not the far-off result of the impending sacrifice. It was to date from the present hour and to begin in the sacrifice. God will glorify Him "straightway." "Yet *a little while*" was He to be with His disciples. Therefore does He tenderly address them, recognising their incompetence, their inability to stand alone, as "little children"; and in view of the exhibition of bad feeling, and even of treachery, which the Twelve had at that very hour given, His commandment, "Love one another," comes with a tenfold significance. I am leaving you, He says: put away, then, all heart-burnings and jealousies;

cling together; do not let quarrels and envyings divide you. This was to be their safeguard when He left them and went where they could not come. "A new commandment I give unto you, That ye love one another; as I have loved you, that ye also love one another. By this shall all men know that ye are My disciples, if ye have love one to another."

The commandment to love our neighbour as ourselves was no new commandment. But to love "as I have loved you" was so new that its practice was enough to identify a man as a disciple of Christ. The manner and the measure of the love that is possible and that is commanded could not even be understood until Christ's love was revealed. But probably what Jesus had even more directly in view was the love that was to bind His followers together[1] and make them one solid body. It was on their mutual attachment that the very existence of the Christian Church depended; and this love of men to one another springing out of the love of Christ for them, and because of their acknowledgment and love of a common Lord, was a new thing in the world. The bond to Christ proved itself stronger than all other ties, and those who cherished a common love to Him were drawn to one another more closely than even to blood relations. In fact, Christ, by His love for men, has created a new bond, and that the strongest by which men can be bound to one another. As the Christian Church is a new institution upon earth, so is the principle which forms it a new principle. The principle has, indeed, too often been hidden from sight, if not smothered, by the institution; too little has love been regarded as the one

---

[1] "That ye love *one another*" is the twice-expressed commandment.

thing by which the disciple of Christ is to be recognised, the one note of the true Church. But that this form of love was a new thing upon earth is apparent.[1]

Tenderly as Jesus made the announcement of His departure, it filled the minds of the disciples with consternation. Even the buoyant and hardy Peter felt for the moment staggered by the intelligence, and still more by the announcement that he was not able to accompany his Lord. He was assured that one day he should follow Him, but at present this was impossible. This, Peter considered a reflection upon his courage and fidelity; and although his headlong self-confidence had only a few minutes before been so severely rebuked, he exclaims, "Lord, why cannot I follow Thee now? I will lay down my life for Thy sake." This was the true expression of Peter's present feeling, and he was allowed in the end to give proof that these vehement words were not mere bluster. But as yet he had not at all apprehended the separateness of his Lord and the uniqueness of His work. He did not know precisely what Jesus alluded to, but he thought a strong arm would not be out of place in any conflict that was coming. The offers which even true fidelity makes are often only additional hindrances to our Lord's purposes, and additional burdens for Him to bear. On Himself alone must He depend. No

---

[1] "Any Church that professes to be *the* Church of Christ cannot be that Church. The true Church refuses to be circumscribed or parted by any denominational wall. It knows that Christ is repudiated when His people are repudiated. Not even a Biblical creed can yield satisfactory evidence that a specified Church is the true Church. True Christians are those who love one another across denominational differences, and exhibit the spirit of Him who gave Himself to death upon the cross that His murderers might live."

man can counsel Him, and none can aid save by first receiving from Him His own spirit.

Peter thus rebuked falls into unwonted silence, and takes no further part in the conversation. The rest, knowing that Peter has more courage than any of them, fear that if he is thus to fall it cannot be hopeful for themselves. They feel that if they are left without Jesus they have no strength to make head against the rulers, no skill in argument such as made Jesus victorious when assailed by the scribes, no popular eloquence which might enable them to win the people. Eleven more helpless men could not well be. "Sheep without a shepherd" was not too strong an expression to depict their weakness and want of influence, their incompetence to effect anything, their inability even to keep together. Christ was their bond of union and the strength of each of them. It was to be with Him that they had left all. And in forsaking all—father and mother, wife and children, home and kindred and calling—they had found in Christ that hundredfold more even in this life which He had promised. He had so won their hearts, there was about Him something so fascinating, that they felt no loss when they enjoyed His presence, and feared no danger in which He was their leader. They had perhaps not thought very definitely of their future; they felt so confident in Jesus that they were content to let Him bring in His kingdom as He pleased; they were so charmed with the novelty of their life as His disciples, with the great ideas that dropped from His lips, with the wonderful works He did, with the new light He shed upon all the personages and institutions of the world, that they were satisfied to leave their hope undefined. But all this satisfaction and secret assurance of hope depended on Christ. As yet He had not given to *them* anything which could enable them to make any mark upon the world. They were still very ignorant, so that any lawyer could entangle and puzzle them. They had not received from Christ any influential position in society from which they could sway men. There were no great visible institutions with which they could identify themselves and so become conspicuous.

It was with dismay, therefore, that they heard that He was going where they could not accompany Him. A cloud of gloomy foreboding gathered on their faces as they lay round the table and fixed their eyes on Him as on one whose words they would interpret differently if they could. Their anxious looks are not disregarded. "Let not your heart be troubled," He says: "believe in God, and in Me, too, believe." Do not give way to disturbing thoughts; do not suppose that only failure, disgrace, helplessness, and calamity await you. Trust God. In this, as in all matters, He is guiding and ruling and working His own good ends through all present evil. Trust Him, even when you cannot penetrate the darkness. It is His part to bring you successfully through; it is your part to follow where He leads. Do not question and debate and vex your soul, but leave all to Him. "Why art thou cast down, O my soul? and why art thou disquieted within me? Hope thou in God; for I shall yet praise Him who is the health of my countenance and my God."

"And in Me, too, trust." I would not leave you had I not a purpose to serve. It is not to secure My own safety or happiness I go. It is not to occupy the sole available room in My Father's house. There are many rooms there, and I go to prepare a place for you.

Trust Me. In order that they may fully understand the reasonableness of His departure He assures them, first of all, that it has a purpose. The parent mourns over the son who in mere waywardness leaves his home and his occupation; but with very different feelings does he follow one who has come to see that the greater good of the family requires that he should go, and who has carefully ascertained where and how he can best serve those he leaves behind. To such an absence men can reconcile themselves. The parting is bitter, but the greater good to be gained by it enables them to approve its reasonableness and to submit. And what our Lord says to His disciples is virtually this: I have not wearied of earth and tired of your company, neither do I go because I must. I could escape Judas and the Jews. But I have a purpose which requires that I should go. You have not found Me impulsive, neither am I now acting without good reason. Could I be of more use to you by staying, I would stay.

This is a new kind of assertion to be made by human lips: "I am going into the other world to effect a a purpose." Often the sense of duty has been so strong in men that they have left this world without a murmur. But no one has felt so clear about what lies beyond, or has been so confident of his own power to effect any change for the better in the other world, that he has left this for a sphere of greater usefulness. This is what Christ does.

But He also explains what His purpose is: "In My Father's house are many mansions. I go to prepare a place for you." The Father's house was a new figure for heaven. The idea of God's house was, however, familiar to the Jews. But in the Temple the freedom and familiarity which we associate with home were absent. It was only when One came who felt that His real home was in God that the Temple could be called "the Father's house." Yet there is nothing that the heart of man more importunately craves than the freedom and ease which this name implies. To live unafraid of God, not shrinking from Him, but so truly at one with Him that we live as one household brightened by His presence—this is the thirst for God which is one day felt in every heart. And on His part God has many mansions in His house, proclaiming that He desires to have us at home with Him; that He wishes us to know and trust Him, not to change our countenances when we meet Him at a corner, save by an added brightness of joy. And this is what we have to look forward to—that after all our coldness and distrust have been removed and our hearts thawed by His presence, we shall live in the constant enjoyment of a Father's love, feeling ourselves more truly at home with Him than with any one else, delighting in the perfectness of His sympathy and the abundance of His provision.

Into this intimacy with God, this freedom of the universe, this sense that "all things are ours" because we are His, this entirely attractive heaven, we are to be introduced by Christ. "I go to prepare a place for you." It is He who has transformed the darkness of the grave into the bright gateway of the Father's home, where all His children are to find eternal rest and everlasting joy. As an old writer says, "Christ is the quartermaster who provides quarters for all who follow Him." He has gone on before to make ready for those whom He has summoned to come after Him.

If we ask why it was needful that Christ should

go forward thus, and what precisely He had to do in the way of preparation, the question may be answered in different ways. These disciples in after-years compared Christ's passing into the Father's presence to the high priest's entrance within the veil to present the blood of sprinkling and to make intercession. But in the language of Christ there is no hint that such thoughts were in His mind. It is the Father's house that is in His mind, the eternal home of men; and He sees the Father welcoming Him as the leader of many brethren, and with gladness in His heart going from room to room, always adding some new touch for the comfort and surprise of the eagerly expected children. If God, like a grieved and indignant father whose sons have preferred other company to his, had dismantled and locked the rooms that once were ours, Christ has made our peace, and has given to the yearning heart of the Father opportunity to open these rooms once more and deck them for our home-coming. With the words of Christ there enters the spirit a conviction that when we pass out of this life we shall find ourselves as much fuller of life and deeper in joy as we are nearer to God, the source of all life and joy; and that when we come to the gates of God's dwelling it will not be as the vagabond and beggar unknown to the household and who can give no good account of himself, but as the child whose room is ready for him, whose coming is expected and prepared for, and who has indeed been sent for.

This of itself is enough to give us hopeful thoughts of the future state. Christ is busied in preparing for us what will give us satisfaction and joy. When we expect a guest we love and have written for, we take pleasure in preparing for his reception,—we hang in his room the picture he likes; if he is infirm, we wheel in the easiest chair; we gather the flowers he admires and set them on his table; we go back and back to see if nothing else will suggest itself to us, so that when he comes he may have entire satisfaction. This is enough for us to know—that Christ is similarly occupied. He knows our tastes, our capabilities, our attainments, and he has identified a place as ours and holds it for us. What the joys and the activities and occupations of the future shall be we do not know. With the body we shall lay aside many of our appetites and tastes and proclivities, and what has here seemed necessary to our comfort will at once become indifferent. We shall not be able to desire the pleasures that now allure and draw us. The need of shelter, of retirement, of food, of comfort, will disappear with the body; and what the joys and the requirements of a spiritual body will be we do not know. But we do know that at home with God the fullest life that man can live will certainly be ours.

It is a touching evidence of Christ's truthfulness and fidelity to His people that is given in the words, " If it were not so, I would have told you "—that is to say, if it had not been possible for you to follow Me into the Father's presence and find a favourable reception there, I would have told you this long ago. I would not have taught you to love Me, only to have given you the grief of separation. I would not have encouraged you to hope for what I was not sure you are to receive. He had all along seen how the minds of the disciples were working; He had seen that by being admitted to familiarity with Him they had learnt to expect God's eternal favour; and had this been a deceitful expectation He would have undeceived them. So it is with

Him still. The hopes His word begets are not vain These dreams of glory that pass before the spirit that listens to Christ and thinks of Him are to be realised. If it were not so, He would have told us. We ourselves feel that we are scarcely acting an honest part when we allow persons to entertain false hopes, even when these hopes help to comfort and support them, as in the case of persons suffering from disease. So our Lord does not beget hopes He cannot satisfy. If there were still difficulties in the way of our eternal happiness, He would have told us of these. If there were any reason to despair, He Himself would have been the first to tell us to despair. If eternity were to be a blank to us, if God were inaccessible, if the idea of a perfect state awaiting us were mere talk, He would have told us so.

Neither will the Lord leave His disciples to find their own way to the Father's home: "If I go and prepare a place for you, I will come again, and receive you unto Myself; that where I am, there ye may be also." Present separation was but the first step towards abiding union. And as each disciple was summoned to follow Christ in death, he recognised that this was the summons, not of an earthly power, but of his Lord; he recognised that to him the Lord's promise was being kept, and that he was being taken into eternal union with Jesus Christ. From many all the pain and darkness of death have been taken away by this assurance. They have accepted death as the needful transition from a state in which much hinders fellowship with Christ to a state in which that fellowship is all in all.

## IX.

*THE WAY, THE TRUTH, AND THE LIFE.*

"Thomas saith unto Him, Lord, we know not whither Thou goest; how know we the way? Jesus saith unto him, I am the Way, and the Truth, and the Life: no one cometh unto the Father, but by Me. If ye had known Me, ye would have known My Father also: from henceforth ye know Him, and have seen Him."—JOHN xiv. 5-7.

## IX.

### THE WAY, THE TRUTH, AND THE LIFE.

IT surprises us to find that words which have become familiar and most intelligible to us should have been to the Apostles obscure and puzzling. Apparently they were not yet persuaded that their Master was shortly to die; and, accordingly, when He spoke of going to His Father's house, it did not occur to them that He meant passing into the spiritual world. His assuring words, "Where I am, there ye shall be also," therefore fell short. And when He sees their bewilderment written on their faces, He tentatively, half interrogatively, adds, "And whither I go ye know, and the way ye know."[1] Unless they knew where He was going, there was less consolation even in the promise that He would come for them after He had gone and prepared a place for them. And when He thus challenges them candidly to say whether they understood where He was going, and where He would one day take them also, Thomas, always the mouthpiece for the despondency of the Twelve, at once replies, "Lord, we know not whither Thou goest; and how can we know the way?"

This interruption by Thomas gives occasion to the

---

[1] Or, "And whither I go ye know the way."

great declaration, "I am the Way, and the Truth, and the Life: no man cometh unto the Father, but by Me." It is, then, to the Father that Christ is the Way. And He is the Way by being the Truth and the Life. We must first, then, consider in what sense He is the Truth and the Life.

I. I am the Truth. Were these words merely equivalent to "I speak the truth," it would be much to know this of One who tells us things of so measureless a consequence to ourselves. The faith of the disciples was being strained by what He had just been saying to them. Here was a man in most respects like themselves: a man who got hungry and sleepy, a man who was to be arrested and executed by the rulers, assuring them that He was going to prepare for them everlasting habitations, and that He would return to take them to these habitations. He saw that they found it hard to believe this. Who does not find it hard to believe all our Lord tells us of our future? Think how much we trust simply to His word. If He is not true, then the whole of Christendom has framed its life on a false issue, and is met at death by blank disappointment. Christ has aroused in our minds by His promises and statements a group of ideas and expectations which nothing but His word could have persuaded us to entertain. Nothing is more remarkable about our Lord than the calmness and assurance with which He utters the most astounding statements. The ablest and most enlightened men have their hesitations, their periods of agonising doubt, their suspense of judgment, their laboured inquiries, their mental conflicts. With Jesus there is nothing of this. From first to last He sees with perfect clearness to the utmost bound of human thought, knows with absolute certainty whatever is essential for us to know. His is not the assurance of ignorance, nor is it the dogmatism of traditional teaching, nor the evasive assurance of a superficial and reckless mind. It is plainly the assurance of One who stands in the full noon of truth and speaks what He knows.

But in His endeavours to gain the confidence of men there is discernible no anger at their incredulity. Again and again He brings forward reasons why His word should be believed. He appeals to their knowledge of His candour : " If it were not so, I would have told you." It was the *truth* He came into the world to bear witness to. Lies enough were current already. He came to be the Light of the world, to dispel the darkness and bring men into the very truth of things. But with all His impressiveness of asseveration there is no anger, scarcely even wonder that men did not believe, because He saw as plainly as we see that to venture our eternal hope on His word is not easy. And yet He answered promptly and with authority the questions which have employed the lifetime of many and baffled them in the end. He answered them as if they were the very alphabet of knowledge. These alarmed and perturbed disciples ask Him : " Is there a life beyond ? is there another side of death ? " " Yes," He says, " through death I go to the Father." " Is there," they ask, " for us also a life beyond ? shall such creatures as we find sufficient and suitable habitation and welcome when we pass from this warm, well-known world ? " " In My Father's house," He says, " are many mansions." Confronted with the problems that most deeply exercise the human spirit, He without faltering pronounces upon them. For every question which our most anxious and trying experiences dictate

He has the ready and sufficient answer. "He is the Truth."

But more than this is contained in His words. He says not merely "I speak the truth," but "I am the Truth." In His person and work we find all truth that it is essential to know. He is the true Man, the revelation of perfect manhood, in whom we see what human life truly is. In His own history He shows us our own capacities and our own destiny. An angel or an inanimate law might *tell* us the truth about human life, but Christ is the Truth. He is man like ourselves. If we are extinguished at death, so is He. If for us there is no future life, neither is there for Him. He is Himself human.

Further and especially, He is the truth about God: "If ye had known Me, ye had known My Father also." Strenuous efforts are being made in our day to convince us that all our search after God is vain, because by the very nature of the case it is impossible to know God. We are assured that all our imaginations of God are but a reflection of ourselves magnified infinitely; and that what results from all our thinking is not God, but only a magnified man. We form in our thoughts an ideal of human excellence—perfect holiness and perfect love; and we add to this highest moral character we can conceive a supernatural power and wisdom, and this we call God. But this, we are assured, is but to mislead ourselves; for what we thus set before our minds as Divine is not God, but only a higher kind of man. But God is not a higher kind of man: He is a different kind of being—a Being to whom it is absurd to ascribe intelligence, or will, or personality, or anything human.

We have felt the force of what is thus urged; and

feeling most deeply that for us the greatest of all questions is, What is God? we have been afraid lest, after all, we have been deluding ourselves with an image of our own creating very different from the reality. We have felt that there is a great truth lying at the heart of what is thus urged, a truth which the Bible makes as much of as philosophy does—the truth that we cannot find out God, cannot comprehend Him. We say certain things about Him, as that He is a Spirit; but which of us knows what a pure spirit is, which of us can conceive in our minds a distinct idea of what we so freely speak of as a spirit? Indeed, it is because it is impossible for us to have any sufficient idea of God as He is in Himself that He has become man and manifested Himself in flesh.

This revelation of God in man implies that there is an affinity and likeness between God and man—that man is made in God's image. Were it not so, we should see in Christ, not God at all, but only man. If God is manifest in Christ, it is because there is that in God which can find suitable expression in a human life and person. In fact, this revelation takes for granted that in a sense it is quite true that God is a magnified Man—that He is a Being in whom there is much that resembles what is in man. And it stands to reason that this must be so. It is quite true that man can only conceive what is like himself; but that is only half the truth. It is also true that God can only create what is consistent with His own mind. In His creatures we see a reflection of Himself. And as we ascend from the lowest of them to the highest, we see what He considers the highest qualities. Finding in ourselves these highest qualities—qualities which enable us to understand all lower creatures and to use them—

we gather that in God Himself there must be something akin to our mind and to our inner man.

Christ, then, is "the Truth," because He is the Revealer of God. In Him we learn what God is and how to approach Him. But knowledge is not enough. It is conceivable that we should have learned much about God and yet have despaired of ever becoming like Him. It might gradually have become our conviction that we were for ever shut out from all good, although that is incompatible with a true knowledge of God; for if God is known at all, He must be known as Love, as self-communicating. But the possibility of having knowledge which we cannot use is precluded by the fact that He who is the Truth is also the Life. In Him who is the Revealer we at the same time find power to avail ourselves of the revelation. For:

II. "I am the Life." The declaration need not be restricted to the immediate occasion. Christ imparts to men power to use the knowledge of the Father He gives them. He gives men desire, will, and power to live with God and in God. But is not all life implied in this? This is life as men are destined to know it.

In every man there is a thirst for life. Everything that clogs, impedes, or retards life we hate; sickness, imprisonment, death, whatever diminishes, enfeebles, limits, or destroys life, we abhor. Happiness means abundant life, great vitality finding vent for itself in healthy ways. Great scope or opportunity of living to good purpose is useless to the invalid who has little life in himself; and, on the other hand, abundant vitality is only a pain to the man who is shut up and can spend his energy only in pacing a cell eight feet by four. Our happiness depends upon these two conditions—perfect energy and infinite scope.

But can we assure ourselves of either? Is not the one certainty of life, as we know it, that it must end? Is it not certain that, no matter what energy the most vigorous of us enjoy, we shall all one day "lie in cold obstruction"? Naturally we fear that time, as if all life were then to end for us. We shrink from that apparent termination, as if beyond it there could be but a shadowy, spectral life in which nothing is substantial, nothing lively, nothing delightsome, nothing strong. That state which we shrink from our Lord chooses as a condition of perfect life, abundant and untrammelled. And what He has chosen for Himself He means to bestow upon us.

Why should we find it so hard to believe in that abundant life? There is a sufficient source of physical life which upholds the universe and is not burdened, which in continuance and exuberantly brings forth life in inconceivably various forms. The world around us indicates a source of life which seems always to grow and expand rather than to be exhausted. So there is a source of spiritual life, a force sufficient to uphold all men in righteousness and in eternal vitality of spirit, and which can give birth to ever new and varied forms of heroic, holy, godly living—a force which is ever pressing forward to find expression through all moral beings, and capable of making all human action as perfect, as beautiful, and infinitely more significant than the products of physical life which we see around us. If the flowers profusely scattered by the wayside are marvels of beauty, if the bodily frame of man and of the other animals is continually surprising us with some new revelation of exquisite arrangement of parts, if nature is so lavish and so perfect in physical life, may we not believe that there is as rich a fountain of moral and spiritual life? Nay, "the youths may faint and be weary, and the young men utterly fall," physical life may fail and in the nature of things must fail, "but they that wait upon the Lord shall renew their strength, they shall run and not be weary."

It is Jesus Christ who brings us into connection with this source of life eternal—He bears it in His own person. In Him we receive a new spirit; in Him our motive to live for righteousness is continually renewed; we are conscious that in Him we touch what is undying and never fails to renew spiritual life in us. Whatever we need to give us true and everlasting life we have in Christ. Whatever we need to enable us to come to the Father, whatever we shall need between this present stage of experience and our final stage, we have in Him.

The more, then, we use Christ, the more life we have. The more we are with Him and the more we partake of His Spirit, the fuller does our own life become. It is not by imitating successful men we become influential for good, but by living with Christ. It is not by adopting the habits and methods of saints we become strong and useful, but by accepting Christ and His Spirit. Nothing can take the place of Christ. Nothing can take His words and say to us, "I am the Life." If we wish life, if we see that we are doing little good and desire energy to overtake the good that needs to be done, it is to Him we must go. If we feel as if all our efforts were vain, and as if we could not bear up any longer against our circumstances or against our wicked nature, we can receive fresh vigour and hopefulness only from Christ. We need not be surprised at our failures if we are not receiving from Christ the life that is in Him. And nothing can give us the life that is in Him but our own personal application to Him, our direct dealing with Himself. Ordinances and sacraments help to bring Him clearly before us, but they are not living and cannot give us life. It is only in so far as through and in them we reach Christ and receive Him that we partake of that highest of all forms of life—the life that is in Him, the living One, by whom all things were made, and who in the very face of death can say, "Because I live ye shall live also."

III. Being the Revealer of the Father, and giving men power to approach God and live in Him, Jesus legitimately designates Himself "the Way." Jesus never says "I am the Father"; He does not even say "I am God," for that might have produced misunderstanding. He uniformly speaks as if there were One on whom He Himself leant, and to whom He prayed, and with whom, as with another person, He had fellowship. "I am the Way," He says; and a way implies a goal beyond itself, some further object to which it leads and brings us. He is not the Being revealed, but the Revealer; not the terminal object of our worship, but the image of the invisible God, the Priest, the Sacrifice.

Christ announces Himself to Thomas as the Way, in order to remove from the mind of the disciple the uncertainty he felt about the future. He knew there were heights of glory and blessedness to which the Messiah would certainly attain, but which seemed dim and remote and even quite unattainable to sinful men. Jesus defines at once the goal and the way. All our vague yearnings after what will satisfy us He reduces to this simple expression: "the Father." This, He implies, is the goal and destiny of man; to come to the Father, who embraces in His loving care all our wants, our incapacities, our sorrows ; to reach and abide in a love that is strong, wise, educative, imperishable ; to reach this love and be so transformed by it as to feel more at home with this perfectly holy God than with any besides. And to bring us to this goal is the function of Christ, the Way. It is His to bring together what is highest and what is lowest. It is His to unite those who are separated by the most real obstacles : to bring us, weak and unstable and full of evil imaginings, into abiding union with the Supreme, glad to be conformed to Him and to accomplish His purposes. In proclaiming Himself "the Way," Christ pronounces Himself able to effect the most real union between parties and conditions as separate as heaven and earth, sin and holiness, the poor creature I know myself to be and the infinite and eternal God who is so high I cannot know Him.

Further, the way to which we commit ourselves when we seek to come to the Father through Christ is a *Person*. "*I* am the Way." It is not a cold, dead road we have to make the most of for ourselves, pursuing it often in darkness, in weakness, in fear. It is a living way—a way that renews our strength as we walk in it, that enlivens instead of exhausting us, that gives direction and light as we go forward. Often we seem to find our way barred ; we do not know how to get farther forward ; we wonder if there is no book in which we can find direction ; we long for some wise guide who could show us how to proceed. At such times Christ would have us hear Him saying, "I am the Way. If you abide in Me, if you continue in My love, you are in the way and must be carried forward to all good." Often we seem to lose ourselves and cannot tell whether our faces and our steps are directed aright or not; we become doubtful whether we have been making any progress or have not rather been going back. Often we lose heart and begin to doubt whether it is possible for us men ever to reach any purer, higher life; we are going we say, we know not whither; this life is full of blunders and failures. Many of the best and most earnest and gifted men have owned their ignorance of the purpose of life and of its end. No voice comes to us out of the unseen world to give us assurance that there is life there. How can lonely, ignorant, irresolute, weak, and helpless creatures such as we are ever attain to anything we can call blessedness? To all such gloom and doubting Christ, with the utmost confidence, says, "I am the Way. Wherever you are, at whatever point of experience, at whatever stage of sin, this way begins where you are, and you have but to take it and it leads to God, to that unknown Highest you yearn for even while you shrink from Him. From your person, as you are at this moment, there leads a way to the Father."

# X.
## *THE FATHER SEEN IN CHRIST.*

"Philip saith unto Him, Lord, show us the Father, and it sufficeth us. Jesus saith unto him, Have I been so long time with you, and dost thou not know Me, Philip? he that hath seen Me hath seen the Father; how sayest thou, Show us the Father? Believest thou not that I am in the Father, and the Father in Me? the words that I say unto you I speak not from Myself: but the Father abiding in Me doeth His works. Believe Me that I am in the Father, and the Father in Me: or else believe Me for the very works' sake. Verily, verily, I say unto you, He that believeth on Me, the works that I do shall he do also; and greater works than these shall he do; because I go unto the Father. And whatsoever ye shall ask in My name, that will I do, that the Father may be glorified in the Son. If ye shall ask Me anything in My name, that will I do. If ye love Me, ye will keep My commandments. And I will pray the Father, and He shall give you another Comforter, that He may be with you for ever, even the Spirit of truth: whom the world cannot receive; for it beholdeth Him not, neither knoweth Him: ye know Him; for He abideth with you, and shall be in you. I will not leave you desolate: I come unto you. Yet a little while, and the world beholdeth Me no more; but ye behold Me: because I live, ye shall live also. In that day ye shall know that I am in My Father, and ye in Me, and I in you. He that hath My commandments, and keepeth them, he it is that loveth me: and he that loveth Me shall be loved of My Father and I will love him, and will manifest Myself unto him."—JOHN xiv. 8-21.

## X.

#### THE FATHER SEEN IN CHRIST.

A THIRD interruption on the part of one of the disciples gives the Lord occasion to be still more explicit. Philip is only further bewildered by the words, " from henceforth ye know the Father and have seen Him." He catches, however, at the idea that the Father can be seen, and eagerly exclaims, " Lord, show us the Father, and it sufficeth us." In this exclamation there may be a little of that vexed and almost irritated feeling that every one at times has felt in reading the words of Christ. We feel as if He might have made things plainer. We unconsciously reproach Him with making a mystery, with going about and about a subject and refusing to speak straight at it. Philip felt that if Christ could show the Father, then there was no need of any more enigmatical talk.

Ignorant as this request may be, it sprang from the thirst for God which was felt by an earnest and godly man. It arose from the craving that now and again visits every soul to get to the heart of all mystery. Here in this life we are much in the dark. We feel ourselves to be capable of better enjoyments, of a higher life. The whole creation groaneth and travaileth, as if striving towards some better and more satisfying state. There is a something not yet attained which we feel we must reach. Were this life all, we should pronounce existence a failure. And yet there is great uncertainty over our future. There is no familiar intercourse with those who have passed on and are now in the other world. We have no opportunity of informing ourselves of their state and occupations. We go on in great darkness and often with a feeling of great insecurity and trepidation; feeling lost, in darkness, not knowing whither we are going, not sure that we are in the way to life and happiness. Why, we are tempted to ask, should there be so much uncertainty? Why should we live so remote from the centre of things, and have to grope our way to life and light, clouded by doubts, beset by misleading and disturbing influences? "*Show* us the Father," we are tempted to say with Philip—show us the Father and it sufficeth us. Show us the Supreme. Show us the eternal One who governs all. Take us but once to the centre of things and show us the Father in whom we live. Take us for once behind the scenes and let us see the hand that moves all things; let us know all that can be known, that we may see what it is we are going to, and what is to become of us when this visible world is done. Give us assurance that behind all this dumb, immovable mask of outward things there is a living God whose love we can trust and whose power can preserve us to life everlasting.

To Philip's eager request Jesus replies: "Have I been so long time with you, and hast thou not known Me, Philip? He that hath seen Me hath seen the Father; how sayest thou, Show us the Father?" And it is thus our Lord addresses all whose unsatisfied craving finds voice in Philip's request. To all who crave some more immediate, if not more sensible manifestation of God, to all who live in doubt and feel as if more might be done to give us certitude regarding the relation we hold to God and to the future, Christ says: No further revelation is to be made, because no further revelation is needed or can be made. All has been shown that can be shown. There is no more of the Father you can see than you have seen in Me. God has taken that form which is most comprehensible to you—your own form, the form of man. You have seen the Father. I am the truth, the reality. It is no longer a symbol telling you something about a distant God, but the Father Himself is in Me, speaking and acting among you through Me.

What do we find in Christ? We find perfection of moral character, superiority to circumstances, to the elements, to disease, to death. We find in Him One who forgives sin and brings peace of conscience, who bestows the Holy Spirit and leads to perfect righteousness. We cannot imagine anything in God which is not made present to us in Christ. In any part of the universe we should feel secure with Christ. In the most critical spiritual emergency we should have confidence that He could right matters. In the physical and in the spiritual world He is equally at home and equally commanding. We can believe Him when He says that he that has seen Him has seen the Father.

What precisely does this utterance mean? Does it only mean that Jesus in His holy and loving ways and in the whole of His character was God's very image? As you might say of a son who strongly resembles his father, "If you have seen the one, you have seen the other." It is true that the self-sacrifice and humility and devotedness of Jesus did give men new views of the true character of God, that His conduct was an exact transcript of God's mind and conveyed to men new thoughts of God.

But it is plain that the connection between Jesus and God was a different *kind* of connection from that which subsists between every man and God. Every man might in a sense say, "I am in the Father and the Father in me." But plainly the very fact that Jesus said to Philip, "Believest thou not that I am in the Father and the Father in Me?" is proof that it was not this ordinary connection He had in view. Philip could have had no difficulty in perceiving and acknowledging that God was in Jesus as He is in every man. But if that were all that Jesus meant, then it was wholly out of place to appeal to the works the Father had given Him to do in proof of this assertion.

When, therefore, Jesus said, "He that hath seen Me hath seen the Father," He did not merely mean that by His superior holiness He had revealed the Father as no other man had done (although even this would be a most surprising assertion for any mere man to make—that He was so holy that whoever had seen Him had seen the absolutely holy God), but He meant that God was present with Him in a special manner.

So important was it that the disciples should firmly grasp the truth that the Father was in Christ that Jesus proceeds to enlarge upon the proof or evidence of this. In the course of doing so He imparts to them three assurances fitted to comfort them in the prospect of His departure: first, that so far from being weakened by His going to the Father, they will do greater works than even those which had proved that the Father was present with Him; second, that He would not leave them friendless and without support, but would send them the Paraclete, the Spirit of truth, who should abide with them; and third, that although the world would not see Him, they would, and would recognise that He was the maintainer of their own life.

But all this experience would serve to convince them that the Father was in Him. He had, He says, lived among them as the representative of the Father, uttering His will, doing His works. These works might have convinced them even if they were not spiritual enough to perceive that His words were Divine utterances. But a time was coming when a satisfying conviction of the truth that God had been present with them in the presence of Jesus would be wrought in them. When, after His departure, they found *themselves* doing the works of God, greater works than Jesus had done, when they found that the Spirit of truth dwelt in them, imparting to them the very mind and life of Christ Himself, then they should be certified of the truth that Jesus now declared, that the Father was in Him and He in the Father. "At that day ye shall know that I am in My Father, and you in Me, and I in you." What their understanding could not at present quite grasp, the course of events and their own spiritual experience would make plain to them. When in the prosecution of Christ's instructions they strove to fulfil His commands and carry out His will upon earth, they would find themselves countenanced and supported by powers unseen, would find their life sustained by the life of Christ.

Jesus, then, speaks here of three grades of conviction regarding His claim to be God's representative: three kinds of evidence—a lower, a higher, and the highest. There is the evidence of His miracles, the evidence of His words or His own testimony, and the evidence of the new spiritual life He would maintain in His followers.

Miracles are not the highest evidence, but they are evidence. One miracle might not be convincing evidence. Many miracles of the same kind, such as a number of cures of nervous complaints, or several successful treatments of blind persons, might only indicate superior knowledge of morbid conditions and of remedies. A physician in advance of his age might accomplish wonders. Or had all the miracles of Jesus been such as the multiplication of the loaves and fishes, it might, with a shade of plausibility, have been urged that this was legerdemain. But what we see in Jesus is not power to perform an occasional wonder to make men stare or to win for Himself applause, but power as God's representative on earth to do whatever is needful for the manifestation of God's presence and for the fulfilment of God's will. It may surely at this time of day be taken for granted that Jesus was serious and true. The works are given Him by the Father to do: it is as an exhibition of God's power He performs them. They are therefore performed not in one form only, but in every needed form. He shows command over all nature, and gives evidence that spirit is superior to matter and rules it.

The miracles of Christ are also convincing because they are performed by a miraculous Person. That an ordinary man should seem to rule nature, or should exhibit wonders on no adequate occasion, must always seem unlikely, if not incredible. But that a Person notoriously exceptional, being what no other man has ever been, should do things that no other man has done, excites no incredulity. That Christ was supremely and absolutely holy no one doubts ; but this itself is a miracle ; and that this miraculous Person should act miraculously is not unlikely. Moreover, there was adequate occasion both for the miracle of Christ's person and the miracle of His life and separate acts. There was an end to be served so great as to justify this interruption of the course of things as managed by men. If miracles are possible, then they could never be more worthily introduced. If at any time it might seem appropriate and needful that the unseen, holy, and loving God should assert His power over all that touches us His children, so as to give us the consciousness of His presence and of His faithfulness, surely that time was precisely then when Christ came forth from the Father to reveal His holiness and His love, to show men that supreme power and supreme holiness and love reside together in God.

At present men are swinging from an excessive exaltation of miracles to an excessive depreciation of them. They sometimes speak as if no one could work a miracle, and sometimes as if any one could work a miracle. Having discovered that miracles do not convince every one, they leap to the conclusion that they convince no one ; and perceiving that Christ does not place them on the highest platform of evidence, they proceed to put them out of court altogether. This is inconsiderate and unwise. The miracles of Christ are appealed to by Himself as evidence of His truth; and looking at them in connection with His person, His life, and His mission or object, considering their character as works of compassion, and their instructive revelation of the nature and purpose of Him who did them, we cannot, I think, but feel that they carry in them a very strong claim upon our most serious attention and do help us to trust in Christ.

But Christ Himself, in the words before us, expects that those who have listened to His teaching and seen His life should need no other evidence that God is in Him and He in God—should not require to go down and back to the preliminary evidence of miracles which may serve to attract strangers. And, obviously, we get closer to the very heart of any person, nearer to the very core of their being, through their ordinary and habitual demeanour and conversation than by considering their exceptional and occasional acts. And it is a great tribute to the power and beauty of Christ's personality that it actually is not His miracles which solely or chiefly convince us of His claims upon our confidence, but rather His own character as it shines through His talks with His disciples and with all men He met. This, we feel, is the Person for us. Here we have the human ideal. The characteristics here disclosed are those which ought everywhere to prevail.

But the crowning evidence of Christ's unity with the Father can be enjoyed only by those who share His life. The conclusive evidence which for ever scatters doubt and remains abidingly as the immovable ground of confidence in Christ is our individual acceptance of His Spirit. Christ's life in God, His identification with the ultimate source of life and power, is to become one of the unquestioned facts of consciousness, one of the immovable data of human existence. We shall one day be as sure of His unity with the Father, and that in Christ our life is hid in God, as we are sure that now we are alive. Faith in Christ is to become an unquestioned certainty. How then is this assurance to be attained? It is to be attained when we ourselves as Christ's agents do greater works than He Himself did, and when by the power of His spiritual presence with us we live as He lived.

Christ calls our attention to this with His usual formula when about to declare a surprising but important truth: "Verily, verily, I say unto you, He that believeth on Me shall do greater works than these." Beginning with such evidence and such trust as we can attain, we shall be encouraged by finding the practical strength which comes of union with Christ. It speedily became apparent to the disciples that our Lord meant what He said when He assured them that they would do greater works than He had done. His miracles had amazed them and had done much good. And yet, after all, they were necessarily very limited in number, in the area of their exercise, and in the permanence of their results. Many were healed; but many, many more remained diseased. And even those who were healed were not rendered permanently unassailable by disease. The eyes of the blind which were opened for a year or two must close shortly in death. The paralysed, though sent from Christ's presence healed, must yield to the debilitating influences of age and betake themselves again to the crutch or the couch. Lazarus given back for a time to his sorrowing sisters must again, and this time without recall, own the power of death. And how far did the influence of Christ penetrate into these healed persons? Did they all obey His words and sin no more? or did some worse thing than the disease He freed them from fall upon some of them? Was there none who used his restored eyesight to minister to sin, his restored energies to do more wickedness than otherwise would have been possible? In one word, the miracles of

Christ, great as they were and beneficent as they were, were still confined to the body, and did not directly touch the spirit of man.

But was this the object of Christ's coming? Did He come to do a little less than several of the great medical discoverers have done? Assuredly not. These works of healing which He wrought on the bodies of men were, as John regularly calls them, "signs"; they were not acts terminating in themselves, and finding their full significance in the happiness communicated to the healed persons; they were signs pointing to a power over men's spirits, and suggesting to men analogous but everlasting benefits. Christ wrought His miracles that men, beginning with what they could see and appreciate, might be led on to believe in and trust Him for power to help them in all their matters. And now He expressly announces to His disciples that these works which He had been doing were not miracles of the highest kind; that miracles of the highest kind were works of healing and renewal wrought not on the bodies but on the souls of men, works whose effects would not be deleted by disease and death, but would be permanent, works which should not be confined to Palestine, but should be coextensive with the human race. And these greater works He would now proceed to accomplish through His disciples. By His removal from earth His work was not to be stopped, but to pass into a higher stage. He had come to earth not to make a passing display of Divine power, not to give a tantalising glimpse of what the world might be were His power acting freely and continuously in it; but He had come to lead us to apprehend the value of spiritual health and to trust Him for that. And now that He had won men's trust and taught a few to love Him and to value His Spirit, He removes Himself from their sight, and puts Himself beyond the reach of those who merely sought for earthly benefits, that He may through the Spirit come to all who understood how much greater are spiritual benefits.

This crowning evidence of Christ's being with the Father and in Him the disciples very soon enjoyed. On the day of Pentecost they found such results following from their simple word as had never followed the word of Christ. Thousands were renewed in heart and life. And from that day to this these greater works have never ceased. And why? "Because I go to the Father." And two reasons are given in these simple words. In the first place, no such results could be accomplished by Christ because not till He died was the Father's love fully known. It was the death and resurrection of Christ that convinced men of the truth of what Christ had proclaimed in His life and in His words regarding the Father. The tender compunction which was stirred by His death gave a purchase to the preacher of repentance which did not previously exist. It is Christ's death and resurrection which have been the converting influence through all the ages, and these Christ Himself could not preach. It was only when He had gone to the Father that the greater works of His kingdom could be done. Besides, it was only then that the greater works could be understood and longed for. The fact is, that the death and resurrection of Christ radically altered men's conceptions of the spiritual world, and gave them a belief in a future life of the spirit such as they previously had not and could not have. When men came experimentally into contact with One who had passed through death, and who now entered the unseen world full of plans and of vitality to execute them, a new sense of the value of spiritual benefits was born within them. The fact of being associated with a living Christ at God's right hand has refined the spiritual conceptions of men, and has given a quality to holiness which was not previously conspicuous. The spiritual world is now real and near, and men no longer think of Christ as a worker of miracles on physical nature, but as the King of the world unseen and the willing Source of all spiritual good. We sometimes wonder Christ preached so little and spoke so little as men do now in directing sinners to Him; but He knew that while He lived this was almost useless, and that events would proclaim Him more effectually than any words.

But when Christ gives as a reason for the greater works of His disciples that He Himself went to the Father, He also means that, being with the Father, He would be in the place of power, able to respond to the prayers of His people. "I go unto the Father, and whatsoever ye shall ask in My name that will I do." No man in Christ's circumstances would utter such words at random. They are uttered with a perfect knowledge of the difficulties and in absolute good faith. But praying "in Christ's name" is not so easy an achievement as we are apt to think. Praying in Christ's name means, no doubt, that we go to God, not in our own name, but in His. He has given us power to use His name, as when we send a messenger we bid him use our name. Sometimes when we send a person to a friend we are almost afraid to give him our name, knowing that our friend will be anxious for our sakes to do all he can and perhaps too much for the applicant. And in going to God in the name of Christ, as those who can plead His friendship and are identified with Him, we know we are sure of a loving and liberal reception.

But praying in Christ's name means more than this. It means that we pray for such things as will promote Christ's kingdom. When we do anything in another's name, it is for him we do it. When we take possession of a property or a legacy in the name of some society, it is not for our own private advantage but for the society we take possession. When an officer arrests any one in the Queen's name, it is not to satisfy his private malice he does so; and when he collects money in the name of government, it is not to fill his own pocket. Yet how constantly do we overlook this obvious condition of acceptable prayer! To pray in Christ's name is to seek what He seeks, to ask aid in promoting what He has at heart. To come in Christ's name and plead selfish and worldly desires is absurd. To pray in Christ's name is to pray in the spirit in which He Himself prayed and for objects He desires. When we measure our prayers by this rule, we cease to wonder that so few seem to be answered. Is God to answer prayers that positively lead men away from Him? Is He to build them up in the presumption that happiness can be found in the pursuit of selfish objects and worldly comfort? It is when a man stands, as these disciples stood, detached from worldly hopes and finding all in Christ, so clearly apprehending the sweep and benignity of Christ's will as to see that it comprehends all good to man, and that life can serve no purpose if it do not help to fulfil that will—it is then a man prays with assurance and finds his prayer answered. Christ had won the love of these men and knew that their chief desire would be to serve Him, that their prayers would always be that they might fulfil His purposes. Their fear was, not that He would summon them to live wholly for the ends for which He had lived, but that when He was gone they should find themselves unfit to contend with the world.

And therefore He gives them the final encouragement that He would still be with them, not indeed in a visible form apparent to all eyes, but in a valid and powerful spiritual manner appreciable by those who loved Christ and strove to do His will. "If ye love Me, keep My commandments. And I will pray the Father, and He shall give you another Comforter," another *Advocate*, one *called to* your aid, and who shall so effectually aid you that in His presence and help you will know Me present with you. "I will not leave you comfortless, like orphans: *I* will come to you." Christ Himself was still to be with them. He was not merely to leave them His memory and example, but was to be with them, sustaining and guiding and helping them even as He had done. The only difference was to be this—that whereas up to this time they had verified His presence by their senses, seeing His body, hearing His words, and so forth, they should henceforward verify His presence by a spiritual sense which the world of those who did not love Him could not make use of. "Yet a little while, and the world seeth Me no more; but ye see Me: because I live, ye shall live also." They would find that their life was bound up in His; and as that new life of theirs grew strong and proved itself victorious over the world and powerful to subdue men's hearts to Christ and win the world to Christ's kingdom, they should feel a growing persuasion, a deepening consciousness, that this life of theirs was but the manifestation of the continued life of Christ. "At that day they would know that Christ was in the Father, and they in Him, and He in them."

Consciousness, then, of Christ's present life and of His close relation to ourselves is to be won only by loving Him and living in Him and for Him. Lower grades of faith there are on which most of us stand, and by which, let us hope, we are slowly ascending to this assured and ineradicable consciousness. Drawn to Christ we are by the beauty of His life, by His evident mastery of all that concerns us, by His knowledge, by the revelation He makes; but doubts assail us, questionings arise, and we long for the full assurance of the personal love of God and of the continued personal life and energy of Christ which would give us an immovable ground to stand on. According to Christ's explanation given in this passage to His disciples, this deepest conviction, this unquestionable consciousness of His presence, is attained only by those who proceed upon the lower grades of faith, and with true love for Him seek to find their life in Him. It is a conviction which can only be won experimentally. The disciples passed from the lower to the higher faith at a bound. The sight of the risen Lord, the new world vividly present to them in His person, gave their devotedness an impulse which carried them at once and for ever to certainty. There are many still who are so drawn by spiritual affinity to Christ that unhesitatingly and unrepentingly they give themselves wholly to Him, and have the reward of a conscious life in Christ. Others have more slowly to win their way upwards, fighting against unbelief, striving to give themselves more undividedly to Christ, and encouraging themselves with the hope that from their hearts also all doubts will one day for ever vanish. Certain it is that Christ's life can only be given to those who are willing to receive it—certain it is that only those who seek to do His work seek to be sustained by His life. If we are not striving to attain those ends which He gave His life to accomplish, we cannot be surprised if we are not sensible of receiving His aid. If we aim at worldly ends, we shall need no other energy than what the world supplies; but if we throw ourselves heartily into the Christian order of things and manner of life, we shall at once be sensible of our need of help, and shall know whether we receive it or not.

Christ's promise is explicit—a promise given as the stay of His friends in their bitterest need: "He that hath My commandments, and keepeth them, he it is that loveth Me: and he that loveth Me shall be loved of My Father, and I will love Him, and will manifest Myself to him." It will still be a spiritual manifestation which can be perceived only by those whose spirits are exercised to discern such things; but it will be absolutely satisfying. We shall find one day that Christ's work has been successful, that He has brought men and God into a perfect harmony. "That day" shall arrive for us also, when we shall find that Christ has actually accomplished what He undertook, and has set our life and ourselves on an enduring foundation—has given us eternal life in God, a life of perfect joy. Things are under God's guidance progressive, and Christ is the great means He uses for the progress of all that concerns ourselves. And what Christ has done is not to be fruitless or only half effective; He will see of the travail of His soul and be satisfied—satisfied because in us the utmost of happiness and the utmost of good have been attained, because greater and richer things than man has conceived have been made ours.

These utterances are fitted to dispel a form of unbelief which seriously hinders many sincere inquirers. It arises from the difficulty of believing in Christ as now alive and able to afford spiritual assistance. Many persons who enthusiastically admit the perfectness of Christ's character and of the morality He taught, and who desire above all else to make that morality their own, are yet unable to believe that He can give them any real and present assistance in their efforts after holiness. A teacher is a very different thing from a Saviour. They are satisfied with Christ's teaching; but they need more than teaching—they need not only to see the road, but to be enabled to follow it. Unless a man can find some real connection between himself and God, unless he can rely upon receiving inward support from God, he feels that there is nothing which can truly be called salvation.

This form of unbelief assails almost every man. Very often it results from the slow-growing conviction that the Christian religion is not working in ourselves the definite results we expected. When we read the New Testament, we see the reasonableness of faith, we cannot but subscribe to the *theory* of Christianity; but when we endeavour to practise it we fail. We have tried it, and it does not seem to work. At first we think this is something peculiar to ourselves, and that through some personal carelessness or mistake we have failed to receive all the benefit which others receive. But as time goes on the suspicion strengthens in some minds that faith is a delusion : prayer seems to be unanswered ; effort seems to be unacknowledged. The power of an almighty spirit within the human spirit cannot be traced. Perhaps this suspicion, more than all other causes put together, produces undecided, heartless Christians.

What, then, is to be said in view of such doubts? Perhaps it may help us past them if we consider that spiritual things are spiritually discerned, and that the one proof of His ascension to God's right hand which Christ Himself promised was the bestowal of His Spirit. If we find that, however slowly, we are coming into a truer harmony with God; if we find that we can more cordially approve the Spirit of Christ, and give to that Spirit a more real place in our life; if we are finding that we can be satisfied with very little in the way of selfish and worldly advancement, and that it is a greater satisfaction to us to do good than to get good; if we find ourselves in any degree more patient, more temperate, more humble,—then Christ is manifesting in us His present life in the only way in which He promised to do so. Even if we have more knowledge, more perception of what moral greatness is, if we see through the superficial formalisms which once passed for religion with us, this is a step in the right direction, and if wisely used may be the foundation of a superstructure of intelligent service and real fellowship with God. Every discovery and abandonment of error, every unmasking of delusion, every attainment of truth, is a step nearer to permanent reality, and is a true spiritual gain; and if in times past we have had little experience of spiritual joy and confidence, if our thoughts have been sceptical and questioning and perplexed, all this may be the needful preliminary to a more independent and assured and truer faith, and may be the very best proof that Christ is guiding our mind and attending to our prayers. It is for "the world" to refuse to believe in the Spirit, because "it beholdeth Him not, neither knoweth Him."

It may also be said that to think of Christ as a good man who has passed away like other good men, leaving an influence and no more behind Him, to think of Him as lying still in His tomb outside Jerusalem, is to reverse not only the belief of those who knew Christ best, but the belief of godly men in all ages. For in all ages both before and after Christ it has been the clear conviction of devout souls that God sought them much more ardently and persistently than they sought God. The truth which shines most conspicuously in the experience of all the saved is that they were saved by God and not by themselves. If human experience is to be trusted at all, if it in any case reflects the substantial verities of the spiritual world, then we may hold it as proved in the uniform experience of men that God somehow communicated to them a living energy, and not only taught them what to do, but gave them strength to do it. If under the Christian dispensation we are left to make the best we can for ourselves of the truth taught by Christ and of the example He set us in His life and death, then the Christian dispensation, so far from being an advance on all that went before, fails to supply us with that very thing which is sought through all religions—actual access to a living source of spiritual strength. I believe that the resurrection of Christ is established by stronger evidence than exists for any other historical fact; but apart altogether from the historical evidence, the entire experience of God's people goes to show that Christ, as the mediator between God and man, as the representative of God and the channel of

His influence upon us, must be now alive, and must be in a position to exert a personal care and a personal influence, and to yield a present and inward assistance. Were it otherwise, we should be left without a Saviour to struggle against the enemies of the soul in our own strength, and this would be a complete reversal of the experience of all those who in past ages have been engaged in the same strife and have been victorious.

# XI.

*THE BEQUEST OF PEACE.*

"Judas (not Iscariot) saith unto Him, Lord, what is come to pass that Thou wilt manifest Thyself unto us, and not unto the world? Jesus answered and said unto him, If a man love Me, he will keep My word : and My Father will love him, and We will come unto him, and make our abode with him. He that loveth Me not keepeth not My words : and the word which ye hear is not Mine, but the Father's who sent Me. These things have I spoken unto you, while yet abiding with you. But the Comforter, even the Holy Spirit, whom the Father will send in My name, He shall teach you all things, and bring to your remembrance all that I said unto you. Peace I leave with you; My peace I give unto you : not as the world giveth, give I unto you. Let not your heart be troubled, neither let it be fearful. Ye heard how I said to you, I go away, and I come unto you. If ye loved Me, ye would have rejoiced, because I go unto the Father : for the Father is greater than I. And now I have told you before it come to pass, that, when it is come to pass, ye may believe. I will no more speak much with you, for the prince of the world cometh : and he hath nothing in Me ; but that the world may know that I love the Father, and as the Father gave Me commandment, even so I do. Arise, let us go hence."
—JOHN xiv. 22-31.

## XI.

### THE BEQUEST OF PEACE.

THE encouraging assurances of our Lord are interrupted by Judas Thaddeus. As Peter, Thomas, and Philip had availed themselves of their Master's readiness to solve their difficulties, so now Judas utters his perplexity. He perceives that the manifestation of which Jesus has spoken is not public and general, but special and private; and he says, "Lord, what has happened, that Thou art to manifest Thyself to us, and not to the world?" It would seem as if Judas had been greatly impressed by the public demonstration in favour of Jesus a day or two previously, and supposed that something must have occurred to cause Him now to wish to manifest Himself only to a select few.

Apparently Judas' construction of the future was still entangled with the ordinary Messianic expectation. He thought Jesus, although departing for a little, would return speedily in outward Messianic glory, and would triumphantly enter Jerusalem and establish Himself there. But how this could be done privately he could not understand. And if Jesus had entirely altered His plan, and did not mean immediately to claim Messianic supremacy, but only to manifest Himself to a few, was this possible?

By His reply our Lord shows for the hundredth time that outward proclamation and external acknowledgment were not in His thoughts. It is to the individual and in response to individual love He will manifest Himself. It is therefore a spiritual manifestation He has in view. Moreover, it was not to a specially privileged few, whose number was already complete, that He would manifest Himself. Judas supposed that to him and his fellow-Apostles, "us," Jesus would manifest Himself, and over against this select company he set "the world." But this mechanical line of demarcation our Lord obliterates in His reply, "If *any man* loveth Me, ... We will come to him." He enounces the great spiritual law that they who seek to have Christ's presence manifested to them must love and obey Him. He that longs for more satisfying knowledge of spiritual realities, he that thirsts for certainty and to see God as if face to face, must expect no sudden or magical revelation, but must be content with the true spiritual education which proceeds by loving and living. To the disciples the method might seem slow—to us also it often seems slow; but it is the method which nature requires. Our knowledge of God, our belief that in Christ we have a hold of ultimate truth and are living among eternal verities, grow with our love and service of Christ. It may take us a lifetime—it will take us a lifetime—to learn to love Him as we ought, but others have learned and we also may learn, and there is no possible experience so precious to us.

It is, then, to those who serve Him that Christ manifests Himself, and manifests Himself in an abiding, spiritual, influential manner. That those who do not serve Him do not believe in His presence and power is to be expected. But were those who have served Him asked if they had become more convinced of His spiritual and effectual presence, their voice would be that this promise had been fulfilled. And this is the very citadel of the religion of Christ. If Christ does not now abide with and energetically aid those who serve Him, then their faith is vain. If His spiritual presence with them is not manifested in spiritual results, if they have no evidence that He is personally and actively employed in and with them, their faith is vain. To believe in a Christ long since removed from earth and whose present life cannot now influence or touch mankind is not the faith which Christ Himself invites. And if His promise to abide with those who love and serve Him is not actually performed, Christendom has been produced by a mistake and has lived on a delusion.

At this point (ver. 25) Jesus pauses; and feeling how little He had time to say of what was needful, and how much better they would understand their relation to Him after He had finally passed from their bodily sight, He says : " These things I have spoken to you, while yet I remain with you; but the Paraclete, the Holy Spirit, which the Father will send in My name, He will teach you all things, and will remind you of all that I have said to you." Jesus cannot tell them all He would wish them to know; but the same Helper whom He has already promised will especially help them by giving them understanding of what has already been told them, and by leading them into further knowledge. He is to come "in the name" of Jesus—that is to say, as His representative—and to carry on His work in the world.[1]

---

[1] " In this designation of the teaching Spirit as holy, there lie lessons for two classes of people. All fanatical professions of possessing Divine

Here, then, the Lord predicts that one day His disciples will know more than He has taught them. They were to advance in knowledge beyond the point to which He had brought them. His teaching would necessarily be the foundation of all future attainment, and whatever would not square with that they must necessarily reject; but they were to add much to the foundation He had laid. We cannot therefore expect to find in the teaching of Jesus all that His followers ought to know regarding Himself and His connection with them. All that is absolutely necessary we shall find there; but if we wish to know all that He would have us know, we must look beyond. The teaching which we receive from the Apostles is the requisite and promised complement of the teaching which Christ Himself delivered. He being the subject taught as much as the teacher, and His whole experience as living, dying, rising, and ascending, constituting the facts which Christian teaching was to explain, it was impossible that He Himself should be the final teacher. He could not at once be text and exposition. He lived among men, and by His teaching shed much light on the significance of His life; He died, and was not altogether silent regarding the meaning of His death, but it was enough that He furnished matter for His Apostles to explain, and confined Himself to sketching the mere outline of Christian truth.

Again and again throughout this last conversation

---

illumination, which are not warranted and sealed by purity of life, are lies or self-delusion. And, on the other hand, cold-blooded intellectualism will never force the locks of the palace of Divine truth; but they that come there must have clean hands and a pure heart; and only those who have the love and the longing for goodness will be wise scholars in Christ's school."—MACLAREN.

Jesus tries to break off, but finds it impossible. Here (ver. 27), when He has assured them that, although He Himself leaves them in ignorance of many things, the Spirit will lead them into all truth, He proceeds to make His parting bequest. He would fain leave them what will enable them to be free from care and distress; but He has none of those worldly possessions which men usually lay up for their children and those dependent on them. House, lands, clothes, money, He had none. He could not even secure for those who were to carry on His work an exemption from persecution which He Himself had not enjoyed. He did not leave them, as some initiators have done, stable though new institutions, an empire of recent origin but already firmly established. "Not as the world giveth, give I unto you."

But He does give them that which all other bequests aim at producing: "Peace I leave with you." Men may differ as to the best means of attaining peace, or even as to the kind of peace that is desirable, but all agree in seeking an untroubled state. We seek a condition in which we shall have no unsatisfied desires gnawing at our heart and making peace impossible, no stings of conscience, dipped in the poison of past wrong-doing, torturing us hour by hour, no foreboding anxiety darkening and disturbing a present which might otherwise be peaceful. The comprehensive nature of this possession is shown by the fact that peace can be produced only by the contribution of past, present, and future. As health implies that all the laws which regulate bodily life are being observed, and as it is disturbed by the infringement of any one of these, so peace of mind implies that in the spiritual life all is as it should be. Introduce remorse or an evil conscience, and you destroy peace; introduce fear or anxiety, and peace is impossible. Introduce anything discordant, ambition alongside of indolence, a sensitive conscience alongside of strong passions, and peace takes flight. He, therefore, who promises to give peace promises to give unassailable security, inward integrity and perfectness, all which goes to make up that perfect condition in which we shall be for ever content to abide.

Jesus further defines the peace which He was leaving to the disciples as that peace which He had Himself enjoyed: "*My* peace I give unto you,"—as one hands over a possession he has himself tested, the shield or helmet that has served him in battle. "That which has protected Me in a thousand fights I make over to you." The peace which Christ desires His disciples to enjoy is that which characterised Himself; the same serenity in danger, the same equanimity in troublous circumstances, the same freedom from anxiety about results, the same speedy recovery of composure after anything which for a moment ruffled the calm surface of His demeanour. This is what He makes over to His people; this is what He makes possible to all who serve Him.

There is nothing which more markedly distinguishes Jesus and proves His superiority than His calm peace in all circumstances. He was poor, and might have resented the incapacitating straitness of poverty. He was driven from place to place, His purpose and motives were suspected, His action and teaching resisted, the good He strove to do continually marred; but He carried Himself through all with serenity. It is said that nothing shakes the nerve of brave men so much as fear of assassination: our Lord lived among bitterly hostile men, and was again and again on the brink of being made away with, but He was imperturbably resolute to do the work given Him to do. Take Him at an unguarded moment, tell Him the boat is sinking underneath Him, and you find the same undisturbed composure. He was never troubled at the results of His work or about His own reputation; when He was reviled, He reviled not again.

This unruffled serenity was so obvious a characteristic of the demeanour of Jesus, that as it was familiar to His friends, so it was perplexing to His judges. The Roman governor saw in His bearing an equanimity so different from the callousness of the hardened criminal and from the agitation of the self-condemned, that he could not help exclaiming in astonishment, "Dost Thou not know that I have power over Thee?" Therefore without egotism our Lord could speak of "My peace." The world had come to Him in various shapes, and He had conquered it. No allurement of pleasure, no opening to ambition had distracted Him and broken up His serene contentment; no danger had filled His spirit with anxiety and fear. On one occasion only could He say, "Now is My soul troubled." Out of all that life had presented to Him He had wrought out for Himself and for us peace.

By calling it specifically "My peace" our Lord distinguishes it from the peace which men ordinarily pursue. Some seek it by accommodating themselves to the world, by fixing for themselves a low standard and disbelieving in the possibility of living up to any high standard in this world. Some seek peace by giving the fullest possible gratification to all their desires; they seek peace in external things—comfort, ease, plenty, pleasant connections. Some stifle anxiety about worldly things by impressing on themselves that fretting does no good, and that what cannot be cured must be endured; and any anxiety that might arise about their spiritual condition they stifle by the imagination that God is too great or too good to deal strictly with their shortcomings. Such kinds of peace, our Lord implies, are delusive. It is not outward things which can give peace of mind, no more than it is a soft couch which can give rest to a fevered body. Restfulness must be produced from within.

There are, in fact, two roads to peace—we may conquer or we may be conquered. A country may always enjoy peace, if it is prepared always to submit to indignities, to accommodate itself to the demands of stronger parties, and absolutely to dismiss from its mind all ideas of honour or self-respect. This mode of obtaining peace has the advantages of easy and speedy attainment—advantages to which every man naturally attaches too high a value. For in the individual life we are daily choosing either the one peace or the other; the unrighteous desires which distract us we are either conquering or being conquered by. We are either accepting the cheap peace that lies on this side of conflict, or we are attaining or striving towards the peace that lies on the other side of conflict. But the peace we gain by submission is both short-lived and delusive. It is short-lived, for a gratified desire is like a relieved beggar, who will quickly find his way back to you with his request rather enlarged than curtailed; and it is delusive, because it is a peace which is the beginning of bondage of the worst kind. Any peace that is worth the having or worth the speaking about lies beyond, at the other side of conflict. We cannot long veil this from ourselves: we may decline the conflict and put off the evil day; but still we are conscious that we have not the peace our natures crave until we subdue the evil that is in us. We look and look for peace to distil upon us from without, to rise and shine upon us as to-morrow's sun, without effort of our own, and yet we know that such expectation is the merest delusion, and that peace must begin within, must be found in ourselves and not in our circumstances. We know that until our truest purposes are in thorough harmony with our conscientious convictions we have no right to peace. We know that we can have no deep and lasting peace until we are satisfied with our own inward state, or are at least definitely on the road to satisfaction.

Again, the peace of which Christ here speaks may be called His, as being wrought out by Him, and as being only attainable by others through His communication of it to them. We do at first inquire with surprise how it is possible that any one can bequeath to us his own moral qualities. This, in fact, is what one often wishes were possible—that the father who by long discipline, by many painful experiences, has at last become meek and wise, could transmit these qualities to his son who has life all before him. As we read the notices of those who pass away from among us, it is the loss of so much moral force we mourn; it may be, for all we know, as indispensable elsewhere, but nevertheless it is our loss, a loss for which no work done by the man, nor any works left behind him, compensate; for the man is always, or generally, greater than his works, and what he has done only shows us the power and possibilities that are in him. Each generation needs to raise its own good men, not independent, certainly, of the past, but not altogether inheriting what past generations have done; just as each new year must raise its own crops, and only gets the benefit of past toil in the shape of improved land, good seed, better implements and methods of agriculture. Still, there is a transmission from father to son of moral qualities. What the father has painfully acquired may be found in the son by inheritance. And this is *analogous* to the transfusion of moral qualities from Christ to His people. For it is true of all the graces of the Christian, that they are first acquired by Christ, and only from Him derived to the Christian. It is of His fulness we all receive, and grace for grace. He is the Light at whom we must all kindle, the Source from whom all flows.

How, then, does Christ communicate to us His peace or any of His own qualities—qualities in some instances acquired by personal experience and personal effort? He gives us peace, first, by reconciling us to God by removing the burden of our past guilt and giving us access to God's favour. His work sheds quite a new light upon God; reveals the fatherly love of God following us into our wandering and misery, and claiming us in our worst estate as His, acknowledging us and bidding us hope. Through Him we are brought back to the Father. He comes with this message from God, that He loves us. Am I, then, troubled about the past, about what I have done? As life goes on, do I only see more and more clearly how thoroughly I have been a wrong-doer? Does the present, as I live through it, only shed a brighter and brighter light on the evil of the past? Do I fear the future as that which can only more and more painfully evolve the consequences of my past wrong-doing? Am I gradually awaking to the full and awful import of being a sinner? After many years of a Christian profession, am I coming at last to see that above all else my life has been a life of sin, of shortcoming or evasion of duty, of deep consideration for my own pleasure or my own purpose, and utter or comparative regardlessness of God? Are the slowly evolving circumstances of my life at length effecting what no preaching has ever effected? are they making me understand that sin is the real evil, and that I am beset by it and my destiny entangled and ruled by it? To me, then, what offer could be more appropriate than the offer of peace? From all fear of God and of myself I am called to peace in Christ.

Reconcilement with God is the foundation, manifestly and of course, of all peace; and this we have as Christ's direct gift to us. But this fundamental peace, though it will eventually pervade the whole man, does in point of fact only slowly develop into a peace such as our Lord Himself possessed. The peace which our Lord spoke of to His disciples, peace amidst all the ills of life, can only be attained by a real following of Christ, and a hearty and profound acceptance of His principles and spirit. And it is not the less His gift because we have thus to work for it, to alter or be altered wholly in our own inward being. It is not therefore a deceptive bequest. When the father gives his son a good education, he cannot do so irrespective of the hard work of the son himself. When the general promises victory to his men, they do not expect to have it without fighting. And our Lord does not upset or supersede the fundamental laws of our nature and of our spiritual growth. He does not make effort of our own unnecessary; He does not give us a ready-made character irrespective of the laws by which character grows, irrespective of deep-seated thirst for holiness in ourselves and long-sustained conflict with outward obstacles and internal weaknesses and infidelities.

But He helps us to peace, not only though primarily by bringing us back to God's favour, but also by showing us in His own person and life how peace is attained and preserved, and by communicating to us His Spirit to aid us in our efforts to attain it. He found out more perfectly than any one else the secret of peace; and we are stirred by His example and success, not only as we are stirred by the example of any dead saint or sage with whom we have no present personal living fellowship, but as we are stirred by the example of a living Father who is always with us to infuse new heart into us, and to give us effectual counsel and aid. While we put forth our own efforts to win this self-conquest, and so school all within us as to enter into peace, Christ is with us securing that our efforts shall not be in vain, giving us the fixed and clear idea of peace as our eternal condition, and giving us also whatever we need to win it.

These words our Lord uttered at a time when, if ever, He was not likely to use words of course, to adopt traditional and misleading phrases. He loved the men He was speaking to, He knew He was after this to have few more opportunities of speaking with them, His love interpreted to Him the difficulties and troubles which would fall upon them, and this was the armour which He knew would bear them scathless through all. That His promise was fulfilled we know. We do not know what became of the majority of the Apostles, whether they did much or little; but if we look at the men who stood out prominently in the early history of the Church, we see how much they stood in need of this peace and how truly they received it. Look at

Stephen, sinking bruised and bleeding under the stones of a cursing mob, and say what characterises him—what makes his face shine and his lips open in prayer for his murderers? Look at Paul, driven out of one city, dragged lifeless out of another, clinging to a spar on a wild sea, stripped by robbers, arraigned before magistrate after magistrate—what keeps his spirit serene, his purpose unshaken through a life such as this? What put into his lips these valued words and taught him to say to others, " Rejoice evermore, and let the peace of God which passeth understanding keep your heart and mind"? It was the fulfilment of this promise—a promise which is meant for us as for them. It will be fulfilled in us as in these men, not by a mere verbal petition, not by a craving however strong, or a prayer however sincere, but by a true and profound acceptance of Christ, by a conscientious following of Him as our real leader, as that One from whom we take our ideas of life, of what is worthy and what is unworthy.

# XII.
## THE VINE AND THE BRANCHES.

"Arise, let us go hence. I am the true Vine, and My Father is the Husbandman. Every branch in Me that beareth not fruit, He taketh it away: and every branch that beareth fruit, He cleanseth it, that it may bear more fruit. Already ye are clean because of the word which I have spoken unto you. Abide in Me, and I in you. As the branch cannot bear fruit of itself, except it abide in the vine; so neither can ye, except ye abide in Me. I am the Vine, ye are the branches: He that abideth in Me, and I in him, the same beareth much fruit: for apart from Me ye can do nothing. If a man abide not in Me, he is cast forth as a branch, and is withered; and they gather them, and cast them into the fire, and they are burned. If ye abide in Me, and My words abide in you, ask whatsoever ye will, and it shall be done unto you. Herein is My Father glorified, that ye bear much fruit; and so shall ye be My disciples. Even as the Father hath loved Me, I also have loved you: abide ye in My love. If ye keep My commandments, ye shall abide in My love; even as I have kept My Father's commandments, and abide in His love. These things have I spoken unto you, that My joy may be in you, and that your joy may be fulfilled. This is My commandment, that ye love one another, even as I have loved you."—JOHN xiv. 31—xv. 12.

## XII.

### THE VINE AND THE BRANCHES.

LIKE a friend who cannot tear himself away and has many more last words after he has bid us good-bye, Jesus continues speaking to the disciples while they are selecting and putting on their sandals and girding themselves to face the chill night air. He had to all appearance said all He meant to say. He had indeed closed the conversation with the melancholy words, "Henceforth I will not talk much with you." He had given the signal for breaking up the feast and leaving the house, rising from table Himself and summoning the rest to do the same. But as He saw their reluctance to move, and the alarmed and bewildered expression that hung upon their faces, He could not but renew His efforts to banish their forebodings and impart to them intelligent courage to face separation from Him. All He had said about His spiritual presence with them had fallen short: they could not as yet understand it. They were possessed with the dread of losing Him whose future was their future, and with the success of whose plans all their hopes were bound up. The prospect of losing Him was too dreadful; and though He had assured them He would still be with them, there was an appearance of mystery and unreality about that presence which prevented them from trusting it. They knew they could effect nothing if He left them: their work was done, their hopes blighted.

As Jesus, then, rises, and as they all fondly cluster round Him, and as He recognises once more how much He is to these men, there occurs to His mind an allegory which may help the disciples to understand better the connection they have with Him, and how it is still to be maintained. It has been supposed that this allegory was suggested to Him by some vine trailing round the doorway or by some other visible object, but such outward suggestion is needless. Recognising their fears and difficulties and dependence on Him as they hung upon Him for the last time, what more natural than that He should meet their dependence and remove their fears of real separation by saying, " I am the Vine, ye the branches"? What more natural, when He wished to set vividly before them the importance of the work He was bequeathing to them, and to stimulate them faithfully to carry on what He had begun, than to say, "I am the Vine, ye the fruit-bearing branches: abide in Me, and I in you"?

Doubtless our Lord's introduction of the word "true" or "real"—"I am the true Vine"—implies a comparison with other vines, but not necessarily with any vines then outwardly visible. Much more likely is it that as He saw the dependence of His disciples upon Him, He saw new meaning in the old and familiar idea that Israel was the vine planted by God. He saw that in Himself[1] and His disciples all that had been suggested by this figure was in reality accomplished. God's intention in creating man was ful-

---

[1] That the vine was a recognised symbol of the Messiah is shown by Delitzsch in the *Expositor*, 3rd series, vol. iii., pp. 68, 69. See also his *Iris*, pp. 180-190. F. Tr.

filled. It was secured by the life of Christ and by the attachment of men to Him that the purpose of God in creation would bear fruit. That which amply satisfied God was now in actual existence in the person and attractiveness of Christ. Seizing upon the figure of the vine as fully expressing this, Christ fixes it for ever in the mind of His disciples as the symbol of His connection with them, and with a few decisive strokes He gives prominence to the chief characteristics of this connection.

I. The first idea, then, which our Lord wished to present by means of this allegory is, that He and His disciples together form one whole, neither being complete without the other. The vine can bear no fruit if it has no branches; the branches cannot live apart from the vine. Without the branches the stem is a fruitless pole; without the stem the branches wither and die. Stem and branches together constitute one fruit-bearing tree. I, for my part, says Christ, am the Vine; ye are the branches, neither perfect without the other, the two together forming one complete tree, essential to one another as stem and branches.

The significance underlying the figure is obvious, and no more welcome or animating thought could have reached the heart of the disciples as they felt the first tremor of separation from their Lord. Christ, in His own visible person and by His own hands and words, was no longer to extend His kingdom on earth. He was to continue to fulfil God's purpose among men, no longer however in His own person, but through His disciples. They were now to be His branches, the medium through which He could express all the life that was in Him, His love for man, His purpose to lift and save the world. Not with His own lips was He any longer to tell men of holiness and of God, not with His own hand was He to dispense blessing to the needy ones of earth, but His disciples were now to be the sympathetic interpreters of His goodness and the unobstructed channels through which He might still pour out upon men all His loving purpose. As God the Father is a Spirit and needs human hands to do actual deeds of mercy for Him, as He does not Himself in His own separate personality make the bed of the sick poor, but does it only through the intervention of human charity, so can Christ speak no audible word in the ear of the sinner, nor do the actual work required for the help and advancement of men. This He leaves to His disciples, His part being to give them love and perseverance for it, to supply them with all they need as His branches.

This, then, is the last word of encouragement and of quickening our Lord leaves with these men and with us: I leave you to do all for Me; I entrust you with this gravest task of accomplishing in the world all I have prepared for by My life and death. This great end, to attain which I thought fit to leave the glory I had with the Father, and for which I have spent all—this I leave in your hands. It is in this world of men the whole results of the Incarnation are to be found, and it is on you the burden is laid of applying to this world the work I have done. You live for Me. But on the other hand I live for you. "Because I live, ye shall live also." I do not really leave you. If I say, "Abide in Me," I none the less say, "and I in you." It is in you I spend all the Divine energy you have witnessed in my life. It is through you I live. I am the Vine, the life-giving Stem, sustaining and quickening you. Ye are the branches, effecting what I intend, bearing the fruit for the sake of which I have been planted in the world by My Father, the Husbandman.

II. The second idea is that this unity of the tree is formed by unity *of life*. It is a unity brought about, not by mechanical juxtaposition, but by organic relationship. "As the branch cannot bear fruit of itself, but must abide in the vine, so neither can ye except ye abide in Me." A ball of twine or a bag of shot cannot be called a whole. If you cut off a yard of the twine, the part cut off has all the qualities and properties of the remainder, and is perhaps more serviceable apart from the rest than in connection with it. A handful of shot is more serviceable for many purposes than a bagful, and the quantity you take out of the bag retains all the properties it had while in the bag; because there is *no common life* in the twine or in the shot, making all the particles one whole. But take anything which is a true unity or whole—your body, for example. Different results follow here from separation. Your eye is useless taken from its place in the body. You can lend a friend your knife or your purse, and it may be more serviceable in his hands than in yours; but you cannot lend him your arms or your ears. Apart from yourself, the members of your body are useless, because here there is one common life forming one organic whole.

It is thus in the relation of Christ and His followers. He and they together form one whole, *because* one common *life* unites them. "*As* the branch cannot bear fruit of itself, so neither can ye." Why can the branch bear no fruit except it abide in the vine? Because it is a *vital* unity that makes the tree one. And what is a vital unity between persons? It can be nothing else than a spiritual unity—a unity not of a bodily kind, but inward and of the spirit. In other words, *it is a unity of purpose and of resources for attaining that purpose.* The branch is one with the tree because it draws its life from the tree and bears the fruit proper to the tree. We are one with Christ when we adopt His purpose in the world as the real governing aim of our life, and when we renew our strength for the fulfilment of that purpose by fellowship with His love for mankind and His eternal purpose to bless men.

We must be content, then, to be branches. We must be content not to stand isolated and grow from a private root of our own. We must utterly renounce selfishness. Successful selfishness is absolutely impossible. The greater the apparent success of selfishness is, the more gigantic will the failure one day appear. An arm severed from the body, a branch lopped off the tree, is the true symbol of the selfish man. He will be left behind as the true progress of mankind proceeds, with no part in the common joy, stranded and dying in cold isolation. We must learn that our true life can only be lived when we recognise that we are parts of a great whole, that we are here not to prosecute any private interest of our own and win a private good for ourselves, but to forward the good that others share in and the cause that is common.

How this unity is formed received no explanation on this occasion. The manner in which men become branches of the true Vine was not touched upon in the allegory. Already the disciples were branches, and no explanation was called for. It may, however, be legitimate to gather a hint from the allegory itself regarding the formation of the living bond between Christ and His people. However ignorant we may be of the propagation of fruit trees and the processes of grafting we can at any rate understand that no mere tying of a branch to a tree, bark to bark, would effect anything save the withering of the branch. The branch, if it is to be fruitful, must form a solid part of the tree, must be grafted so as to become of one structure and life with the stem. It must be cut through, so as to lay bare the whole interior structure of it, and so as to leave open all the vessels that carry the sap ; and a similar incision must be made in the stock upon which the branch is to be grafted, so that the cut sap-vessels of the branch may be in contact with the cut sap-vessels of the stock. Such must be our grafting into Christ. It must be a laying bare of our inmost nature to His inmost nature, so that a vital connection may be formed between these two. What we expect to receive by being connected with Christ is the very Spirit which made Him what He was. We expect to receive into the source of conduct in us all that was the source of conduct in Him. We wish to be in such a connection with Him that His principles, sentiments, and aims shall become ours.

On His side Christ has laid bare His deepest feelings and spirit. In His life and in His death He submitted to that severest operation which seemed to be a maiming of Him, but which in point of fact was the necessary preparation for His receiving fruitful branches. He did not hide the true springs of His life under a hard and rough bark ; but submitting Himself to the Husbandman's knife, He has suffered us through His wounds to see the real motives and vital spirit of His nature— truth, justice, holiness, fidelity, love. Whatever in this life cut our Lord to the quick, whatever tested most thoroughly the true spring of His conduct, only more clearly showed that deepest within Him and strongest within Him lay holy love. And He was not shy of telling men His love for them : in the public death He died He loudly declared it, opening His nature to the gaze of all. And to this open heart He declined to receive none ; as many as the Father gave Him were welcome ; He had none of that aversion we feel to admit all and sundry into close relations with us. He at once gives His heart and keeps back nothing to Himself; He invites us into the closest possible connection with Him, with the intention that we should grow to Him and for ever be loved by Him. Whatever real, lasting, and influential connection can be established between two persons, this He wishes to have with us. If it is possible for two persons so to grow together that separation in spirit is for ever impossible, it is nothing short of this Christ seeks.

But when we turn to the cutting of the branch, we see reluctance and vacillation and much to remind us that, in the graft we now speak of, the Husbandman has to deal, not with passive branches which cannot shrink from his knife, but with free and sensitive human beings. The hand of the Father is on us to sever us from the old stock and give us a place in Christ, but we feel it hard to be severed from the root we have grown from and to which we are now so firmly attached. We refuse to see that the old tree is doomed to the axe, or after we have been inserted into Christ we loosen ourselves again and again, so that morning by morning as the Father visits His tree He finds us dangling useless with signs of withering already upon us. But in the end the Vinedresser's patient skill prevails. We submit ourselves to those incisive operations of God's providence or of His gentler but effective word which finally sever us from what we once clung to. We are impelled to lay bare our heart to Christ and seek the deepest and truest and most influential union.

And even after the graft has been achieved the husbandman's care is still needed that the branch may "abide in the vine," and that it may "bring forth more fruit." There are two risks—the branch may be loosened, or it may run to wood and leaves. Care is taken when a graft is made that its permanent participation in the life of the tree be secured. The graft is not only tied to the tree, but the point of juncture is cased in clay or pitch or wax, so as to exclude air, water, or any disturbing influence. Analogous spiritual treatment is certainly requisite if the attachment of the soul to Christ is to become solid, firm, permanent. If the soul and Christ are to be really one, nothing must be allowed to tamper with the attachment. It must be sheltered from all that might rudely impinge upon it and displace the disciple from the attitude towards Christ he has assumed. When the graft and the stock have grown together into one, then the point of attachment will resist any shock; but, while the attachment is recent, care is needed that the juncture be hermetically secluded from adverse influences.

The husbandman's care is also needed that after the branch is grafted it may bring forth fruit increasingly. Stationariness is not to be tolerated. As for fruitlessness, that is out of the question. More fruit each season is looked for, and arranged for by the vigorous prunings of the husbandman. The branch is not left to nature. It is not allowed to run out in every direction, to waste its life in attaining size. Where it seems to be doing grandly and promising success, the knife of the vinedresser ruthlessly cuts down the flourish, and the fine appearance lies withering on the ground. But the vintage justifies the husbandman.

III. This brings us to the third idea of the allegory—that the result aimed at in our connection with Christ is fruit-bearing. The allegory bids us think of God as engaged in the tendance and culture of men with the watchful, fond interest with which the vinedresser tends his plants through every stage of growth and every season of the year, and even when there is nothing to be done gazes on them admiringly and finds still some little attention he can pay them; but all in the hope of fruit. All this interest collapses at once, all this care becomes a foolish waste of time and material, and reflects discredit and ridicule on the vinedresser, if there is no fruit. God has prepared for us in this life a soil than which nothing can be better for the production of the fruit He desires us to yield; He has made it possible for every man to serve a good purpose; He does His part not with reluctance, but, if we may say so, as His chief interest; but all in the expectation of fruit. We do not spend days of labour and nights of anxious thought, we do not lay out all we have at command, on that which is to effect nothing and give no satisfaction to ourselves or any one else; and neither does God. He did not make this world full of men for want of something better to do, as a mere idle pastime. He made it that the earth might yield her increase, that each of us might bring forth fruit. Fruit alone can justify the expense put upon this world. The wisdom, the patience, the love that have guided all things through the slow-moving ages will be justified in the product. And what this product is we already know: it is the attainment of moral perfection by created beings. To this all that has been made and done in the past leads up. "The whole creation groaneth and travaileth,"—for what? "For the manifestation of the sons of God." The lives and acts of good men are the adequate return for all past outlay, the satisfying fruit.

The production of this fruit became a certainty when Christ was planted in the world as a new moral stem. He was sent into the world not to make some magnificent outward display of Divine power, to carry us to some other planet, or alter the conditions of life here. God might have departed from His purpose of filling this earth with holy men, and might have used it for some easier display which for the moment might have seemed more striking. He did not do so. It was human obedience, the fruit of genuine human righteousness, of the love and goodness of men and women, that He was resolved to reap from earth. He was resolved to train men to such a pitch of goodness that in a world contrived to tempt there should be found nothing so alluring, nothing so terrifying, as to turn men from the straight path. He was to produce a race of men who, while still in the body, urged by appetites, assaulted by passions and cravings, with death threatening and life inviting, should prefer all suffering rather than flinch from duty, should prove themselves actually superior to every assault that can be made on virtue, should prove that spirit is greater than matter. And God set Christ in the world to be the living type of human perfection, to attract men by their love for Him to His kind of life, and to furnish them with all needed aid in becoming like Him—that as Christ had kept the Father's commandments, His disciples should keep His commandments, that thus a common understanding, an identity of interest and moral life, should be established between God and man.

Perhaps it is not pressing the figure too hard to remark that the fruit differs from timber in this respect—that it enters into and nourishes the life of man. No doubt in this allegory fruit-bearing primarily and chiefly indicates that God's purpose in creating man is satisfied. The tree He has planted is not barren, but fruitful. But certainly a great distinction between the selfish and the unselfish man, between the man who has private ambitions and the man who labours for the public good, lies in this—that the selfish man seeks to erect a monument of some kind for himself, while the unselfish man spends himself in labours that are not conspicuous, but assist the life of his fellows. An oak carving or a structure of hard wood will last a thousand years and keep in memory the skill of the designer: fruit is eaten and disappears, but it passes into human life, and becomes part of the stream that flows on for ever. The ambitious man longs to execute a monumental work, and does not much regard whether it will be for the good of men or not; a great war will serve his turn, a great book, anything conspicuous. But he who is content to be a branch of the True Vine will not seek the admiration of men, but will strive to introduce a healthy spiritual life into those he can reach, even although in order to do so he must remain obscure and must see his labours absorbed without notice or recognition.

Does the teaching of this allegory, then, accord with the facts of life as we know them? Is it a truth, and a truth we must act upon, that apart from Christ we can do nothing? In what sense and to what extent is association with Christ really necessary to us?

Something may of course be made of life apart from Christ. A man may have much enjoyment and a man may do much good apart from Christ. He may be an inventor, who makes human life easier or safer or fuller of interest. He may be a literary man, who by his writings enlightens, exhilarates, and elevates mankind. He may, with entire ignorance or utter disregard of Christ, toil for his country or for his class or for his cause. But the best uses and ends of human life cannot be attained apart from Christ. Only in Him does the reunion of man with God seem attainable, and only in Him do God and God's aim and work in the world become intelligible. He is as necessary for the spiritual life of men as the sun is for this physical life. We may effect something by candle-light; we may be quite proud of electric light, and think we are getting far towards independence; but what man in his senses will be betrayed by these attainments into thinking we may dispense with the sun? Christ holds the key to all that is most permanent in human endeavour, to all that is deepest and best in human character. Only in Him can we take our place as partners with God in what He is really doing with this world. And only from Him can we draw courage, hopefulness, love to prosecute this work. In Him God does reveal Himself, and in Him the fulness of God is found by us. He is in point of fact the one moral stem apart from whom we are not bearing and cannot bear the fruit God desires.

If, then, we are not bringing forth fruit, it is because there is a flaw in our connection with Christ; if we are conscious that the results of our life and activity are not such results as He designs, and are in no sense traceable to Him, this is because there is something about our adherence to Him that is loose and needs rectification. Christ calls us to Him and makes us sharers in His work; and he who listens to this call and counts it enough to be a branch of this Vine and do His will is upheld by Christ's Spirit, is sweetened by His meekness and love, is purified by His holy and fearless rectitude, is transformed by the dominant will of this Person whom he has received deepest into his soul, and does therefore bring forth, in whatever place in life he holds, the same kind of fruit as Christ Himself would bring forth; it is indeed Christ who brings forth these fruits, Christ at a few steps removed—for every Christian learns, as well as Paul, to say, "Not I, but Christ in me." If, then, the will of Christ is not being fulfilled through us, if there is good that it belongs to us to do, but which remains undone, then the point of juncture with Christ is the point that needs looking to. It is not some unaccountable blight that makes us useless; it is not that we have got the wrong piece of the wall, a situation in which Christ Himself could bear no precious fruit. The Husbandman knew His own meaning when He trained us along that restricted line and nailed us down; He chose the place for us, knowing the quality of fruit He desires us to yield. The reason of our fruitlessness is the simple one, that we are not closely enough attached to Christ.

 How, then, is it with ourselves? By examining the results of our lives, would any one be prompted to exclaim, "These are trees of *righteousness*, the planting of the Lord that He may be glorified"? For this examination is made, and made not by one who chances to pass, and who, being a novice in horticulture, might be deceived by a show of leaves or poor fruit, or whose examination might terminate in wonder at the slothfulness or mismanagement of the owner who allowed such trees to cumber his ground; but the examination is made by One who has come for the express purpose of gathering fruit, who knows exactly what has been spent upon us and what might have been made of our opportunities, who has in His own mind a definite idea of the fruit that should be found, and who can tell by a glance whether such fruit actually exists or no. To this infallible Judge of produce what have we to offer? From all our busy engagement in many affairs, from all our thought, what has resulted that we can offer as a satisfactory return for all that has been spent upon us? It is deeds of profitable service such as men of large and loving nature would do that God seeks from us. And He recognises without fail what is love and what only seems so. He infallibly detects the corroding spot of selfishness that rots the whole fair-seeming cluster. He stands undeceivable before us, and takes our lives precisely for what they are worth.

It concerns us to make such inquiries, for fruitless branches cannot be tolerated. The purpose of the tree is fruit. If, then, we would escape all suspicion of our own state and all reproach of fruitlessness, what we have to do is, not so much to find out new rules for conduct, as to strive to renew our hold upon Christ and intelligently to enter into His purposes. "Abide in Him." This is the secret of fruitfulness. All that the branch needs is in the Vine; it does not need to go beyond the Vine for anything. When we feel the life of Christ ebbing from our soul, when we see our leaf fading, when we feel sapless, heartless for Christian duty, reluctant to work for others, to take anything to do with the relief of misery and the repression of vice, there is a remedy for this state, and it is to renew our fellowship with Christ—to allow the mind once again to conceive clearly the worthiness of His aims, to yield the heart once again to the vitalising influence of His love, to turn from the vanities and futilities with which men strive to make life seem important to the reality and substantial worth of the life of Christ. To abide in Christ is to abide by our adoption of His view of the true purpose of human life after testing it by actual experience; it is to abide by our trust in Him as the true Lord of men, and as able to supply us with all that we need to keep His commandments. And thus abiding in Christ we are sustained by Him; for He abides in us, imparts to us, His branches now on earth, the force which is needful to accomplish His purposes.

## XII.

*NOT SERVANTS, BUT FRIENDS.*

"Greater love hath no man than this, that a man lay down his life for his friends. Ye are My friends, if ye do the things which I command you. No longer do I call you servants; for the servant knoweth not what his lord doeth: but I have called you friends; for all things that I heard from My Father I have made known unto you. Ye did not choose Me, but I chose you, and appointed you, that ye should go and bear fruit, and that your fruit should abide: that whatsoever ye shall ask of the Father in My name, He may give it you. These things I command you, that ye may love one another."—JOHN xv. 13-17.

## XIII.

### NOT SERVANTS, BUT FRIENDS.

THESE words of our Lord are the charter of our emancipation. They give us entrance into true freedom. They set us in the same attitude towards life and towards God as Christ Himself occupied. Without this proclamation of freedom and all it covers we are the mere drudges of this world,—doing its work, but without any great and far-reaching aim that makes it worth doing; accepting the tasks allotted to us because we must, not because we will; living on because we happen to be here, but without any part in that great future towards which all things are running on. But this is of the very essence of slavery. For our Lord here lays His finger on the sorest part of this deepest of human sores when He says, "The slave knows not what his master does." It is not that his back is torn with the lash, it is not that he is underfed and overworked, it is not that he is poor and despised; all this would be cheerfully undergone to serve a cherished purpose and accomplish ends a man had chosen for himself. But when all this must be endured to work out the purposes of another, purposes never hinted to him, and with which, were they hinted, he might have no sympathy, this is slavery, this is to be treated as a tool for accomplishing aims chosen by another, and to be robbed of all that constitutes manhood. Sailors and soldiers have sometimes mutinied when subjected to similar treatment, when no inkling has been given them of the port to which they are shipped or the nature of the expedition on which they are led. Men do not feel degraded by any amount of hardship, by going for months on short rations or lying in frost without tents; but they do feel degraded when they are used as weapons of offence, as if they had no intelligence to appreciate a worthy aim, no power of sympathising with a great design, no need of an interest in life and a worthy object on which to spend it, no share in the common cause. Yet such is the life with which, apart from Christ, we must perforce be content, doing the tasks appointed us with no sustaining consciousness that our work is part of a great whole working out the purposes of the Highest. Even such a spirit as Carlyle is driven to say: "Here on earth we are soldiers, fighting in a foreign land, that understand not the plan of campaign and have no need to understand it, seeing what is at our hand to be done,"—excellent counsel for slaves, but not descriptive of the life we are meant for, nor of the life our Lord would be content to give us.

To give us true freedom, to make this life a thing we choose with the clearest perception of its uses and with the utmost ardour, our Lord makes known to us all that He heard of the Father. What He had heard of the Father, all that the Spirit of the Father had taught Him of the need of human effort and of human righteousness, all that as He grew up to manhood He recognised of the deep-seated woes of humanity, and all that He was prompted to do for the relief of these woes, He made known to His disciples. The irresistible call to self-sacrifice and labour for the relief of men which He heard and obeyed, He made known and He makes known to all who follow Him. He did not allot clearly defined tasks to His followers; He did not treat them as slaves, appointing one to this and another to that: He showed them His own aim and His own motive, and left them as His friends to be attracted by the aim that had drawn Him, and to be ever animated with the motive that sufficed for Him. What had made His life so glorious, so full of joy, so rich in constant reward, He knew would fill their lives also; and He leaves them free to choose it for themselves, to stand before life as independent, unfettered, undriven men, and choose without compulsion what their own deepest convictions prompted them to choose. The "friend" is not compelled blindly to go through with a task whose result he does not understand or does not sympathise with; the friend is invited to share in a work in which he has a direct personal interest and to which he can give himself cordially. All life should be the forwarding of purposes we approve, the bringing about of ends we earnestly desire: all life, if we are free men, must be matter of choice, not of compulsion. And therefore Christ, having heard of the Father that which made Him feel straitened until the great aim of His life could be accomplished, which made Him press forward through life attracted and impelled by the consciousness of its infinite value as achieving endless good, imparts to us what moved and animated Him, that we may freely choose as He chose and enter into the joy of our Lord.

This, then, is the point of this great utterance: Jesus takes our lives up into partnership with His own.

He sets before us the same views and hopes which animated Himself, and gives us a prospect of being useful to Him and in His work. If we engage in the work of life with a dull and heartless feeling of its weariness, or merely for the sake of gaining a livelihood, if we are not drawn to labour by the prospect of result, then we have scarcely entered into the condition our Lord opens to us. It is for the merest slaves to view their labour with indifference or repugnance. Out of this state our Lord calls us, by making known to us what the Father made known to Him, by giving us the whole means of a free, rational, and fruitful life. He gives us the fullest satisfaction moral beings can have, because He fills our life with intelligent purpose. He lifts us into a position in which we see that we are not the slaves of fate or of this world, but that *all things are ours*, that we, through and with Him, are masters of the position, and that so far from thinking it almost a hardship to have been born into so melancholy and hopeless a world, we have really the best reason and the highest possible object for living. He comes among us and says, "Let us all work together. Something can be made of this world. Let us with heart and hope strive to make of it something worthy. Let unity of aim and of work bind us together." This is indeed to redeem life from its vanity.

He says this, and lest any should think, "This is fantastic; how can such an one as I am forward the work of Christ? It is enough if I get from Him salvation for myself," He goes on to say, "Ye have not chosen Me, but I have chosen you, and ordained you that ye should go and bring forth fruit, and that your fruit should remain. It was," He says, "precisely in view of the eternal results of your work that I selected you and called you to follow Me." It was true then, and it is true now, that the initiative in our fellowship with Christ is with Him. So far as the first disciples were concerned Jesus might have spent His life making ploughs and cottage furniture. No one discovered Him. Neither does any one now discover Him. It is He who comes and summons us to follow and to serve Him. He does so because He sees that there is that which we can do which no one else can: relationships we hold, opportunities we possess, capacities for just this or that, which are our special property into which no other can possibly step, and which, if we do not use them, cannot otherwise be used.

Does He, then, point out to us with unmistakable exactness what we are to do, and how we are to do it? Does He lay down for us a code of rules so multifarious and significant that we cannot mistake the precise piece of work He requires from us? He does not. He has but one sole commandment, and this is no commandment, because we cannot keep it on compulsion, but only at the prompting of our own inward spirit: He bids us love one another. He comes back and back to this with significant persistence, and declines to utter one other commandment. In love alone is sufficient wisdom, sufficient motive, and sufficient reward for human life. It alone has adequate wisdom for all situations, new resource for every fresh need, adaptability to all emergencies, an inexhaustible fertility and competency; it alone can bring the capability of each to the service of all. Without love we beat the air.

That love is our true life is shown further by this— that it is its own reward. When a man's life is in any intelligible sense proceeding from love, when this is his chief motive, he is content with living, and looks for no reward. His joy is already full; he does not ask, What shall I be the better of thus sacrificing myself? what shall I gain by all this regulation of my life? what good return in the future shall I have for all I am losing now? He cannot ask these questions, if the motive of his self-sacrificing life be love; just as little as the husband could ask what reward he should have for loving his wife. A man would be astounded and would scarcely know what you meant if you asked him what he expected to get by loving his children or his parents or his friends. Get? Why he does not expect to get anything; he does not love for an object: he loves because he cannot help it; and the chief joy of his life is in these unrewarded affections. He no longer looks forward and thinks of a fulness of life that is to be; he already lives and is satisfied with the life he has. His happiness is present; his reward is that he may be allowed to express his love, to feed it, to gratify it by giving and labouring and sacrificing. In a word, he finds in love eternal life—life that is full of joy, that kindles and enlivens his whole nature, that carries him out of himself and makes him capable of all good.

This truth, then, that whatever a man does from love is its own reward, is the solution of the question whether virtue is its own reward. Virtue is its own reward when it is inspired by love. Life is its own reward when love is the principle of it. We know that we should always be happy were we always loving. We know that we should never weary of living nor turn with distaste from our work were all our work only the expression of our love, of our deep, true, and well-directed regard for the good of others. It is when we disregard our Lord's one commandment and try some other kind of virtuous living that joy departs from our life, and we begin to hope for some future reward which may compensate for the dulness of the present—as if a change of time could change the essential conditions of life and happiness. If we are not joyful now, if life is dreary and dull and pointless to us, so that we crave the excitement of a speculative business, or of boisterous social meetings, or of individual success and applause, then it should be quite plain to us that as yet we have not found life, and have not the capacity for eternal life quickened in us. If we are able to love one human being in some sort as Christ loved us—that is to say, if our affection is so fixed upon any one that we feel we could give our life for that person—let us thank God for this; for this love of ours gives us the key to human life, and will better instruct us in what is most essential to know, and lead us on to what is most essential to be and to do than any one can teach us. It is profoundly and widely true, as John says, that every one that loveth is born of God and knoweth God. If we love one human being, we at least know that a life in which love is the main element needs no reward and looks for none. We see that God looks for no reward, but is eternally blessed because simply God is eternally love. Life eternal must be a life of love, of delight in our fellows, of rejoicing in their good and seeking to increase their happiness.

Sometimes, however, we find ourselves grieving at the prosperity of the wicked: we think that they should be unhappy, and yet they seem more satisfied than ourselves. They pay no regard whatever to the law of life laid down by our Lord; they never dream of living for others; they have never once proposed to themselves to consider whether His great law, that a man must lose his life if he is to have it eternally, has any application to them; and yet they seem to enjoy life as much as anybody can. Take a man who has a good constitution, and who is in easy circumstances, and who has a good and pure nature; you will often see such a man living with no regard to the Christian rule, and yet enjoying life thoroughly to the very end. And of course it is just such a spectacle, repeated everywhere throughout society, that influences men's minds and tempts all of us to believe that such a life is best after all, and that selfishness as well as unselfishness can be happy; or at all events that we can have as much happiness as our own disposition is capable of by a self-seeking life. Now, when we are in a mood to compare our own happiness with that of other men, our own happiness must obviously be at a low ebb; but when we resent the prosperity of the wicked, we should remember that, though they may flourish like the green bay tree, their fruit does not remain: living for themselves, their fruit departs with themselves, their good is interred with their bones. But it is also to be considered that we should never allow ourselves to get the length of putting this question or of comparing our happiness with that of others. For we can only do so when we are ourselves disappointed and discontented and have missed the joy of life; and this again can be only when we have ceased to live lovingly for others.

But this one essential of Christian service and human freedom—how are we to attain it? Is it not the one thing which seems obstinately to stand beyond our grasp? For the human heart has laws of its own, and cannot love to order or admire because it ought But Christ brings, in Himself, the fountain out of which our hearts can be supplied, the fire which kindles all who approach it. No one can receive His love without sharing it. No one can dwell upon Christ's love for him and treasure it as his true and central possession without finding his own heart enlarged and softened. Until our own heart is flooded with the great and regenerating love of Christ, we strive in vain to love our fellows. It is when we fully admit it that it overflows through our own satisfied and quickened affections to others.

And perhaps we do well not too curiously to question and finger our love, making sure only that we are keeping ourselves in Christ's fellowship and seeking to do His will. Affection, indeed, induces companionship, but also companionship produces affection, and the honest and hopeful endeavour to serve Christ loyally will have its reward in a deepening devotion. It is not the recruit but the veteran whose heart is wholly his chief's. And he who has long and faithfully served Christ will not need to ask where his heart is. We hate those whom we have injured, and we love those whom we have served; and if by long service we can win our way to an intimacy with Christ which no longer needs to question itself or test its soundness, in that service we may most joyfully engage. For what can be a happier consummation than to find ourselves finally overcome by the love of Christ, drawn with all the force of a Divine attraction, convinced that here is our rest, and that this is at once our motive and our reward?

# XIV.

## THE SPIRIT CHRIST'S WITNESS.

"If the world hateth you, ye know that it hath hated Me before it hated you. If ye were of the world, the world would love its own: but because ye are not of the world, but I chose you out of the world, therefore the world hateth you. Remember the word that I said unto you, A servant is not greater than his lord. If they persecuted Me, they will also persecute you; if they kept My word, they will keep yours also. But all these things will they do unto you for My name's sake, because they know not Him that sent Me. If I had not come and spoken unto them, they had not had sin: but now they have no excuse for their sin. He that hateth Me hateth My Father also. If I had not done among them the works which none other did, they had not had sin: but now have they both seen and hated both Me and My Father. But this cometh to pass, that the word may be fulfilled that is written in their law, They hated Me without a cause. But when the Comforter is come, whom I will send unto you from the Father, even the Spirit of truth, which proceedeth from the Father, He shall bear witness of Me: and ye also bear witness, because ye have been with Me from the beginning. These things have I spoken unto you, that ye should not be made to stumble. They shall put you out of the synagogues: yea, the hour cometh, that whosoever killeth you shall think that he offereth service unto God. And these things will they do, because they have not known the Father, nor Me. But these things have I spoken unto you, that when their hour is come, ye may remember them, how that I told you. And these things I said not unto you from the beginning, because I was with you. But now I go unto Him that sent Me; and none of you asketh Me, Whither goest Thou? But because I have spoken these things unto you, sorrow hath filled your heart. Nevertheless I tell you the truth; It is expedient for you that I go away: for if I go not away, the Comforter will not come unto you; but if I go, I will send Him unto you. And He, when He is come, will convict the world in respect of sin, and of righteousness, and of judgment: of sin, because they believe not on Me; of righteousness, because I go to the Father, and ye behold Me no more; of judgment, because the prince of this world hath been judged. I have yet many things to say unto you, but ye cannot bear them now. Howbeit when He, the Spirit of truth, is come, He shall guide you into all the truth: for He shall not speak from Himself; but what things soever He shall hear, these shall He speak: and He shall declare unto you the things that are to come. He shall glorify Me: for He shall take of Mine, and shall declare it unto you. All things whatsoever the Father hath are Mine: therefore said I, that He taketh of Mine, and shall declare it unto you."—JOHN xv. 18—xvi. 15.

## XIV.

### *THE SPIRIT CHRIST'S WITNESS.*

HAVING shown His disciples that by them only can His purposes on earth be fulfilled, and that He will fit them for all work that may be required of them, the Lord now adds that their task will be full of hazard and hardship: "They shall put you out of the synagogues: yea, the time cometh that whosoever killeth you will think that he offereth service unto God." This was but a dreary prospect, and one to make each Apostle hesitate, and in the privacy of his own thoughts consider whether he should face a life so devoid of all that men naturally crave. To live for great ends is no doubt animating, but to be compelled in doing so to abandon all expectation of recognition, and to lay one's account for abuse, poverty, persecution, calls for some heroism in him that undertakes such a life. He forewarns them of this persecution, that when it comes they may not be taken aback and fancy that things are not falling out with them as their Lord anticipated. And He offers them two strong consolations which might uphold and animate them under all they should be called upon to suffer.

I. "If the world hateth you, ye know that it hath hated Me before it hated you. If ye were of the world, the world would love its own; but because ye are not of the world, but I chose you out of the world, therefore the world hateth you." Persecution is thus turned into a joy, because it is the testimony paid by the world to the disciples' identity with Christ. The love of the world would be a sure evidence of their unfaithfulness to Christ and of their entire lack of resemblance to Him; but its hate was the tribute it would pay to their likeness to Him and successful promotion of His cause. They might well question their loyalty to Christ, if the world which had slain Him fawned upon them. The Christian may conclude he is reckoned a helpless and harmless foe if he suffers no persecution, if in no company he is frowned upon or felt to be uncongenial, if he is treated by the world as if its aims were his aims and its spirit his spirit. No faithful follower of Christ who mixes with society can escape every form of persecution. It is the seal which the world puts on the choice of Christ. It is proof that a man's attachment to Christ and endeavour to forward His purposes have been recognised by the world. Persecution, then, should be welcome as the world's testimony to the disciple's identity with Christ.

No idea had fixed itself more deeply in the mind of John than this of the identity of Christ and His people. As he brooded upon the life of Christ and sought to penetrate to the hidden meanings of all that appeared on the surface, he came to see that the unbelief and hatred with which He was met was the necessary result of goodness presented to worldliness and selfishness. And as time went on he saw that the experience of Christ was exceptional only in degree, that His experience was and would be repeated in every one who sought to live in His Spirit and to do His will. The future of the Church accordingly presented itself to him as a history of conflict, of extreme cruelty on the part of the world and quiet conquering endurance on the part of Christ's people. And it was this which he embodied in the Book of Revelation. This book he wrote as a kind of detailed commentary on the passage before us, and in it he intended to depict the sufferings and final conquest of the Church. The one book is a reflex and supplement to the other; and as in the Gospel he had shown the unbelief and cruelty of the world against Christ, so in the Revelation he shows in a series of strongly coloured pictures how the Church of Christ would pass through the same experience, would be persecuted as Christ was persecuted, but would ultimately conquer. Both books are wrought out with extreme care and finished to the minutest detail, and both deal with the cardinal matters of human history—sin, righteousness, and the final result of their conflict. Underneath all that appears on the surface in the life of the individual and in the history of the race there are just these abiding elements—sin and righteousness. It is the moral value of things which in the long run proves of consequence, the moral element which ultimately determines all else.

II. The second consolation and encouragement the Lord gave them was that they would receive the aid of a powerful champion—*the* Paraclete, the one effectual, sufficient Helper. "When the Paraclete is come, whom I will send unto you from the Father, even the Spirit of truth, which proceedeth from the Father, he shall bear witness of Me: and ye also bear witness, because ye have been with Me from the beginning." Inevitably the disciples would argue that, if the words and works of Jesus Himself had not broken down the unbelief of the world, it was not likely that anything which they could say or do would have that effect. If the impressive presence of Christ Himself had not attracted and convinced all men, how was it possible that mere telling about what He had said and done and been would convince them? And He has just been reminding them how little effect His own words and works had had. "If I had not come and spoken unto them, they had not had sin: . . . if I had not done among them the works which none other did, they had not had sin: but now have they both seen and hated both Me and My Father." What power, then, could break down this obstinate unbelief?

Our Lord assures them that together with their witness-bearing there will be an all-powerful witness— "the Spirit of truth"; one who could find access to the hearts and minds to which they addressed themselves and carry truth home to conviction. It was on this account that it was "expedient" that their Lord should depart, and that His visible presence should be superseded by the presence of the Spirit. It was necessary that His death, resurrection, and ascension to the right hand of the Father should take place, in order that His supremacy might be secured. And in order that He might be everywhere and inwardly present with men, it was necessary that He should be visible nowhere on earth. The inward spiritual presence depended on the bodily absence.

Before passing to the specific contents of the Spirit's testimony, as stated in vv. 8-11, it is necessary to gather up what our Lord indicates regarding the Spirit Himself and His function in the Christian dispensation. First, the Spirit here spoken of is a personal existence. Throughout all that our Lord says in this last conversation regarding the Spirit personal epithets are applied to Him, and the actions ascribed to Him are personal actions. He is to be the substitute of the most marked and influential Personality with whom the disciples had ever been brought in contact. He is to supply His vacated place. He is to be to the disciples as friendly and staunch an ally and a more constantly present and efficient teacher than Christ Himself. What as yet was not in their minds He was to impart to them; and He was to mediate and maintain communication between the absent Lord and themselves. Was it possible that the disciples should think of the Spirit otherwise than as a conscious and energetic Person when they heard Him spoken of in such words as these: " Howbeit when He, the Spirit of truth, is come, He shall guide you into all the truth: for He shall not speak from Himself; but what things soever He shall hear, these shall He speak: and He shall declare unto you the things that are to come. He shall glorify Me: for He shall take of Mine, and shall declare it unto you"? From these words it would seem as if the disciples were justified in expecting the presence and aid of One who was very closely related to their Lord, but yet distinct from Him, who could understand their state of mind and adapt Himself to them, who is not identical with the Master they are losing, and yet comes into still closer contact with them. What underlies this, and what is the very nature of the Spirit and His relation to the Father and the Son, we do not know; but our Lord chose these expressions which to our thought involve personality because this is the truest and safest form under which we can now conceive of the Spirit.

The function for the discharge of which this Spirit is necessary is the "glorification" of Christ. Without

Him the manifestation of Christ will be lost. He is needed to secure that the world be brought into contact with Christ, and that men recognise and use Him. This is the most general and comprehensive aspect of the Spirit's work: "He shall glorify Me" (ver. 14). In making this announcement our Lord assumes that position of commanding importance with which this Gospel has made us familiar. The Divine Spirit is to be sent forth, and the direct object of His mission is the glorifying of Christ. The meaning of Christ's manifestation is the essential thing for men to understand. In manifesting Himself He has revealed the Father. He has in His own person shown what a Divine nature is; and therefore in order to His glorification all that is required is that light be shed upon what He has done and been, and that the eyes of men be opened to see Him and His work. The recognition of Christ and of God in Him is the blessedness of the human race; and to bring this about is the function of the Spirit. As Jesus Himself had constantly presented Himself as the revealer of the Father and as speaking His words, so, in "a rivalry of Divine humility," the Spirit glorifies the Son and speaks "what He shall hear."

To discharge this function a twofold ministry is undertaken by the Spirit: He must enlighten the Apostles, and He must convince the world.

He must enlighten the Apostles. From the nature of the case much had to be left unsaid by Christ. But this would not prevent the Apostles from understanding what Christ had done, and what applications His work had to themselves and their fellow-men. "I have yet many things to say unto you, but ye cannot bear them now. Howbeit when He, the Spirit of truth, is come, He will guide you into all the truth." A great untravelled country lay before them. Their Master had led them across its border, and set their faces in the right direction; but who was to find a way for them through all its intricacies and perplexities? The Spirit of truth, He who is Himself perfect knowledge and absolute light, "will guide you"; He will go before you and show you your way.[1] There may be no sudden impartation of truth, no lifting of the mist that hangs on the horizon, no consciousness that now you have mastered all difficulties and can see your way to the end; there may be no violation of the natural and difficult processes by which men arrive at truth; the road may be slow, and sometimes there may even be an appearance of ignominious defeat by those who use swifter but more precarious means of advance; much will depend on your own patience and wakefulness and docility; but if you admit the Spirit, He will guide you into all the truth.

This promise does not involve that the Apostles, and through them all disciples, should know everything. "All the truth" is relative to the subject taught. All that they need to know regarding Christ and His work for them they will learn. All that is needed to glorify Christ, to enable men to recognise Him as the manifestation of God, will be imparted. To the truth which the Apostles learn, therefore, nothing need be added. Nothing essential has been added. Time has now been given to test this promise, and what time has shown is this—that while libraries have been written on what the Apostles thought and taught, their teaching remains as the sufficient guide into all the truth regard-

---

[1] ὁδηγήσει.

ing Christ. Even in non-essentials it is marvellous how little has been added. Many corrections of misapprehensions of their meaning have been required, much laborious inquiry to ascertain precisely what they meant, much elaborate inference and many buildings upon their foundations; but in their teaching there remain a freshness and a living force which survive all else that has been written upon Christ and His religion.

This instruction of the Apostles by the Spirit was to recall to their minds what Christ Himself had said, and was also to show them things to come. The changed point of view introduced by the dispensation of the Spirit and the abolition of earthly hopes would cause many of the sayings of Jesus which they had disregarded and considered unintelligible to spring into high relief and ray out significance, while the future also would shape itself quite differently in their conception. And the Teacher who should superintend and inspire this altered attitude of mind is the Spirit.[1]

Not only must the Spirit enlighten the Apostles; He must also convince the world. "He shall bear witness of Me," and by His witness-bearing the testimony of the Apostles would become efficacious. They had a natural fitness to witness about Christ, "because they had been with Him from the beginning." No more trustworthy witnesses regarding what Christ had said or done or been could be called than those men with whom He had lived on terms of intimacy. No men could more certainly testify to the identity of the risen Lord. But the significance of the facts they spoke of

---

[1] Godet says: "The saying xiv. 26 gives the formula of the inspiration of our Gospels; ver. 13 gives that of the inspiration of the Epistles and the Apocalypse."

could best be taught by the Spirit. The very fact of the Spirit's presence was the greatest evidence that the Lord had risen and was using "all power in heaven" in behalf of men. And possibly it was to this Peter referred when he said: "We are His witnesses of these things; and so is also the Holy Ghost, whom God hath given to them that obey Him." Certainly the gifts of the Holy Ghost, the power to speak with tongues or to work miracles of healing, were accepted by the primitive Church as a seal of the Apostolic word and as the appropriate evidence of the power of the risen Christ.

But it is apparent from our Lord's description of the subject-matter of the Spirit's witness that here He has especially in view the function of the Spirit as an inward teacher and strengthener of the moral powers. He is the fellow-witness of the Apostles, mainly and permanently, by enlightening men in the significance of the facts reported by them, and by opening the heart and conscience to their influence.

The subject-matter of the Spirit's testimony is three-fold: "He will convict the world in respect of sin, and of righteousness, and of judgment."

I. He should convict the world of sin. No conviction cuts so deeply and produces results of such magnitude as the conviction of sin. It is like subsoil ploughing: it turns up soil that nothing else has got down to. It alters entirely a man's attitude towards life. He cannot know himself a sinner and be satisfied with that condition. This awakening is like the waking of one who has been buried in a trance, who wakes to find himself bound round with grave-clothes, hemmed in with all the insignia of corruption, terror and revulsion distracting and overwhelming his soul. In spirit he has been far away, weaving perhaps a paradise out of his fancies, peopling it with choice and happy society, and living through scenes of gorgeous beauty and comfort in fulness of interest and life and felicity; but suddenly comes the waking, a few brief moments of painful struggle and the dream gives place to the reality, and then comes the certain accumulation of misery till the spirit breaks beneath its fear. So does the strongest heart groan and break when it wakes to the full reality of sin, when the Spirit of Christ takes the veil from a man's eyes and gives him to see what this world is and what he has been in it, when the shadows that have occupied him flee away and the naked inevitable reality confronts him.

Nothing is more overwhelming than this conviction, but nothing is more hopeful. Given a man who is alive to the evil of sin and who begins to understand his errors, and you know some good will come of that. Given a man who sees the importance of being in accord with perfect goodness and who feels the degradation of sin, and you have the germ of all good in that man. But how were the Apostles to produce this? how were they to dispel those mists which blurred the clear outline of good and evil, to bring to the self-righteous Pharisee and the indifferent and worldly Sadducee a sense of their own sin? What instrument is there which can introduce to every human heart, howsoever armoured and fenced round, this healthy revolution? Looking at men as they actually are, and considering how many forces are banded together to exclude the knowledge of sin, how worldly interest demands that no brand shall be affixed to this and that action, how the customs we are brought up in require us to take a lenient view of this and that immorality, how we deceive ourselves by sacrificing sins we do not care for in order to retain sins that are in our blood, how the resistance of certain sins makes us a prey to self-righteousness and delusion—considering what we have learnt of the placidity with which men content themselves with a life they know is not the highest, does there seem to be any instrument by which a true and humbling sense of sin can be introduced to the mind?

Christ, knowing that men were about to put Him to death because He had tried to convict them of sin, confidently predicts that His servants would by His Spirit's aid convince the world of sin and of this in particular—that they had not believed in Him. That very death which chiefly exhibits human sin has, in fact, become the chief instrument in making men understand and hate sin. There is no consideration from which the deceitfulness of sin will not escape, nor any fear which the recklessness of sin will not brave, nor any authority which self-will cannot override but only this: Christ has died for me, to save me from my sin, and I am sinning still, not regarding His blood, not meeting His purpose. It was when the greatness and the goodness of Christ were together let in to Peter's mind that he fell on his face before Him, saying, "Depart from me, O Lord, for I am a sinful man." And the experience of thousands is recorded in that more recent confession:

"In evil long I took delight, unawed by shame or fear,
Till a new object struck my sight and stopped my wild career:
I saw One hanging on a tree in agonies and blood,
Who fixed His languid eyes on me as near His cross I stood.
Sure never till my latest breath can I forget that look;
It seemed to charge me with His death, though not a word He
    spoke."

Of other convictions we may get rid ; the consequences

of sin we may brave, or we may disbelieve that in our case sin will produce any very disastrous fruits; but in the death of Christ we see, not what sin may possibly do in the future, but what it actually has done in the past. In presence of the death of Christ we cannot any longer make a mock of sin or think lightly of it, as if it were on our own responsibility and at our own risk we sinned.

But not only does the death of Christ exhibit the intricate connections of our sin with other persons and the grievous consequence of sin in general, but also it exhibits the enormity of this particular sin of rejecting Christ. " He will convince the world of sin, *because they believe not on Me.*" It was this sin in point of fact which cut to the heart the crowd at Jerusalem first addressed by Peter. Peter had nothing to say of their looseness of life, of their worldliness, of their covetousness : he did not go into particulars of conduct calculated to bring a blush to their cheeks; he took up but one point, and by a few convincing remarks showed them the enormity of crucifying the Lord of glory. The lips which a few days before had cried out "Crucify Him, crucify Him!" now cried, Men and brethren, what shall we do, how escape from the crushing condemnation of mistaking God's image for a criminal? In that hour Christ's words were fulfilled; they were convinced of sin because they believed not on Him.

This is ever the damning sin—to be in presence of goodness and not to love it, to see Christ and to see Him with unmoved and unloving hearts, to hear His call without response, to recognise the beauty of holiness and yet turn away to lust and self and the world. This is the condemnation—that light is come into the world and we have loved darkness rather than the light. "If I had not come and spoken unto them, they had not had sin: but now they have no cloke for their sin. He that hateth Me, hateth My Father also." To turn away from Christ is to turn away from absolute goodness. It is to show that however much we may relish certain virtues and approve particular forms of goodness, goodness absolute and complete does not attract us.

II. The conviction of righteousness is the complement, the other half, of the conviction of sin. In the shame of guilt there is the germ of the conviction of righteousness. The sense of guilt is but the acknowledgment that we ought to be righteous. No guilt attaches to the incapable. The sting of guilt is poisoned with the knowledge that we were capable of better things. Conscience exclaims against all excuses that would lull us into the idea that sin is insuperable, and that there is nothing better for us than a moderately sinful life. When conscience ceases to condemn, hope dies. A mist rises from sin that obscures the clear outline between its own domain and that of righteousness, like the mist that rises from the sea and mingles shore and water in one undefined cloud. But let it rise off the one and the other is at once distinctly marked out; and so in the conviction of sin there is already involved the conviction of righteousness. The blush of shame that suffuses the face of the sinner as the mist-dispelling Sun of righteousness arises upon him is the morning flush and promise of an everlasting day of righteous living.

For each of us it is of the utmost importance to have a fixed and intelligent persuasion that righteousness is what we are made for. The righteous Lord loveth righteousness and made us in His image to widen the joy of rational creatures. He waits for righteousness and cannot accept sin as an equally grateful fruit of men's lives. And though in the main perhaps our faces are turned towards righteousness, and we are on the whole dissatisfied and ashamed of sin, yet the conviction of righteousness has much to struggle against in us all. Sin, we unconsciously plead, is so finely interwoven with all the ways of the world that it is impossible to live wholly free from it. As well cast a sponge into the water and command that it absorb none nor sink as put me in the world and command that I do not admit its influences or sink to its level. It presses in on me through all my instincts and appetites and hopes and fears; it washes ceaselessly at the gateways of my senses, so that one unguarded moment and the torrent bursts in on me and pours over my wasted bulwarks, resolves, high aims, and whatever else. It is surely not now and here that I am expected to do more than learn the rudiments of righteous living and make small experiments in it; endeavours will surely stand for accomplishment, and pious purposes in place of heroic action and positive righteousness. Men take sin for granted and lay their account for it. Will not God also, who remembers our frailty, consider the circumstances and count sin a matter of course? Such thoughts haunt and weaken us; but every man whose heart is touched by the Spirit of God clings to this as his hopeful prayer: "Teach me to do Thy will, for Thou art my God: Thy Spirit is good; lead me into the land of uprightness."

But, after all, it is by fact men are convinced; and were there no facts to appeal to in this matter conviction could not be attained. It does seem that we are made for righteousness, but sin is in this world so universal that there must surely be some way of accounting for it which shall also excuse it. Had righteousness been to be our life, surely some few would have attained it. There must be some necessity of sin, some impossibility of attaining perfect righteousness, and therefore we need not seek it. Here comes in the proof our Lord speaks of: " The Spirit will convince of righteousness, because I go to the Father." Righteousness has been attained. There has lived One, bone of our bone, and flesh of our flesh, tempted in all points like as we are, open to the same ambitious views of life, growing up with the same appetites and as sensitive to bodily pleasure and bodily pain, feeling as keenly the neglect and hatred of men, and from the very size of His nature and width of His sympathy tempted in a thousand ways we are safe from, and yet in no instance confounding right and wrong, in no instance falling from perfect harmony with the Divine will to self-will and self-seeking; never deferring the commandments of God to some other sphere or waiting for holier times; never forgetting and never renouncing the purpose of God in His life; but at all times, in weariness and lassitude, in personal danger and in domestic comfort, putting Himself as a perfect instrument into God's hand, ready at all cost to Himself to do the Father's will. Here was One who not only recognised that men are made to work together with God, but who actually did so work; who not only approved, as we all approve, of a life of holiness and sacrifice, but actually lived it; who did not think the trial too great, the privation and risk too dreadful, the self-effacement too humbling; but who met life with all it brings to all of us—its conflict, its interests, its opportunities, its allurements, its snares, its hazards. But while out of this material we fail to make a perfect life, He by His integrity of purpose and devotedness and love of good fashioned a perfect life. Thus He simply by living accomplished what the law with its commands and threats had not accomplished: He condemned sin in the flesh.

But it was open to those whom the Apostles addressed to deny that Jesus had thus lived; and therefore the conviction of righteousness is completed by the evidence of the resurrection and ascension of Christ. "Of righteousness, because I go to My Father, and ye see Me no more." Without holiness no man shall see God. It was this that the Apostles appealed to when first moved to address their fellow-men and proclaim Christ as the Saviour. It was to His resurrection they confidently appealed as evidence of the truth of His claim to have been sent of God. The Jews had put Him to death as a deceiver; but God proclaimed His righteousness by raising Him from the dead. "Ye denied the Holy One and the Just, and desired a murderer to be granted unto you, and killed the Prince of life whom God hath raised from the dead, whereof we are witnesses."

Probably, however, another idea underlies the words "because I go to My Father, and ye see Me no more." So long as Christ was on earth the Jews believed that Jesus and His followers were plotting a revolution: when He was removed beyond sight such a suspicion became ludicrous. But when His disciples could no longer see Him, they continued to serve Him and to strive with greater zeal than ever to promote His cause. Slowly then it dawned on men's minds that righteousness was what Christ and His Apostles alone desired and sought to establish on earth. This new spectacle of men devoting their lives to the advancement of righteousness, and confident they could establish a kingdom of righteousness and actually establishing it—this spectacle penetrated men's minds, and gave them a new sense of the value of righteousness, and quite a new conviction of the possibility of attaining it.

III. The third conviction by which the Apostles were to prevail in their preaching of Christ was the conviction "of judgment, because the prince of this world is judged." Men were to be persuaded that a distinction is made between sin and righteousness, that in no case can sin pass for righteousness and righteousness for sin. The world that has worldly ends in view and works towards them by appropriate means, disregarding moral distinctions, will be convicted of enormous error. The Spirit of truth will work in men's minds the conviction that all and every sin is mistake and productive of nothing good, and can in no instance accomplish what righteousness would have accomplished. Men will find, when truth shines in their spirit, that they have not to await a great day of judgment in the end, when the good results of sin shall be reversed and reward allotted to those who have done righteously, but that judgment is a constant and universal element in God's government and to be found everywhere throughout it, distinguishing between sin and righteousness in every present instance, and never for one moment allowing to sin the value or the results which only righteousness has. In the minds of men who have been using the world's unrighteous methods and living for the world's selfish ends, the conviction is to be wrought that no good can come of all that— that sin is sin and not valid for any good purpose. Men are to recognise that a distinction is made between human actions, and that condemnation is pronounced on all that are sinful.

And this conviction is to be wrought in the light of the fact that in Christ's victory the prince of this world is judged. The powers by which the world is actually led are seen to be productive of evil, and not the powers by which men can permanently be led or should at any time have been led. The prince of this world was judged by Christ's refusal throughout His life to be in anything guided by him. The motives by which the world is led were not Christ's motives.

But it is in the death of Christ the prince of this world was especially judged. That death was brought about by the world's opposition to unworldliness. Had the world been seeking spiritual beauty and prosperity, Christ would not have been crucified. He was crucified because the world was seeking material gain and worldly glory, and was thereby blinded to the highest form of goodness. And unquestionably the very fact that worldliness led to this treatment of Christ is its most decided condemnation. We cannot think highly of principles and dispositions which so blind men to the highest form of human goodness and lead them to actions so unreasonable and wicked. As an individual will often commit one action which illustrates his whole character, and flashes sudden light into the hidden parts of it, and discloses its capabilities and possible results, so the world has in this one act shown what worldliness essentially is and at all times is capable of. No stronger condemnation of the influences which move worldly men can be found than the crucifixion of Christ.

But, besides, the death of Christ exhibits in so touching a form the largeness and power of spiritual beauty, and brings so vividly home to the heart the charm of holiness and love, that here more than anywhere else do men learn to esteem beauty of character and holiness and love more than all the world can yield them. We feel that to be wholly out of sympathy with the qualities and ideas manifested in the Cross would be a pitiable condition. We adopt as our ideal the kind of glory there revealed, and in our hearts condemn the opposed style of conduct that the world leads to. As we open our understanding and conscience to the meaning of Christ's love and sacrifice and devotedness to God's will, the prince of this world is judged and condemned within us. We feel that to yield to the powers that move and guide the world is impossible for us, and that we must give ourselves to this Prince of holiness and spiritual glory.

In point of fact the world is judged. To adhere to worldly motives and ways and ambitions is to cling to a sinking ship, to throw ourselves away on a justly doomed cause. The world may trick itself out in what delusive splendours it may; it is judged all the same, and men who are deluded by it and still in one way or other acknowledge the prince of this world destroy themselves and lose the future.

Such was the promise of Christ to His disciples. Is it fulfilled in us? We may have witnessed in others the entrance and operation of convictions which to all appearance correspond with those here described. We may even have been instrumental in producing these convictions. But a lens of ice will act as a burning-glass, and itself unmelted will fire the tinder to which it transmits the rays. And perhaps we may be able to say with much greater confidence that we have done good than that we are good. Convinced of sin we may be, and convinced of righteousness we may be—so far at least as to feel most keenly that the distinction between sin and righteousness is real, wide, and of eternal consequence—but is the prince of this world judged? has the power that claims us as the servants of sin and mocks our strivings after righteousness been, so far as we can judge from our own experience, defeated? For this is the final test of religion, of our faith in Christ, of the truth of His words and the efficacy of His work. Does He accomplish in me what He promised?

Now, when we begin to doubt the efficacy of the Christian method on account of its apparent failure in our own case, when we see quite clearly how it ought to work and as clearly that it has not worked, when this and that turns up in our life and proves beyond controversy that we are ruled by much the same motives and desires as the world at large, two subjects of reflection present themselves. First, have we remembered the word of Christ, "The servant is not greater than his Lord"? Are we so anxious to be His servants that we would willingly sacrifice whatever stood in the way of our serving Him? Are we content to be as He was in the world? There are always many in the Christian Church who are, first, men of the world, and, secondly, varnished with Christianity; who do not seek first the kingdom of God and His righteousness; who do not yet understand that the *whole* of life must be consecrated to Christ and spring from His will, and who therefore without compunction do make themselves greater in every worldly respect than their professed Lord. There are also many in the Christian Church at all times who decline to make more of this world than Christ Himself did, and whose constant study it is to put all they have at His disposaL Now, we cannot too seriously inquire to which of these classes we belong. Are we making a *bonâ-fide* thing of our attachment to Christ? Do we feel it in every part of our life? Do we strive, not to minimise our service and His claims, but to be wholly His? Have His words, "The servant is not greater than his Lord," any meaning to us at all? Is His service truly the main thing we seek in life? I say we should seriously inquire if this is so; for not hereafter, but now, are we finally determining our relation to all things by our relation to Christ.

But, secondly, we must beware of disheartening ourselves by hastily concluding that in our case Christ's grace has failed. If we may accept the Book of Revelation as a true picture, not merely of the conflict of the Church, but also of the conflict of the individual, then only in the end can we look for quiet and achieved victory—only in the closing chapters does conflict cease and victory seem no more doubtful. If it is to be so with us, the fact of our losing some of the battles must not discourage us from continuing the campaign. Nothing is more painful and humbling than to find ourselves falling into unmistakable sin after much concernment with Christ and His grace; but the very resentment we feel and the deep and bitter humiliation must be used as incentive to further effort, and must not be allowed to sound permanent defeat and surrender to sin.

# XV.
## LAST WORDS.

" A little while, and ye behold Me no more ; and again a little while, and ye shall see Me. Some of His disciples therefore said one to another, What is this that He saith unto us, A little while, and ye behold Me not; and again a little while, and ye shall see Me : and, Because I go to the Father? They said therefore, What is this that He saith, A little while? We know not what He saith. Jesus perceived that they were desirous to ask Him, and He said unto them. Do ye inquire among yourselves concerning this, that I said, A little while, and ye behold Me not, and again a little while, and ye shall see Me? Verily, verily, I say unto you, that ye shall weep and lament, but the world shall rejoice : ye shall be sorrowful, but your sorrow shall be turned into joy. A woman when she is in travail hath sorrow, because her hour is come : but when she is delivered of the child, she remembereth no more the anguish, for the joy that a man is born into the world. And ye therefore now have sorrow: but I will see you again, and your heart shall rejoice, and your joy no one taketh away from you. And in that day ye shall ask Me nothing. Verily, verily, I say unto you, If ye shall ask anything of the Father, He will give it you in My name. Hitherto have ye asked nothing in My name : ask, and ye shall receive, that your joy may be fulfilled. These things have I spoken unto you in proverbs: the hour cometh, when I shall no more speak unto you in proverbs, but shall tell you plainly of the Father. In that day ye shall ask in My name : and I say not unto you, that I will pray the Father for you ; for the Father Himself loveth you, because ye have loved Me, and have believed that I came forth from the Father. I came out from the Father, and am come into the world : again, I leave the world, and go unto the Father. His disciples say, Lo, now speakest Thou plainly, and speakest no proverb. Now know we that Thou knowest all things, and needest not that any man should ask Thee : by this we believe that Thou camest forth from God. Jesus answered them, Do ye now believe? Behold, the hour cometh, yea, is come, that ye shall be scattered, every man to his own, and shall leave Me alone : and yet I am not alone, because the Father is with Me. These things have I spoken unto you, that in Me ye may have peace. In the world ye have tribulation: but be of good cheer; I have overcome the world."—JOHN xvi. 16-33.

## XV.

### *LAST WORDS.*

IN the intercourse of Jesus with His disciples He at all times showed one of the most delightful qualities of a friend—a quick and perfect apprehension of what was passing in their mind. They did not require to bring their mental condition before Him by laboured explanations. He knew what was in man, and He especially knew what was in them. He could forecast the precise impression which His announcements would make upon them, the doubts and the expectations they would give rise to. Sometimes they were surprised at this insight, always they profited by it. In fact, on more occasions than one this insight convinced them that Jesus had this clear knowledge of men given to Him that He might effectually deal with all men. It seemed to them, as of course it is, one of the essential equipments of One who is to be a real centre for the whole race and to bring help to each and all men. How could a person who was deficient in this universal sympathy and practical understanding of the very thoughts of each of us offer himself as our helper? There is therefore evidence in the life of Jesus that He was never non-plussed, never at a loss to understand the kind of man He had to do with. There is evidence of this, and it would seem that we all receive this evidence ; for are we not conscious that our spiritual condition is understood, our thoughts traced, our difficulties sympathised with? We may feel very unlike many prominent Christians ; we may have no sympathy with a great deal that passes for Christian sentiment; but Christ's sympathy is universal, and nothing human comes wrong to Him. Begin with Him as you are, without professing to be, though hoping to be, different from what you are, and by the growth of your own spirit in the sunshine of His presence and under the guidance of His intelligent sympathy your doubts will pass away, your ungodliness be renounced. He is offered for your help as the essential condition of your progress and your growth.

Seeing the perplexity which certain of His expressions had created in the minds of His disciples, He proceeds to remove it. They had great need of hopefulness and courage, and He sought to inspire them with these qualities. They were on the edge of a most bitter experience, and it was of untold consequence that they should be upheld in it. He does not hide from them the coming distress, but He reminds them that very commonly pain and anxiety accompany the birth-throes of a new life ; and if they found themselves shortly in depression and grief which seemed inconsolable, they were to believe that this was the path to a new and higher phase of existence and to a joy that would be lasting. Your grief, He says, will shortly end : your joy never. Your grief will soon be taken away: your joy no one shall take away. When Christ rose again, the disciples remembered and understood these words ; and a few chapters further on we find John returning upon the word and saying, "When they saw the Lord, they were glad,"—they had this *joy*. It was a joy to them, because love for Christ and hope in Him were their dominant feelings. They had the joy of having their Friend again, of seeing Him victorious and proved to be all and more than they had believed. They had the first glowing visions of a new world for which the preparation was the life and resurrection of the Son of God. What were they not prepared to hope for as the result of the immeasurably great things they had themselves seen and known? It was a mere question now of Christ's will: of His power they were assured.

The resurrection of Christ was, however, meant to bring lasting joy, not to these men only, but to all. These greatest of all events, the descent to earth of the Son of God with all Divine power and love, and His resurrection as the conqueror of all that bars the path of men from a life of light and joy, became solid facts in this world's history, that all men might calculate their future by such a past, and might each for himself conclude that a future of which such events are the preparation must be great and happy indeed. Death, if not in all respects the most desolating, is the most certain of all human ills. Anguish and mourning it has brought and will bring to many human hearts. Do what we will we cannot save our friends from it; by us it is unconquerable. Yet it is in this most calamitous of human ills God has shown His nearness and His love. It is to the death of Christ men look to see the full brightness of God's fatherly love. It is this darkest point of human experience that God has chosen to irradiate with His absorbing glory. Death is at once our gravest fear and the spring of our hope; it cuts short human intercourse, but in the cross of Christ it gives us a never-failing, divinely loving

Friend. The death of Christ is the great compensation of all the ill that death has brought into human life; and when we see death made the medium of God's clearest manifestation, we are almost grateful to it for affording material for an exhibition of God's love which transforms all our own life and all our own hopes.

Lasting joy is the condition in which God desires us to be, and He has given us cause of joy. In Christ's victory we see all that is needed to give us hopefulness about the future. Each man finds for himself assurance of God's interest in us and in our actual condition: assurance that whatever is needful to secure for us a happy eternity has been done; assurance that in a new heavens and a new earth we shall find lasting satisfaction. This true, permanent, all-embracing joy is open to all, and is actually enjoyed by those who have something of Christ's Spirit, whose chief desire is to see holiness prevail and to keep themselves and others in harmony with God. To such the accomplishment of God's will seems a certainty, and they have learned that the accomplishment of that will means good to them and to all who love God. The holiness and harmony with God that win this joy are parts of it. To be the friends of Christ, imbued with His views of life and of God, this from first to last is a thing of joy.

That which the disciples at length believed and felt to be the culmination of their faith was that Jesus had come forth from God. He Himself more fully expresses what He desired them to believe about Him in the words: "I came forth from the Father, and am come into the world: again I leave the world, and go to the Father." No doubt there is a sense in which any man may use this language of himself. We can all truthfully say we came forth from God and came into the world; and we pass out from the world and return to God. But that the disciples did not understand the words in this sense is obvious from the difficulty they found in reaching this belief. Had Jesus merely meant that it was true of Him, as of all others, that God is the great existence out of whom we spring and to whom we return, the disciples could have found no difficulty and the Jews must all have believed in Him. In some special and exceptional sense, then, He came forth from God. What, then, was this sense?

When Nicodemus came to Jesus, he addressed Him as a teacher "come from God," because, he added, "no man can do these miracles which Thou doest except God be with Him." In Nicodemus' lips, therefore, the words "a teacher come from God" meant a teacher with a Divine mission and credentials. In this sense all the prophets were teachers "come from God." And accordingly many careful readers of the Gospels believe that nothing more than this is meant by any of those expressions our Lord uses of Himself, as "sent from God," "come forth from God," and so on. The only distinction, it is supposed, between Christ and other prophets is that He is more highly endowed, is commissioned and equipped as God's representative in a more perfect degree than Moses or Samuel or Elijah. He had their power to work miracles, their authority in teaching; but having a more important mission to accomplish, He had this power and authority more fully. Now, it is quite certain that some of the expressions which a careless reader might think conclusive in proof of Christ's divinity were not intended to express anything more than that He was God's commissioner. Indeed, it is remarkable how He Himself seems to wish men to believe this above all else—that

He was sent by God. In reading the Gospel of John one is tempted to say that Jesus almost intentionally avoids affirming His divinity explicitly and directly when there seemed opportunity to do so. Certainly His main purpose was to reveal the Father, to bring men to understand that His teaching about God was true, and that He was sent by God.

There are, however, some expressions which unquestionably affirm Christ's pre-existence, and convince us that before He appeared in this world He lived with God. And among these expressions the words He uses in this passage hold a place: "I came forth from the Father, and am come into the world: again, I leave the world, and go to the Father." These words, the disciples felt, lifted a veil from their eyes; they told Him at once that they found an explicitness in this utterance which had been a-wanting in others. And, indeed, nothing could be more explicit: the two parts of the sentence balance and interpret one another. "I leave the world, and go to the Father," interprets "I came forth from the Father, and am come into the world." To say "I leave the world" is not the same as to say "I go to the Father": this second clause describes a state of existence which is entered upon when existence in this world is done. And to say "I came forth from the Father" is not the same as to say "I came into the world"; it describes a state of existence antecedent to that which began by coming into the world.

Thus the Apostles understood the words, and felt therefore that they had gained a new platform of faith. This they felt to be plain-speaking, meant to be understood. It so precisely met their craving and gave them the knowledge they sought, that they felt more than ever Christ's insight into their state of mind and His power to satisfy their minds. At length they are able to say with assurance that He has come forth from God. They are persuaded that behind what they see there is a higher nature, and that in Christ's presence they are in the presence of One whose origin is not of this world. It was this pre-existence of Christ with God which gave the disciples assurance regarding all He taught them. He spoke of what He had seen with the Father.

This belief, however, assured though it was, did not save them from a cowardly desertion of Him whom they believed to be God's representative on earth. They would, when confronted with the world's authorities and powers, abandon their Master to His fate, and "would leave Him alone." He had always, indeed, been alone. All men who wish to carry out some novel design or accomplish some extensive reform must be prepared to stand alone, to listen unmoved to criticism, to estimate at their real and very low value the prejudiced calumnies of those whose interests are opposed to their design. They must be prepared to live without reward and without sympathy, strong in the consciousness of their own rectitude and that God will prosper the right. Jesus enjoyed the affection of a considerable circle of friends; He was not without the comfort and strength which come of being believed in; but in regard to His purpose in life He was always alone. And yet, unless He won men over to His views, unless He made some as ardent as Himself regarding them, His work was lost. This was the special hardship of Christ's solitariness. Those whom He had gathered were to desert Him in the critical hour; but the sore part of this desertion was that they were to go "each to his own"—oblivious, that is to say, of the great cause in which they had embarked with Christ.

At all times this is the problem Christ has to solve: how to prevail upon men to look at life from His point of view, to forget their own things and combine with Him, to be as enamoured of His cause as He Himself is. He looks now upon us with our honest professions of faith and growing regard, and He says: Yes, you believe; but you scatter each to his own at the slightest breath of danger or temptation. This scattering, each to his own, is that which thwarts Christ's purpose and imperils His work. The world with its enterprises and its gains, its glitter and its glory, its sufficiency for the present life, comes in and tempts us; and apart from the common good, we have each our private schemes of advantage. And yet there is nothing more certain than that our ultimate advantage is measured by the measure in which we throw in our lot with Christ —by the measure in which we practically recognise that there is an object for which all men in common can work, and that to scatter "each to his own" is to resign the one best hope of life, the one satisfying and remunerative labour.

In revealing what sustained Himself Christ reveals the true stay of every soul of man. His trial was indeed severe. Brought without a single friend to the bar of unsympathetic and unscrupulous judges: the Friend of man, loving as no other has ever loved, and craving love and sympathy as no other has craved it, yet standing without one pitying eye, without one voice raised in His favour. Alone in a world He came to convince and to win; at the end of His life, spent in winning men, left without one to say He had not lived in vain; abandoned to enemies, to ignorant, cruel, profane men. He was dragged through the streets where He had spoken words of life and healed the sick, but no rescue was attempted. So outcast from all human consideration was He, that a Barabbas found friendly voices where He found none. Hearing the suborned witnesses swear His life away, He heard at the same time His boldest disciple deny that he knew any person of the name of Jesus. But through this abandonment He knew the Father's presence was with Him. "I am not alone, because the Father is with Me."

Times which in their own degree try us with the same sense of solitariness come upon us all. All pain is solitary; you must bear it alone: kind friends may be round you, but they cannot bear one pang for you. You feel how separate and individual an existence you have when your body is racked with pain and healthy people are by your side; and you feel it also when you visit some pained or sorrowing person and sit silently in their presence, feeling that the suffering is theirs and that they must bear it. We should not brood much over any apparent want of recognition we may meet with; all such brooding is unwholesome and weak. Many of our minor sufferings we do best to keep to ourselves and say nothing about them. Let us strive to show sympathy, and we shall feel less the pain of not having it. To a large extent every one must be alone in life—forming his own views of things, working out his own idea of life, conquering his own sins, and schooling his own heart. And every one is more or less misunderstood even by his most intimate friends. He finds himself congratulated on occurrences which are no joy to him, applauded for successes he is ashamed of; the very kindnesses of his friends reveal to him how little they understand his nature. But all this will not deeply affect a healthy-minded man, who recognises that he is in the world to do good, and who is not always craving applause and recognition.

But there are occasional times in which the want of sympathy is crushingly felt. Some of the most painful and enduring sorrows of the human heart are of a kind which forbid that they be breathed to the nearest friend. Even if others know that they have fallen upon us they cannot allude to them; and very often they are not even known. And there are times even more trying, when we have not only to bear a sorrow or an anxiety all our own, but when we have to adopt a line of conduct which exposes us to misunderstanding, and to act continuously in a manner which shuts us off from the sympathy of our friends. Our friends remonstrate and advise, and we feel that their advice is erroneous: we are compelled to go our own way and bear the charge of obstinacy and even of cruelty; for sometimes, like Abraham offering Isaac, we cannot satisfy conscience without seeming to injure or actually injuring those we love.

It is in times like these that our faith is tested. We gain a firmer hold of God than ever before when we in actual life prefer His countenance and fellowship to the approbation and good-will of our friends. When in order to keep conscience clean we dare to risk the good-will of those we depend upon for affection and for support, our faith becomes a reality and rapidly matures. For a time we may seem to have rendered ourselves useless, and to have thrown ourselves out of all profitable relations to our fellow-men: we may be shunned, and our opinions and conduct may be condemned, and the object we had in view may seem to be further off than ever; but such was the experience of Christ also, till even He was forced to cry out, not only Why have ye, My friends, forsaken Me? but "My God, why hast Thou forsaken Me?" But as in His case, so in ours—this is only the natural and necessary path to the perfect justification of ourselves and of the principles our conduct has represented. If in obedience to conscience we are exposed to isolation and the various loss consequent upon it, we are not alone— God is with us. It is in the line of our conduct He is working and will carry out His purposes. And well might such an one be envied by those who have feared such isolation and shrunk from the manifold wretchedness that comes of resisting the world's ways and independently following an unworldly and Christian path.

For really in our own life, as in the life of Christ, all is summed up in the conflict between Christ and the world; and therefore the last words of this His last conversation are: "In the world ye shall have tribulation: but be of good courage. I have overcome the world." When Christ speaks of "the world" as comprising all that was opposed to Him, it is not difficult to understand His meaning. By "the world" we sometimes mean the earth; sometimes all external things, sun, moon, and stars as well as this earth; sometimes we mean the world of men, as when we say "All the world knows" such and such a thing, or as when Christ said "God so loved the world that He gave His only-begotten Son." But much more commonly Christ uses it to denote all in the present state of things which opposes God and leads man away from God. We speak of worldliness as fatal to the spirit, because worldliness means preference for what is external and present to what is inward and both present and future. Worldliness means attachment to things as they are—to the ways of society, to the excitements, the pleasures, the profits, of the present. It means surrender to what appeals to the sense—to comfort to vanity, to ambition, to love of display. Worldliness is the spirit which uses the present world without reference to the lasting and spiritual purposes for the sake of which men are in this world. It ignores what is eternal and what is spiritual; it is satisfied with present comfort, with what brings present pleasure, with what ministers to the beauty of this present life, to the material prosperity of men. And no soul whatsoever or wheresoever situated can escape the responsibility of making his choice between the world and God. To each of us the question which determines all else is, Am I to live for ends which find their accomplishment in this present life, or for ends which are eternal? Am I to live so as to secure the utmost of comfort, of ease, of money, of reputation, of domestic enjoyment, of the good things of this present world? or am I to live so as to do the most I can for the forwarding of God's purposes with men, for the forwarding of spiritual and eternal good? There is no man who is not living for one or other of these ends. Two men enter the same office and transact the same business; but the one is worldly, the other Christian: two men do the same work, use the same material, draw the same salary; but one cherishes a spiritual end, the other a worldly,—the one works, always striving to serve God and his fellows, the other has nothing in view but himself and his own interests. Two women live in the same street, have children at the same school, dress very much alike; but you cannot know them long without perceiving that the one is worldly, with her heart set on position and earthly advancement for her children, while the other is unworldly and prays that her children may learn to conquer the world and to live a stainless and self-sacrificing life though it be a poor one. This is the determining probation of life; this it is which determines what we are and shall be. We are, every one of us, living either with the world as our end or for God. The difficulty of choosing rightly and abiding by our choice is extreme: no man has ever found it easy; for every man it is a sufficient test of his reality, of his dependence on principle, of his moral clear-sightedness, of his strength of character.

Therefore Christ, as the result of all His work, announces that He has "overcome the world." And on the ground of this conquest of His He bids His followers rejoice and take heart, as if somehow His conquest of the world guaranteed theirs, and as if their conflict would be easier on account of His. And so indeed it is. Not only has every one now who proposes to live for high and unworldly ends the satisfaction of knowing that such a life is possible, and not only has he the vast encouragement of knowing that One has passed this way before and attained His end; but, moreover, it is Christ's victory which has really overcome the world in a final and public way. The world's principles of action, its pleasure-seeking, its selfishness, its childish regard for glitter and for what is present to sense, in a word, its worldliness when set over against the life of Christ, is for ever discredited. The experience of Christ in this world reflects such discredit upon merely worldly ways, and so clearly exhibits its blindness, its hatred of goodness, its imbecility when it strives to counterwork God's purposes, that no man who morally has his eyes open can fail to look with suspicion and abhorrence on the world. And the dignity, the love, the apprehension of what is real and abiding in human affairs, and the ready application of His life to a real and abiding purpose—all this, which is so visible in the life of Christ, gives certainty and attractiveness to the principles opposed to worldliness. We have in Christ's life at once an authoritative and an experimental teaching on the greatest of all human subjects—how life should be spent.

Christ has overcome the world, then, by resisting its influence upon Himself, by showing Himself actually superior to its most powerful influences: and His overcoming of the world is not merely a private victory availing for Himself alone, but it is a public good, because in His life the perfect beauty of a life devoted to eternal and spiritual ends is conspicuously shown. The man who can look upon the conflict between the world and Christ as John has shown it, and say, "I would rather be one of the Pharisees than Christ," is hopelessly blind to the real value of human life. But what says our life regarding the actual choice we have made?

# XVI.

*CHRIST'S INTERCESSORY PRAYER.*

"These things spake Jesus; and lifting up His eyes to heaven, He said, Father, the hour is come; glorify Thy Son, that the Son may glorify Thee: even as Thou gavest Him authority over all flesh, that whatsoever Thou hast given Him, to them He should give eternal life. And this is life eternal, that they should know Thee the only true God, and Him whom Thou didst send, even Jesus Christ. I glorified Thee on the earth, having accomplished the work which Thou hast given Me to do. And now, O Father, glorify Thou Me with Thine own self with the glory which I had with Thee before the world was. I manifested Thy name unto the men whom Thou gavest Me out of the world : Thine they were, and Thou gavest them to Me ; and they have kept Thy word. Now they know that all things whatsoever Thou hast given Me are from Thee: for the words which Thou gavest Me I have given unto them ; and they received them, and knew of a truth that I came forth from Thee, and they believed that Thou didst send Me. I pray for them : I pray not for the world, but for those whom Thou hast given Me ; for they are Thine: and all things that are Mine are Thine, and Thine are Mine : and I am glorified in them. And I am no more in the world, and these are in the world, and I come to Thee. Holy Father, keep them in Thy name which Thou hast given Me, that they may be one, even as We are. While I was with them, I kept them in Thy name which Thou hast given Me : and I guarded them, and not one of them perished, but the son of perdition ; that the Scripture might be fulfilled. But now I come to Thee ; and these things I speak in the world, that they may have My joy fulfilled in themselves. I have given them Thy word ; and the world hated them, because they are not of the world, even as I am not of the world. I pray not that Thou shouldest take them from the world, but that Thou shouldest keep them from the evil one. They are not of the world, even as I am not of the world. Sanctify them in the truth : Thy word is truth. As Thou didst send Me into the world, even so sent I them into the world. And for their sakes I sanctify Myself, that they themselves also may be sanctified in truth. Neither for these only do I pray, but for them also that believe on Me through their word ; that they may all be one ; even as Thou, Father, art in Me, and I in Thee, that they also may be in Us : that the world may believe that Thou didst send Me. And the glory which Thou hast given Me I have given unto them ; that they may be one, even as We are one ; I in them, and Thou in Me, that they may be perfected into one ; that the world may know that Thou didst send Me, and lovedst them, even as Thou lovedst Me. Father, that which Thou hast given Me, I will that, where I am, they also may be with Me ; that they may behold My glory, which Thou hast given Me : for Thou lovedst Me before the foundation of the world. O righteous Father, the world knew Thee not, but I knew Thee ; and these knew that Thou didst send Me ; and I made known unto them Thy name, and will make it known ; that the love wherewith Thou lovedst me may be in them, and I in them."—JOHN xvii.

## XVI.

### CHRIST'S INTERCESSORY PRAYER

THIS prayer of Christ is in some respects the most precious relic of the past. We have here the words which Christ addressed to God in the critical hour of His life—the words in which He uttered the deepest feeling and thought of His Spirit, clarified and concentrated by the prospect of death. What a revelation it would be to us had we Christ's prayers from His boyhood onwards ! what a liturgy and promptuary of devotion if we knew what He had desired from His early years—what He had feared, what He had prayed against, what He had never ceased to hope for ; the things that one by one dropped out of His prayers, the things that gradually grew into them ; the persons He commended to the Father and the manner of this commendation ; His prayers for His mother, for John, for Peter, for Lazarus, for Judas ! But here we have a prayer which, if it does not so abundantly satisfy pardonable curiosity, does at least bring us into as sacred a presence. For even among the prayers of Christ this stands by itself as that in which He gathered up the retrospect of His past and surveyed the future of His Church ; in which, as if already dying, He solemnly presented to the Father Himself, His work, and His people. Recognising the grandeur of the occasion, we may be disposed to agree with Melanchthon, who, when giving his last lecture shortly before His death, said: "There is no voice which has ever been heard, either in heaven or in earth, more exalted, more holy, more fruitful, more sublime, than this prayer offered up by the Son of God Himself."

The prayer was the natural conclusion to the conversation which Jesus and the disciples had been carrying on. And as the Eleven saw Him lifting His eyes to heaven, as if the Father He addressed were visible, they no doubt felt a security which had not been imparted by all His promises. And when in after-life they spoke of Christ's intercession, this instance of it must always have risen in memory and have formed all their ideas of that part of the Redeemer's work. It has always been believed that those who have loved and cared for us while on earth continue to do so when through death they have passed nearer to the Source of all love and goodness; this lively interest in us is supposed to continue because it formed so material an element in their life here below; and it was impossible that those who heard our Lord thus awfully commending them to the Father should ever forget this earnest consideration of their state or should ever come to fancy that they were forgotten.

Beginning with prayer for Himself, our Lord passes at the sixth verse into prayer for His disciples, and at the twentieth verse the prayer expands still more widely and embraces the world, all those who should believe on Him.

First, Jesus prays for Himself; and His prayer is, "Father, glorify Thy Son; glorify Thou Me with Thine own self with the glory which I had with Thee before the world was." The work for which He came into the world was done: "I have finished the work which

Thou gavest Me to do." There remains no more reason why He should stay longer on earth; "the hour is come," the hour for closing His earthly career and opening to Him a new period and sphere. He does not wish and does not need a prolongation of life. He has found time enough in less than a half of three-score years and ten to do all He can do on earth. It is character, not time, we need to do our work. To make a deep and abiding impression it is not longer life we need, but intensity. Jesus did not find Himself cramped, limited, or too soon hurried out of life. He viewed death as the suitable timely step, and took it with self-command and in order to pass to something better than earthly life.

How immeasurably beneath this level is the vaunted equanimity of the thinker who says, "Death can be no evil because it is universal"! How immeasurably beneath it is the habit of most of us! Which of us can stand in that clear air on that high point which separates life from what is beyond and can say, "I have finished the work which Thou gavest Me to do"? A broken column is the fit monument of our life, unfinished, frustrated, useless. Wasted energy, ill-repaired blunders, unfulfilled purposes, fruitless years, much that is positively evil, much that was done mechanically and carelessly and for the day; plans ill conceived and worse executed; imperfect ideals of life imperfectly realised; pursuits dictated by uneducated tastes, unchastened whims, accidental circumstances,—such is the retrospect which most of us have as we look back over life. Few men even recognise the reality of life as part of an eternal order, and, of the few who do so, still fewer seriously and persistently aim at fitting in their life as a solid part of that order.

Before we know whether we have finished the work given us to do we must know what that work is. At the outset of his account of Christ's work John gives us his conception of it. "The Word was made flesh, and dwelt among us; and *we beheld His glory*, the glory as of the Only begotten of the Father." This work was now accomplished, and Jesus can say, "I have glorified Thee on the earth"; "I have manifested Thy name unto the men which Thou gavest Me out of the world." We may all add our humble responsive "Amen" to this account of His finished work. John has carried us through the scenes in which Jesus manifested the glory of the Father and showed the full meaning of that name, displaying the Father's love in His self-sacrificing interest in men, the Father's holiness and supremacy in His devoted filial obedience. Never again can men separate the idea of the true God from the life of Jesus Christ; it is in that life we come to know God, and through that life His glory shines. This many a man has felt is the true Divine glory; this God yearning over His lost and wretched children, coming down and sharing in their wretchedness to win them to Himself and blessedness—this is the God for us. This alone is glory such as we bow before and own to be infinitely worthy of trust and adoration, almightiness applying itself to the necessities and fears of the weak, perfect purity winning to itself the impure and the outcast, love showing itself to be Divine by its patience, its humility, its absolute sacrifice. It is Christ who has found entrance for these conceptions of God once for all into the human mind; it is to Christ we owe it that we know a God we can entirely lov and increasingly worship. With the most assured truth He could say, " I have finished the work which

Thou gavest Me to do; I have glorified Thee on the earth; I have manifested Thy name unto the men which Thou gavest Me out of the world."

But Christ recognises a work which ran parallel with this, a work which continually resulted from His manifestation of the Father. By His manifesting the Father He gave eternal life to those who accepted and believed His revelation. The power to reveal the Father which Christ had received He had not on His own account, but that He might give eternal life to men. For "this is life eternal, that they might know Thee the only true God, and Jesus Christ, whom Thou hast sent." Eternal life is not merely life indefinitely prolonged. It is rather life under new conditions and fed from different sources. It can be entered upon now, but a full understanding of it is now impossible. The grub might as well try to understand the life of the butterfly, or the chick in the shell the life of the bird. To know what Christ revealed, this is the birth to life eternal. To know that love and holiness are the governing powers in conformity with which all things are carried onward to their end; to know what God is, that He is a Father who cannot leave us His children of earth behind and pass on to His own great works and purposes in the universe, but stoops to our littleness and delays that He may carry every one of us with Him,—this is life eternal. This it is that subdues the human heart and cleanses it from pride, self-seeking, and lust, and that inclines it to bow before the holy and loving God, and to choose Him and life in Him. This it is that turns it from the brief joys and imperfect meanings of time and gives it a home in eternity—that severs it in disposition and in destiny from the changing, passing world and gives it an eternal inheritance as God's child. To as many as believed Christ, to them He gave power to become the sons of God. To believe Him and to accept the God He reveals is to become a son of God and is to enter into life eternal. To be conquered by the Divine love shown us; to feel that not in worldly ambition or any self-seeking, but only in devotion to interests that are spiritual and general, is the true life for us; to yield ourselves to the Spirit of Christ and seek to be animated and possessed by that Spirit,—this is to throw in our lot with God, to be satisfied in Him, to have eternal life.

The earthly work of Christ, then, being finished, He asks the Father to glorify Him with His own self, with the glory He had with Him before the world was. It seems to me vain to deny that this petition implies on Christ's part a consciousness of a life which He had before He appeared on earth. His mind turns from the present hour, from His earthly life, to eternity, to those regions beyond time into which no created intelligence can follow Him, and in which God alone exists, and in that Divine solitude He claims a place for Himself. If He merely meant that from eternity God had conceived of Him, the ideal man, and if the existence and glory He speaks of were merely existence in God's mind, but not actual, His words do not convey His meaning. The glory which He prayed for now was a conscious, living glory; He did not wish to become extinct or to be absorbed in the Divine being; He meant to continue and did continue in actual, personal, living existence. This was the glory He prayed for, and this therefore must also have been the glory He had before the world was. It was a glory of which it was proper to say, "*I had* it," and not merely God conceived it: it was enjoyed by Christ before the worlds were, and was not only in the mind of God.

What that glory was, who can tell? We know it was a glory not of position only, but of character—a glory which disposed and prepared Him to sympathize with suffering and to give Himself to the actual needs of men. From that glory He came to share with men in their humiliation, to expose Himself to their scorn and abuse, to win them to eternal life and to some true participation in His glory.

But Christ's removal from the earthly and visible life involved a great change in the condition of the disciples. Hitherto He had been present with them day by day, always exhibiting to them spiritual glory, and attracting them to it in His own person. So long as they saw God's glory in so attractive and friendly a form it was not difficult for them to resist the world's temptations. "While I was with them in the world, I kept them in Thy name"—that is, by revealing the Father to them; but "now I am no more in the world, but these are in the world, and I come to Thee. Holy Father, keep through Thine own name those whom Thou hast given Me. Sanctify them through Thy truth: Thy word is truth." Christ had been the Word Incarnate, the utterance of God to men; in Him men recognised what God is and what God wills. And this sanctified them; this marvellous revelation of God and His love for men drew men to Him: they felt how Divine and overcoming a love this was; they adored the name Father which Christ the Son made known to them; they felt themselves akin to God and claimed by Him, and spurned the world; they recognised in themselves that which could understand and be appealed to by such a love as God's. Their glory was to be God's children.

But now the visible image, the Incarnate Word, is withdrawn, and Christ commits to the Father those whom He leaves on earth. "Holy Father," Thou whose holiness moves Thee to keep men separate to Thyself from every evil contagion, "keep through Thine own name those whom Thou hast given Me." It is still by the recognition of God in Christ that we are to be kept from evil, by contemplating and penetrating this great manifestation of God to us, by listening humbly and patiently to this Incarnate Word. Knowledge of the God whose the world and all existence is, knowledge of Him in whom we live and whose holiness is silently judging and ruling all things, knowledge that He who rules all and who is above all gives Himself to us with a love that thinks no sacrifice too great—it is this knowledge of the truth that saves us from the world. It is the knowledge of those abiding realities which Christ revealed, of those great and loving purposes of God to man, and of the certainty of their fulfilment, which recalls us to holiness and to God. There is reality here; all else is empty and delusive.

But these realities are obscured and thrust aside by a thousand pretentious frivolities which claim our immediate attention and interest. We are in the world, and day by day the world insists that we shall consider it the great reality. Christ had conquered it and was leaving it. Why, then, did He not take with Him all whom He had won to Himself out of the world? He did not do so because they had a work to accomplish which could only be accomplished in the world. As He had consecrated Himself to the work of making known the Father, so must they consecrate themselves to the same work. As Christ in His own person and life had brought clear before their minds the presence of the Father, so must they by their person and life manifest in the world the existence and the grace of Christ. They must make permanent and universal the revelation He had brought, that all the world might believe that He was the true representative of God. Christ had lighted them, and with their light they were to kindle all men, till the world was full of light. A share in this work is given to each of us. We are permitted to mediate between God and men, to carry to some the knowledge which gives life eternal. It is made possible to us to be benefactors in the highest kind, to give to this man and that a God. To parents it is made possible to fill the opening and hungry mind of their child with a sense of God which will awe, restrain, encourage, gladden him all his life through. To relieve the wants of to-day, to refresh any human spirit by kindness, and to forward the interests of any struggler in life is much; but it is little compared with the joy and solid utility of disclosing to a human soul that which he at last recognises as Divine, and before which at last he bows in spontaneous adoration and absolute trust. To the man who has long questioned whether there is a God, who has doubted whether there is any morally perfect Being, any Spirit existent greater and purer than man, you have but to show Christ, and through His unconquerable love and untemptable holiness reveal to him a God.

But as it was not by telling men about God that Christ convinced men that somewhere there existed a holy God who cared for them, but by showing God's holiness and love present to them in His own person, so our words may fail to accomplish much if our life does not reveal a presence men cannot but recognise as Divine. It was by being one with the Father Christ revealed Him; it was the Father's will His life exhibited. And the extension of this to the whole world of men is the utmost of Christ's desire. All will be accomplished when all men are one, even as Christ and the Father are already one.

This text is often cited by those who seek to promote the union of churches. But we find it belongs to a very different category and much higher region. That all churches should be under similar government, should adopt the same creed, should use the same forms of worship, even if possible, is not supremely desirable; but real unity of sentiment towards Christ and of zeal to promote His will is supremely desirable. Christ's will is all-embracing; the purposes of God are wide as the universe, and can be fulfilled only by endless varieties of dispositions, functions, organisations, labours. We must expect that, as time goes on, men, so far from being contracted into a narrow and monotonous uniformity, will exhibit increasing diversities of thought and of method, and will be more and more differentiated in all outward respects. If the infinitely comprehensive purposes of God are to be fulfilled, it must be so. But also, if these purposes are to be fulfilled, all intelligent agents must be at one with God, and must be so profoundly in sympathy with God's mind as revealed in Christ that, however different one man's work or methods may be from another's, God's will shall alike be carried out by both. If this will can be more freely carried out by separate churches, then outward separation is no great calamity. Only when outward separation leads one church to despise or rival or hate another is it a calamity. But whether churches abide separate or are incorporated in outward unity, the desirable thing is that they be one in Christ, that they have the same eagerness in His service, that they be as regiments of one army fighting a common foe and supporting one another, diverse in outward appearance, in method, in function, as artillery, infantry, cavalry, engineers, or even as the army and navy of the same country, but fighting for one flag and one cause, and their very diversity more vividly exhibiting their real unity.

But why should unity be the ultimate desire of Christ, the highest point to which the Saviour's wishes for mankind can reach? Because spirit is that which rules; and if we be one with God in spirit the future is ours. This mighty universe in which we find ourselves, apparently governed by forces compared to which the most powerful of human engines are weak as the moth—forces which keep this earth, and orbs immeasurably larger, suspended in space,—this universe is controlled by spirit, is designed for spiritual ends, for ends of the highest kind and which concern conscious and moral beings.

It is as yet only by glimpses we can see the happiness of those who are one with God; it is only by inadequate comparisons and with mental effort we can attain to even a rudimentary conception of the future that awaits those who are thus eternally blessed. Of them well may Paul say, "All things are yours; for ye are Christ's, and Christ is God's." It is for Christ all things are governed by God; to be in Him is to be above the reach of catastrophe—to be, as Christ Himself expresses it, beside Himself on the throne, from which all things are ruled. Having been attracted by His character, by what He is and does, and having sought here on earth to promote His will, we shall be His agents hereafter, but in a life in which spiritual glory irradiates everything, and in which an ecstasy and strength which this frail body could not contain will be the normal and constant index of the life of God in us. To do good, to utter by word or deed the love and power that are in us, is the permanent joy of man. With what alacrity does the surgeon approach the operation he knows will be successful! with what pleasure does the painter put on canvas the idea which fills his mind and which he knows will appeal to every one who sees it! And whoever learns to do good by partaking of God's spirit of communicative goodness will find everlasting joy in imparting what he has and can. He will do so, not with the feeble and hesitating mind and hand which here make almost every good action partly painful, but with a spontaneity and sense of power which will be wholly pleasure; he will know that being one with God he can do good, can accomplish and effect some solid and needful work. Slowly, very slowly, is this arrived at; but time is of no consequence in work that is eternal, so long only as we are sure we do not idly miss present opportunities of learning, so long only as we know that our faces are turned in the right direction, and that a right spirit is in us.

If there lingers in our minds a feeling that the end Christ proposes and utters as His last prayer for men does not draw us with irresistible force, it might be enough to say to our own heart that this is our weakness, that certainly in this prayer we do touch the very central significance of human life, and that however dimly human words may be able to convey thoughts regarding eternity, we have here in Christ's words sufficient indication of the one abiding end and aim of all wisely directed human life. Whatever the future of man is to be, whatever joy *life* is to become, in whatever far-reaching and prolonged experiences we are to learn the fruitfulness and efficacy of God's love, whatever new sources and conditions of happiness we may in future worlds be introduced to, whatever higher energies and richer affections are to be opened in us, all this can only be by our becoming one with God, in whose will the future now lies. And it may also be said, if we think this the prayer of One who was not in the full current of actual human life, and had little understanding of men's ways, that this prayer is fulfilled in very many who are deeply involved and busily occupied in this world. They give their mind to their employment, but their heart goes to higher aims and more enduring results. To do good is to them of greater consequence than to make money. To see the number of Christ's sincere followers increasing is to them truer joy than to see their own business extending. In the midst of their greatest prosperity they recognise that there is something far better than worldly prosperity, and that is, to be kept from the evil that is in the world and to extend the knowledge of God. They feel in common with all men that it is not always easy to remember that great spiritual kingdom with its mighty but unobtrusive interests, but they are kept by the Father's name, and they do on the whole live under the influence of God and hoping in His salvation. And it would help us all to do so were we to believe that Christ's interest in us is such as this prayer reveals, and that the great subject of His intercession is, that **we be kept from the evil that is in the world and be** helpful in the great and enduring work of bringing into truer fellowship men's lives and God's goodness. Alongside of all our profitless labour and unworthiness of aim there runs this lofty aim of Chr'st for us ; and while we are greedily following after pleasure, or thoughtlessly throwing ourselves into mere worldliness, our Lord is praying the Father that we be lifted into harmony with Him and be used as channels of His grace to others.

# XVII.
## *THE ARREST.*

" When Jesus had spoken these words, He went forth with His disciples over the brook Kidron, where was a garden, into the which He entered, Himself and His disciples. Now Judas also, which betrayed Him, knew the place: for Jesus ofttimes resorted thither with His disciples. Judas then, having received the band of soldiers, and officers from the chief priests and the Pharisees, cometh thither with lanterns and torches and weapons. Jesus therefore, knowing all the things that were coming upon Him, went forth, and saith unto them, Whom seek ye? They answered Him, Jesus of Nazareth. Jesus saith unto them, I am He. And Judas also, which betrayed Him, was standing with them. When therefore He said unto them, I am He, they went backward, and fell to the ground. Again therefore He asked them, Whom seek ye? And they said, Jesus of Nazareth. Jesus answered, I told you that I am He: if therefore ye seek Me, let these go their way: that the word might be fulfilled which He spake, Of those whom Thou hast given Me I lost not one. Simon Peter therefore having a sword drew it, and struck the high priest's servant, and cut off his right ear. Now the servant's name was Malchus. Jesus therefore said unto Peter, Put up the sword into the sheath; the cup which the Father hath given Me, shall I not drink it? So the band and the chief captain, and the officers of the Jews, seized Jesus and bound Him, and led Him to Annas first; for he was father-in-law to Caiaphas, which was high priest that year. Now Caiaphas was he which gave counsel to the 'Jews, that it was expedient that one man should die for the people."—JOHN xviii. 1-14.

# XVII.

### THE ARREST.

JESUS having commended to the Father Himself and His disciples, left the city, crossed the Kidron, and entered the Garden of Gethsemane, where He frequently went for quiet and to pass the night. The time He had spent in encouraging His disciples and praying for them Judas had spent in making preparations for His arrest. In order to impress Pilate with the dangerous nature of this Galilean he asks him for the use of the Roman cohort to effect His capture. It was possible His arrest might occasion a tumult and rouse the people to attempt a rescue. Perhaps Judas also had an alarming remembrance of the miraculous power he had seen Jesus put forth, and was afraid to attempt His apprehension with only the understrappers of the Sanhedrim or the Temple guard; so he takes the Roman cohort of five hundred men, or whatever number he would reckon would be more than a match for a miracle. And though the moon was full, he takes the precaution of furnishing the expedition with lanterns and torches, for he knew that down in that deep Kidron gully it was often dark when there was plenty of light above; and might not Jesus hide Himself in some of the shadows, in some thicket or cavern, or in some garden-shed or tower? He could not have made more elaborate preparations had he been wishing to take a thief or to surprise a dangerous chief of banditti in his stronghold.

The futility of such preparations became at once apparent. So far from trying to hide Himself or slip out by the back of the garden, Jesus no sooner sees the armed men than He steps to the front and asks, " Whom seek ye ? " Jesus, in order that He might screen His disciples, wished at once to be identified by His captors themselves as the sole object of their search. By declaring that they sought Jesus of Nazareth, they virtually exempted the rest from apprehension. But when Jesus identified Himself as the person they sought, instead of rushing forward and holding Him fast, as Judas had instructed them, those in front shrank back ; they felt that they had no weapons that would not break upon the calmness of that spiritual majesty ; they went backward and fell to the ground. This was no idle display ; it was not a needless theatrical garnishing of the scene for the sake of effect. If we could imagine the Divine nobility of Christ's appearance at that critical moment when He finally proclaimed His work done and gave Himself up to die, we should all of us sink humbled and overcome before Him. Even in the dim and flickering light of the torches there was that in His appearance which made it impossible for the bluntest and rudest soldier to lay a hand upon Him. Discipline was forgotten ; the legionaries who had thrown themselves on spear-points unawed by the fiercest of foes saw in this unarmed figure something which quelled and bewildered them.

But this proof of His superiority was lost upon His disciples. They thought that armed force should be met by armed force. Recovering from their discomfiture, and being ashamed of it, the soldiers and servants of the Sanhedrim advance to bind Jesus. Peter, who had with some dim presentiment of what was coming possessed himself of a sword, aims a blow at the head of Malchus, who having his hands occupied in binding Jesus can only defend himself by bending his head to one side, and so instead of his life loses only his ear. To our Lord this interposition of Peter seemed as if he were dashing out of His hand the cup which the Father had put into it. Disengaging His hands from those who already held them He said, "Suffer ye thus far"[1] (Permit Me to do this one thing); and laying His hand on the wound He healed it, this forgiving and beneficent act being the last done by His unbound hands—significant, indeed, that such should be the style of action from which they prevented Him by binding His hands. Surely the Roman officer in command, if none of the others, must have observed the utter incongruity of the bonds, the fatuous absurdity and wickedness of tying hands because they wrought miracles of healing.

While our Lord thus calmly resigned Himself to His fate, He was not without an indignant sense of the wrong that was done Him, not only in His being apprehended, but in the manner of it. "Are ye come out as against a thief with swords and with staves? I sat daily teaching in the Temple, and ye laid no hold on Me." Many of the soldiers must have felt how ungenerous it was to treat such a Person as a common felon,—coming upon Him thus in the dead of night, as if He were one who never appeared in the daylight; coming with bludgeons and military aid, as if He were

---

[1] Luke xxii. 51.

likely to create a disturbance. Commonly an arrest is considered to be best made if the culprit is seized red-handed in the very act. Why, then, had they not thus taken Him? They knew that the popular conscience was with Him, and they dared not take Him on the streets of Jerusalem. It was the last evidence of their inability to understand His kingdom, its nature and its aims. Yet surely some of the crowd must have felt ashamed of themselves, and been uneasy till they got rid of their unsuitable weapons, stealthily dropping their sticks as they walked or hurling them deep into the shade of the garden.

This, then, is the result produced by our Lord's labours of love and wisdom. His conduct had been most conciliatory—conciliatory to the point of meekness unintelligible to those who could not penetrate His motives. He had innovated certainly, but His innovations were blessings, and were so marked by wisdom and sanctioned by reason that every direct assault against them had broken down. He did not seek for power further than for the power of doing good. He knew He could lift men to a far other life than they were living, and permission to do so was His grand desire. The result was that He was marked as the object of the most rancorous hatred of which the human heart is capable. Why so? Do we need to ask? What is more exasperating to men who fancy themselves the teachers of the age than to find another teacher carrying the convictions of the people? What is more painful than to find that in advanced life we must revolutionise our opinions and admit the truth taught by our juniors? He who has new truths to declare or new methods to introduce must recognise that he will be opposed by the combined forces of ignorance, pride, self-interest, and sloth. The majority are always on the side of things as they are. And whoever suggests improvement, whoever shows the faultiness and falseness of what has been in vogue, must be prepared to pay the price and endure misunderstanding, calumny, opposition, and ill-usage. If all men speak well of us, it is only while we go with the stream. As soon as we oppose popular customs, explode received opinions, introduce reforms, we must lay our account for ill-treatment. It has always been so, and in the nature of things it must always be so. We cannot commit a crime more truly hated by society than to convince it there are better ways of living than its own and a truth beyond what it has conceived, and it has been the consolation and encouragement of many who have endeavoured to improve matters around them and have met with contempt or enmity that they share the lot of Him whose reward for seeking to bless mankind was that He was arrested as a common felon.

When thus treated, men are apt to be embittered towards their fellows. When all their efforts to do good are made the very ground of accusation against them, there is the strongest provocation to give up all such attempts and to arrange for one's own comfort and safety. This world has few more sufficient tests to apply to character than this; and it is only the few who, when misinterpreted and ill-used by ignorance and malignity, can retain any loving care for others. It struck the spectators, therefore, of this scene in the garden as a circumstance worthy of record, that when Jesus was Himself bound He should shield His disciples. "If ye seek Me, let these go their way." Some of the crowd had perhaps laid hands on the disciples or were showing a disposition to apprehend them as well as their Master. Jesus therefore interferes, reminding His captors that they had themselves said that *He* was the object of this midnight raid, and that the disciples must therefore be scatheless.

In relating this part of the scene John puts an interpretation on it which was not merely natural, but which has been put upon it instinctively by all Christians since. It seemed to John as if, in thus acting, our Lord was throwing into a concrete and tangible form His true substitution in the room of His people. To John these words He utters seem the motto of His work. Had any of the disciples been arrested along with Jesus and been executed by His side as act and part with Him, the view which the Christian world has taken of Christ's position and work must have been blurred if not quite altered. But the Jews had penetration enough to see where the strength of this movement lay. They believed that if the Shepherd was smitten the sheep would give them no trouble, but would necessarily scatter. Peter's flourish with the sword attracted little attention; they knew that great movements were not led by men of his type. They passed him by with a smile and did not even arrest him. It was Jesus who stood before them as alone dangerous. And Jesus on His side knew that the Jews were right, that He was the responsible person, that these Galileans would have been dreaming at their nets had He not summoned them to follow Him. If there was any offence in the matter, it belonged to Him, not to them.

But in Jesus thus stepping to the front and shielding the disciples by exposing Himself, John sees a picture of the whole sacrifice and substitution of Christ. This figure of his Master moving forward to meet the swords and staves of the party remains indelibly stamped upon his mind as the symbol of Christ's whole relation to His people. That night in Gethsemane was to them all the hour and power of darkness; and in every subsequent hour of darkness John and the rest see the same Divine figure stepping to the front, shielding them and taking upon Himself all the responsibility. It is thus Christ would have us think of Him—as our friend and protector, watchful over our interests, alive to all that threatens our persons, interposing between us and every hostile event. If by following Him according to our knowledge we are brought into difficulties, into circumstances of trouble and danger, if we are brought into collision with those in power, if we are discouraged and threatened by serious obstacles, let us be quite sure that in the critical moment He will interpose and convince us that, though He cannot save Himself, He can save others. He will not lead us into difficulties and leave us to find our own way out of them. If in striving to discharge our duty we have become entangled in many distressing and annoying circumstances, He acknowledges His responsibility in leading us into such a condition, and will see that we are not permanently the worse for it. If in seeking to know Him more thoroughly we have been led into mental perplexities, He will stand by us and see that we come to no harm. He encourages us to take this action of His in shielding His disciples as the symbol of what we all may expect He will do for ourselves. In all matters between God and us He interposes and claims to be counted as the true Head who is accountable, as that One who desires to answer all charges that can be made against the rest of us. If therefore, in view of much duty left undone, of many sinful imaginings harboured, of much vileness of conduct and character, we feel that it is ourselves the eye of God is seeking and with *us* He means to take account; if we know not how to answer Him regarding many things that stick in our memory and conscience,—let us accept the assurance here given us that Christ presents Himself as responsible.

It is not without surprise that we read that when Jesus was arrested all the disciples forsook Him and fled. John, indeed, and Peter speedily recovered themselves and followed to the hall of judgment; and the others may not only have felt that they were in danger so long as they remained in His company, but also that by accompanying Him they could not mend matters. Still, the kind of loyalty that stands by a falling cause, and the kind of courage that risks all to show sympathy with a friend or leader, are qualities so very common that one would have expected to find them here. And no doubt had the matter been to be decided in Peter's fashion, by the sword, they would have stood by Him. But there was a certain mysteriousness about our Lord's purpose that prevented His followers from being quite sure where they were being led to. They were perplexed and staggered by the whole transaction. They had expected things to go differently and scarcely knew what they were doing when they fled.

There are times when we feel a slackening of devotion to Christ, times when we are doubtful whether we have not been misled, times when the bond between us and Him seems to be of the slenderest possible description, times when we have as truly forsaken Him as these disciples, and are running no risks for Him, doing nothing to advance His interests, seeking only our own comfort and our own safety. These times will frequently be found to be the result of disappointed expectations. Things have not gone with us in the spiritual life as we expected. We have found things altogether more difficult than we looked for. We do not know what to make of our present state nor what to expect in the future, and so we lose an active interest in Christ and fall away from any hope that is living and influential.

Another point which John evidently desires to bring prominently before us in this narrative is Christ's willingness to surrender Himself; the voluntary character of all He afterwards suffered. It was at this point of His career, at 'His apprehension, this could best be brought out. Afterwards He might say He suffered willingly, but so far as appearances went He had no option. Previous to His apprehension His professions of willingness would not have been attended to. It was precisely now that it could be seen whether He would flee, hide, resist, or calmly yield Himself. And John is careful to bring out His willingness. He went to the garden as usual, "knowing all things that should come upon Him." It would have been easy to seek some safer quarters for the night, but He would not. At the last moment escape from the garden could not have been impossible. His followers could have covered His retreat. But He advances to meet the party, avows Himself to be the man they sought, will not suffer Peter to use his sword, in every way shows that His surrender is voluntary. Still, had He not shown His power to escape, onlookers might have thought this was only the prudent conduct of a brave man who wished to preserve His dignity, and therefore preferred delivering Himself up to being ignominiously dragged from a hiding-place. Therefore it was made plain that if He yielded it was not for want of power to resist.

By a word He overthrew those who came to bind Him, and made them feel ashamed of their preparations. He spoke confidently of help that would have swept the cohort off the field.[1] And thus it was brought out that, if He died, He laid down His life and was not deprived of it solely by the hate and violence of men. The hate and violence were there; but they were not the sole factors. He yielded to these because they were ingredients in the cup His Father wished Him to drink.

The reason of this is obvious. Christ's life was to be all sacrifice, because self-sacrifice is the essence of holiness and of love. From beginning to end the moving spring of all His actions was deliberate self-devotement to the good of men or to the fulfilment of God's will; for these are equivalents. And His death as the crowning act of this career was to be conspicuously a death embodying and exhibiting the spirit of self-sacrifice. He offered Himself on the cross through the eternal Spirit. That death was not compulsory; it was not the outcome of a sudden whim or generous impulse; it was the expression of a constant uniform "eternal" Spirit, which on the cross, in the yielding of life itself, rendered up for men all that was possible. Unwillingly no sacrifice can be made. When a man is taxed to support the poor, we do not call that a sacrifice. Sacrifice must be free, loving, uncompelled; it must be the exhibition in act of love, the freest and most spontaneous of all human emotions. "It is a true Christian instinct in our language which has seized upon the word *sacrifice* to express the self-devotion prompted by an unselfish love for others: we

---

[1] Matt. xxvi. 53.

speak of the *sacrifices* made by a loving wife or mother; and we test the sincerity of a Christian by the *sacrifices* he will make for the love of Christ and the brethren. . . . The reason why Christianity has approved itself a living principle of regeneration to the world is specially because a Divine example and a Divine spirit of self-sacrifice have wrought together in the hearts of men, and thereby an ever-increasing number have been quickened with the desire and strengthened with the will to spend and be spent for the cleansing, the restoration, and the life of the most guilty, miserable, and degraded of their fellows." It was in Christ's life and death this great principle of the life of God and man was affirmed: there self-sacrifice is perfectly exhibited.

It is to this willingness of Christ to suffer we must ever turn. It is this voluntary, uncompelled, spontaneous devotion of Himself to the good of men which is the magnetic point in this earth. Here is something we can cleave to with assurance, something we can trust and build upon. Christ in His own sovereign freedom of will and impelled by love of us has given Himself to work out our perfect deliverance from sin and evil of every kind. Let us deal sincerely with Him, let us be in earnest about these matters, let us hope truly in Him, let us give Him time to conquer by moral means all our moral foes within and without, and we shall one day enter into His joy and His triumph.

But when we thus apply John's words we are haunted with a suspicion that they were perhaps not intended to be thus used. Is John justified in finding in Christ's surrender of Himself to the authorities, on condition that the disciples should escape, fulfilment of the words that of those whom God had given Him He had lost none? The actual occurrence we see here is Jesus arrested as a false Messiah, and claiming to be the sole culprit if any culprit there be. Is this an occurrence that has any bearing upon us or any special instruction regarding the substitution of a sin-bearer in our room? Can it mean that He alone bears the punishment of our sin and that we go free? Is it any more than an illustration of His substitutionary work, one instance out of many of His habit of self-devotion in the room of others? Can I build upon this act in the Garden of Gethsemane and conclude from it that He surrenders Himself that I may escape punishment? Can I legitimately gather from it anything more than another proof of His constant readiness to stand in the breach? It is plain enough that a person who acted as Christ did here is one we could trust; but had this action any special virtue as the actual substitution of Christ in our room as sin-bearer?

It is, I think, well that we should occasionally put to ourselves such questions and train ourselves to look at the events of Christ's life as actual occurrences, and to distinguish between what is fanciful and what is real. So much has been said and written regarding His work, it has been the subject of so much sentiment, the basis of so many conflicting theories, the text of so much loose and allegorising interpretation, that the original plain and substantial fact is apt to be overlaid and lost sight of. And yet it is that plain and substantial reality which has virtue for us, while all else is delusive, howsoever finely sentimental, howsoever rich in coincidences with Old Testament sayings or in suggestions of ingenious doctrine. The subject of substitution is obscure. Inquiry into the Atonement is like the search for the North Pole: approach it from what quarter we may, there are unmistakable indications that a finality exists in that direction; but to make our way to it and take a survey all round it at once is still beyond us. We must be content if we can correct certain variations of the compass and find so much as one open waterway through which our own little vessel can be steered.

Looking, then, at this surrender of Christ in the light of John's comment, we see clearly enough that Christ sought to shelter His disciples at His own expense, and that this must have been the habit of His life. He sought no companion in misfortune. His desire was to save others from suffering. This willingness to be the responsible party was the habit of His life. It is impossible to think of Christ as in any matter sheltering Himself behind any man or taking a second place. He is always ready to bear the burden and the brunt. We recognise in this action of Christ that we have to do with One who shirks nothing, fears nothing, grudges nothing; who will substitute Himself for others wherever possible, if danger is abroad. So far as the character and habit of Christ go, there is unquestionably here manifest a good foundation for His substitution in our stead wheresoever such substitution is possible.

It is also in this scene, probably more than in any other, that we see that the work Christ had come to do was one which He must do entirely by Himself. It is scarcely exaggeration to say He could employ no assistant even in its minor details. He did indeed send forth men to proclaim His kingdom, but it was to proclaim what He *alone did*. In His miracles He did not use His disciples as a surgeon uses His assistants. Here in the garden He explicitly puts the disciples aside and says that this question of the Messiahship is solely His affair. This separate, solitary character of Christ's work is important: it reminds us of the exceptional dignity and greatness of it; it reminds us of the unique insight and power possessed by Him who alone conceived and carried it through.

There is no question, then, of Christ's willingness to be our substitute; the question rather is, Is it possible that He should suffer for our sin and so save us from suffering? and does this scene in the garden help us to answer that question? That this scene, in common with the whole work of Christ, had a meaning and relations deeper than those that appear on the surface none of us doubts. The soldiers who arrested Him, the judges who condemned Him, saw nothing but the humble and meek prisoner, the bar of the Sanhedrim, the stripes of the Roman scourge, the material cross and nails and blood; but all this had relations of infinite reach, meaning of infinite depth. Through all that Christ did and suffered God was accomplishing the greatest of His designs, and if we miss this Divine intention we miss the essential significance of these events. The Divine intention was to save us from sin and give us eternal life. This is accomplished by Christ's surrender of Himself to this earthly life and all the anxiety, the temptation, the mental and spiritual strain which this involved. By revealing the Father's love to us He wins us back to the Father; and the Father's love was revealed in the self-sacrificing suffering He necessarily endured in numbering Himself with sinners. Of Christ's satisfying the law by suffering the penalty under which we lay Paul has much to say. He explicitly affirms that Christ bore and so abolished the curse or penalty of sin. But in this Gospel there may indeed be hints of this same idea, but it is mainly another aspect of the work of Christ which is here presented. It is the exhibition of Christ's self-sacrificing love as a revelation of the Father which is most prominent in the mind of John.

We can certainly say that Christ suffered our penalties in so far as a perfectly holy person can suffer them. The gnawing anguish of remorse He never knew; the haunting anxieties of the wrong-doer were impossible to Him; the torment of ungratified desire, eternal severance from God, He could not suffer; but other results and penalties of sin He suffered more intensely than is possible to us. The agony of seeing men He loved destroyed by sin, all the pain which a sympathetic and pure spirit must bear in a world like this, the contradiction of sinners, the provocation and shame which daily attended Him—all this He bore because of sin and for us, that we might be saved from lasting sin and unrelieved misery. So that even if we cannot take this scene in the garden as an exact representation of the whole substitutionary work of Christ, we can say that by suffering with and for us He has saved us from sin and restored us to life and to God.

# XVIII.
## PETER'S DENIAL AND REPENTANCE.

"'So the band and the chief captain, and the officers of the Jews, seized Jesus and bound Him, and led Him to Annas first; for he was father-in-law to Caiaphas, which was high priest that year. Now Caiaphas was he which gave counsel to the Jews, that it was expedient that one man should die for the people. And Simon Peter followed Jesus, and so did another disciple. Now that disciple was known unto the high priest, and entered in with Jesus into the court of the high priest; but Peter was standing at the door without. So the other disciple, which was known unto the high priest, went out and spake unto her that kept the door, and brought in Peter. The maid therefore that kept the door saith unto Peter, Art thou also one of this man's disciples? He saith, I am not. Now the servants and the officers were standing there, having made a fire of coals; for it was cold; and they were warming themselves: and Peter also was with them, standing and warming himself. . . . Now Simon Peter was standing and warming himself. They said therefore unto him, Art thou also one of His disciples? He denied, and said, I am not. One of the servants of the high priest, being a kinsman of him whose ear Peter cut off, saith, Did not I see thee in the garden with Him? Peter therefore denied again: and straightway the cock crew.'—JOHN xviii. 12-18, 25-27.

# XVIII.

## *PETER'S DENIAL AND REPENTANCE.*

THE examination of Jesus immediately followed His arrest. He was first led to Annas, who at once sent Him to Caiaphas, the high priest, that he might carry out his policy of making one man a scapegoat for the nation.[1] To John the most memorable incident of this midnight hour was Peter's denial of his Master. It happened on this wise. The high priest's palace was built, like other large Oriental houses, round a quadrangular court, into which entrance was gained by a passage running from the street through the front part of the house. This passage or archway is called in the Gospels the "porch," and was closed at the end next the street by a heavy folding gate with a wicket for single persons. This wicket

---

[1] There is a difficulty in tracing the movements of Jesus at this point. John tells us He was led to Annas first, and at ver. 24 he says that Annas sent Him to Caiaphas. We should naturally conclude, therefore, that the preceding examination was conducted by Annas. But Caiaphas has been expressly indicated as chief priest, and it is by the chief priest and in the chief priest's palace the examination is conducted. The name "chief priest" was not confined to the one actually in office, but was applied to all who had held the office, and might therefore be applied to Annas. Possibly the examination recorded vv. 19-23 was before him, and probably he was living with his son-in-law in the palace of the chief priest.

was kept on this occasion by a maid. The interior court upon which this passage opened was paved or flagged and open to the sky, and as the night was cold the attendants had made a fire here. The rooms round the court, in one of which the examination of Jesus was proceeding, were open in front—separated, that is to say, from the court only by one or two pillars or arches and a railing, so that our Lord could see and even hear Peter.

When Jesus was led in bound to this palace, there entered with the crowd of soldiers and servants one at least of His disciples. He was in some way acquainted with the high priest, and presuming on this acquaintanceship followed to learn the fate of Jesus. He had seen Peter following at a distance, and after a little he goes to the gate-keeper and induces her to open to his friend. The maid seeing the familiar terms on which these two men were, and knowing that one of them was a disciple of Jesus, very naturally greets Peter with the exclamation, "Art not thou *also* one of this man's disciples?" Peter, confused by being suddenly confronted with so many hostile faces, and remembering the blow he had struck in the garden, and that he was now in the place of all others where it was likely to be avenged, suddenly in a moment of infatuation, and doubtless to the dismay of his fellow-disciple, denies all knowledge of Jesus. Having once committed himself, the two other denials followed as matter of course.

Yet the third denial is more guilty than the first. Many persons are conscious that they have sometimes acted under what seems an infatuation. They do not plead this in excuse for the wrong they have done. They are quite aware that what has come out of them must have been in them, and that their acts, unaccountable as they seem, have definite roots in their character. Peter's first denial was the result of surprise and infatuation. But an hour seems to have elapsed between the first and the third. He had time to think, time to remember his Lord's warning, time to leave the place if he could do no better. But one of those reckless moods which overtake good-hearted children seems to have overtaken Peter, for at the end of the hour he is talking right round the whole circle at the fire, not in monosyllables and guarded voice, but in his own outspoken way, the most talkative of them all, until suddenly one whose ear was finer than the rest detected the Galilean accent, and says, "You need not deny you are one of this man's disciples, for your speech betrays you." Another, a kinsman of him whose ear Peter had cut off, strikes in and declares that he had seen him in the garden. Peter, driven to extremities, hides his Galilean accent under the strong oaths of the city, and with a volley of profane language asseverates that he has no knowledge of Jesus. At this moment the first examination of Jesus closes and He is led across the court: the first chill of dawn is felt in the air, a cock crows, and as Jesus passes He looks upon Peter; the look and the cock-crow together bring Peter to himself, and he hurries out and weeps bitterly.

The remarkable feature of this sin of Peter's is that at first sight it seems so alien to his character. It was a lie; and he was unusually straightforward. It was a heartless and cruel lie, and he was a man full of emotion and affection. It was a cowardly lie, even more cowardly than common lies, and yet he was exceptionally bold. Peter himself was quite positive that this at least was a sin he would never commit. "Though all men should deny Thee, yet will not I." Neither was this a baseless boast. He was not a mere braggart, whose words found no correspondence in his deeds. Far from it; he was a hardy, somewhat over-venturesome man, accustomed to the risks of a fisherman's life, not afraid to fling himself into a stormy sea, or to face the overwhelming armed force that came to apprehend his Master, ready to fight for him single-handed, and quickly recovering from the panic which scattered his fellow-disciples. If any of his companions had been asked at what point of Peter's character the vulnerable spot would be found, not one of them would have said, "He will fall through cowardice." Besides, Peter had a few hours before been so emphatically warned against denying Christ that he might have been expected to stand firm this night at least.

Perhaps it was this very warning which betrayed Peter. When he struck the blow in the garden, he thought he had falsified his Lord's prediction. And when he found himself the only one who had courage to follow to the palace, his besetting self-confidence returned and led him into circumstances for which he was too weak. He was equal to the test of his courage which he was expecting, but when another kind of test was applied in circumstances and from a quarter he had not anticipated his courage failed him utterly.

Peter probably thought he might be brought bound with his Master before the high priest, and had he been so he would probably have stood faithful. But the devil who was sifting him had a much finer sieve than that to run him through. He brought him to no formal trial, where he could gird himself for a special effort, but to an unobserved, casual questioning by a slave-girl. The whole trial was over before he knew he was being tried. So do our most real trials come; in a business transaction that turns up with others in the day's work, in the few minutes' talk or the evening's intercourse with friends, it is discovered whether we are so truly Christ's friends that we cannot forget Him or disguise that we are His. A word or two with a person he never saw before and would never see again brought the great trial of Peter's life; and as unexpectedly shall we be tried. In these battles we must all encounter, we receive no formal challenge that gives us time to choose our ground and our weapons; but a sudden blow is dealt us, from which we can be saved only by habitually wearing a shirt of mail sufficient to turn it, and which we can carry into all companies.

Had Peter distrusted himself and seriously accepted his Lord's warning, he would have gone with the rest; but ever thinking of himself as able to do more than other men, faithful where others were faithless, convinced where others hesitated, daring where others shrank, he once again thrust himself forward, and so fell. For this self-confidence, which might to a careless observer seem to underprop Peter's courage, was to the eye of the Lord undermining it. And if Peter's true bravery and promptitude were to serve the Church in days when fearless steadfastness would be above all other qualities needed, his courage must be sifted and the chaff of self-confidence thoroughly separated from it. In place of a courage which was sadly tainted with vanity and impulsiveness Peter must acquire a courage based upon recognition of his own weakness and his Lord's strength. And it was this event which wrought this change in Peter's character.

Frequently we learn by a very painful experience that our best qualities are tainted, and that actual disaster has entered our life from the very quarter we least suspected. We may be conscious that the deepest mark has been made on our life by a sin apparently as alien to our character as cowardice and lying were to the too venturesome and outspoken character of Peter. Possibly we once prided ourselves on our honesty, and felt happy in our upright character, plain-dealing, and direct speech; but to our dismay we have been betrayed into double-dealing, equivocation, evasive or even fraudulent conduct. Or the time was when we were proud of our friendships; it was frequently in our mind that, however unsatisfactory in other respects our character might be, we were at any rate faithful and helpful friends. Alas! events have proved that even in this particular we have failed, and have, through absorption in our own interests, acted inconsiderately and even cruelly to our friend, not even recognising at the time how his interests were suffering. Or we are by nature of a cool temperament, and judged ourselves safe at least from the faults of impulse and passion; yet the mastering combination of circumstances came, and we spoke the word, or wrote the letter, or did the deed which broke our life past mending.

Now, it was Peter's salvation, and it will be ours, when overtaken in this unsuspected sin, to go out and weep bitterly. He did not frivolously count it an accident that could never occur again; he did not sullenly curse the circumstances that had betrayed and shamed him. He recognised that there was that in him which could render useless his best natural qualities, and that the sinfulness which could make his strongest natural defences brittle as an egg-shell must be serious indeed. He had no choice but to be humbled before the eye of the Lord. There was no need of words to explain and enforce his guilt: the eye can express what the tongue cannot utter. The finer, tenderer, deeper feelings are left to the eye to express. The clear cockcrow strikes home to his conscience, telling him that the very sin he had an hour or two ago judged impossible is now actually committed. That brief space his Lord had named as sufficient to test his fidelity is gone, and the sound that strikes the hour rings with condemnation. Nature goes on in her accustomed, inexorable, unsympathetic round; but he is a fallen man, convicted in his own conscience of empty vanity, of cowardice, of heartlessness. He who in his own eyes was so much better than the rest had fallen lower than all. In the look of Christ Peter sees the reproachful loving tenderness of a wounded spirit, and understands the dimensions of his sin. That he, the most intimate disciple, should have added to the bitterness of that hour, should not only have failed to help his Lord, but should actually at the crisis of His fate have added the bitterest drop to His cup, was humbling indeed. There was that in Christ's look that made him feel the enormity of his guilt; there was that also that softened him and saved him from sullen despair.

And it is obvious that if we are to rise clear above the sin that has betrayed us we can do so only by as lowly a penitence. We are all alike in this: that we have fallen; we cannot any more with justice think highly of ourselves; we have sinned and are disgraced in our own eyes. In this, I say, we are all alike; that which makes the difference among us is, how we deal with ourselves and our circumstances in connection with our sin. It has been very well said by a keen observer of human nature that " men and women are often more fairly judged by the way in which they bear the burden of their own deeds, the fashion in which they carry themselves in their entanglements, than by the prime act which laid the burden on their lives and made the entanglement fast knotted. The deeper part of us shows in the manner of accepting consequences." The reason of this is that, like Peter, we are often *betrayed* by a weakness; the part of our nature which is least able to face difficulty is assaulted by a combination of circumstances which may never again occur in our life. There was guilt, great guilt it may be, concerned in our fall, but it was not deliberate, wilful wickedness. But in our dealing with our sin and its consequences our whole nature is concerned and searched; the real bent and strength of our will is tried. We are therefore in a crisis, *the* crisis, of our life. Can we accept the situation? Can we humbly, frankly own that, since that evil has appeared in our life, it must have been, however unconsciously, in ourselves first? Can we with the genuine manliness and wisdom of a broken heart say to ourselves and to God, Yes, it is true I am the wretched, pitiful, bad-hearted creature that was capable of doing, and did that thing? I did not think that was my character; I did not think it was in me to sink so very low; but now I see what I am. Do we thus, like Peter, go out and weep bitterly?

Every one who has passed through a time such as this single night was to Peter knows the strain that is laid upon the soul, and how very hard it is to yield utterly. So much rises up in self-defence; so much strength is lost by the mere perplexity and confusion of the thing; so much is lost in the despondency that follows these sad revelations of our deep-seated evil.

What is the use, we think, of striving, if even in the point in which I thought myself most secure I have fallen? What is the meaning of so perplexed and deceiving a warfare? Why was I exposed to so fatal an influence? So Peter, had he taken the wrong direction, might have resented the whole course of the temptation, and might have said, Why did Christ not warn me by His look before I sinned, instead of breaking me by it after? Why had I no inkling of the enormity of the sin before as I have after the sin? My reputation now is gone among the disciples; I may as well go back to my old obscure life and forget all about these perplexing scenes and strange spiritualities. But Peter, though he was cowed by a maid, was man enough and Christian enough to reject such falsities and subterfuges. It is true we did not see the enormity, never do see the enormity, of the sin until it is committed; but is it possible it can be otherwise? Is not this the way in which a blunt conscience is educated? Nothing seems so bad until it finds place in our own life and haunts us. Neither need we despond or sour because we are disgraced in our own eyes, or even in the eyes of others; for we are hereby summoned to build for ourselves a new and different reputation with God and our own consciences—a reputation founded on a basis of reality and not of seeming.

It may be worth while to note the characteristics and danger of that special form of weakness which Peter here exhibited. We commonly call it moral cowardice. It is originally a weakness rather than a positive sin, and yet it is probably as prolific of sin and even of great crime as any of the more definite and vigorous passions of our nature, such as hate, lust, avarice. It is that weakness which prompts a man to avoid difficulties, to escape everything rough and disagreeable, to yield to circumstances, and which above all makes him incapable of facing the reproach, contempt, or opposition of his fellow-men. It is often found in combination with much amiability of character. It is commonly found in persons who have some natural leanings to virtue, and who, if circumstances would only favour them, would prefer to lead, and would lead, at least an inoffensive and respectable, if not a very useful, noble, or heroic life. Finely strung natures that are very sensitive to all impressions from without, natures which thrill and vibrate in response to a touching tale or in sympathy with fine scenery or soft music, natures which are housed in bodies of delicate nervous temperament, are commonly keenly sensitive to the praise or blame of their fellows, and are therefore liable to moral cowardice, though by no means necessarily a prey to it.

The examples of its ill-effects are daily before our eyes. A man cannot bear the coolness of a friend or the contempt of a leader of opinion, and so he stifles his own independent judgment and goes with the majority. A minister of the Church finds his faith steadily diverging from that of the creed he has subscribed, but he cannot proclaim this change because he cannot make up his mind to be the subject of public astonishment and remark, of severe scrutiny on the one side and still more distasteful because ignorant and canting sympathy on the other. A man in business finds that his expenditure exceeds his income, but he is unable to face the shame of frankly lowering his position and curtailing his expenses, and so he is led into dishonest appearances; and from dishonest appearances to fraudulent methods of keeping them up the step, as we all know, is short. Or in trade a man knows that there are shameful, contemptible, and silly practices, and yet he has not moral courage to break through them. A parent cannot bear to risk the loss of his child's goodwill even for an hour, and so omits the chastisement he deserves. The schoolboy, fearing his parents' look of disappointment, says he stands higher in his class than he does ; or fearing to be thought soft and unmanly by his schoolfellows, sees cruelty or a cheat or some wickedness perpetrated without a word of honest anger or manly condemnation. All this is moral cowardice, the vice which brings us down to the low level which bold sinners set for us, or which at any rate sweeps the weak soul down to a thousand perils, and absolutely forbids the good there is in us from finding expression.

But of all the forms into which moral cowardice develops this of denying the Lord Jesus is the most iniquitous and disgraceful. One of the fashions of the day which is most rapidly extending and which many of us have opportunity to resist is the fashion of infidelity. Much of the strongest and best-trained intellect of the country ranges itself against Christianity—that is, against Christ. No doubt the men who have led this movement have adopted their opinions on conviction. They deny the authority of Scripture, the divinity of Christ, even the existence of a personal God, because by long years of painful thought they have been forced to such conclusions. Even the best of them cannot be acquitted of a contemptuous and bitter way of speaking of Christians, which would seem to indicate that they are not quite at ease in their belief. Still, we cannot but think that so far as any men can be quite unbiassed in their opinions, they are so; and we have no right to judge other men for their honestly formed opinions. The moral cowards of whom we speak are not these men, but their followers, persons who with no patience or capacity to understand their reasonings adopt their conclusions because they seem advanced and are peculiar. There are many persons of slender reading and no depth of earnestness who, without spending any serious effort on the formation of their religious belief, presume to disseminate unbelief and treat the Christian creed as an obsolete thing merely because part of the intellect of the day leans in that direction. Weakness and cowardice are the real spring of such persons' apparent advance and new position regarding religion. They are ashamed to be reckoned among those who are thought to be behind the age. Ask them for a reason of their unbelief, and they are either unable to give you any, or else they repeat a time-worn objection which has been answered so often that men have wearied of the interminable task and let it pass unnoticed.

Such persons we aid and abet when we do either of two things: when we either cleave to what is old as unreasoningly as they take up with what is new, refusing to look for fresh light and better ways and acting as if we were already perfect; or when we yield to the current and adopt a hesitating way of speaking about matters of faith, when we *cultivate* a sceptical spirit and seem to connive at if we do not applaud the cold, irreligious sneer of ungodly men. Above all, we aid the cause of infidelity when in our own life we are ashamed to live godly, to act on higher principles than the current prudential maxims, when we hold our allegiance to Christ in abeyance to our fear of our associates, when we find no way of showing that Christ is our Lord and that we delight in opportunities of confessing Him. The confessing of Christ is a duty explicitly imposed on all those who expect that He will acknowledge them as His. It is a duty to which we might suppose every manly and generous instinct in us would eagerly respond, and yet we are often more ashamed of our connection with the loftiest and holiest of beings than of our own pitiful and sin-infected selves, and as little practically stimulated and actuated by a true gratitude to Him as if His death were the commonest boon and as if we were expecting and needing no help from Him in the time that is yet to come.[1]

---

[1] Some of the ideas in this chapter were suggested by a sermon of Bishop Temple's.

## XIX.

### JESUS BEFORE PILATE

"They led Jesus therefore from Caiaphas into the palace. and it was early; and they themselves entered not into the palace, that they might not be defiled, but might eat the Passover. Pilate therefore went out unto them, and saith, What accusation bring ye against this man? They answered and said unto him, If this man were not an evil-doer, we should not have delivered Him up unto thee. Pilate therefore said unto them, Take Him yourselves, and judge Him according to your law. The Jews said unto him, It is not lawful for us to put any man to death : that the word of Jesus might be fulfilled, which He spake, signifying by what manner of death He should die. Pilate therefore entered again into the palace, and called Jesus, and said unto Him, Art Thou the King of the Jews? Jesus answered, Sayest thou this of thyself, or did others tell it thee concerning Me? Pilate answered, Am I a Jew? Thine own nation and the chief priests delivered Thee unto me: what hast Thou done? Jesus answered, My kingdom is not of this world : if My kingdom were of this world, then would My servants fight, that I should not be delivered to the Jews: but now is My kingdom not from hence. Pilate therefore said unto Him, Art Thou a king then? Jesus answered, Thou sayest that I am a king. To this end have I been born, and to this end am I come into the world, that I should bear witness unto the truth. Every one that is of the truth heareth My voice. Pilate saith unto Him, What is truth? And when he had said this, he went out again unto the Jews, and saith unto them, I find no crime in Him. But ye have a custom, that I should release unto you one at the Passover: will ye therefore that I release unto you the King of the Jews? They cried out therefore again, saying, Not this man, but Barabbas. Now Barabbas was a robber. Then Pilate therefore took Jesus, and scourged Him. And the soldiers plaited a crown of thorns, and put it on His head, and arrayed Him in a purple garment; and they came unto Him, and said, Hail, King of the Jews! and they struck Him with their hands. And Pilate went out again, and saith unto them, Behold I bring Him out to you, that ye may know that I find no crime in Him. Jesus therefore came out, wearing the crown of thorns and the purple garment. And Pilate saith unto them, Behold, the man ! When therefore the chief priests and the officers saw Him, they cried out, saying, Crucify Him, crucify Him. Pilate saith unto them, Take Him yourselves, and crucify Him : for I find no crime in Him. The Jews answered him, We have a law, and by that law He ought to die, because He made Himself the Son of God. When Pilate therefore heard this saying he was the more afraid ; and he entered into the palace again, and saith unto Jesus, Whence art Thou ? But Jesus gave him no answer. Pilate therefore saith unto Him, Speakest Thou not unto me ? knowest Thou not that I have power to release Thee, and have power to crucify Thee ? Jesus answered Him, Thou wouldest have no power against Me, except it were given thee from above : therefore he that delivered Me unto thee hath greater sin. Upon this Pilate sought to release Him : but the Jews cried out, saying, If thou release this man, thou art not Cæsar's friend : every one that maketh himself a king speaketh against Cæsar. When Pilate therefore heard these words, he brought Jesus out, and sat down on the judgment-seat at a place called The Pavement, but in Hebrew, Gabbatha. Now it was the preparation of the Passover : it was about the sixth hour. And he saith unto the Jews, Behold, your King ! They therefore cried out, Away with Him, away with Him, crucify Him. Pilate saith unto them, Shall I crucify your King ? The chief priests answered, We have no king but Cæsar. Then therefore he delivered Him unto them to be crucified."—JOHN xviii. 28—xix 16.

# XIX.

## *JESUS BEFORE PILATE.*

JOHN tells us very little of the examination of Jesus by Annas and Caiaphas, but he dwells at considerable length on His trial by Pilate. The reason of this different treatment is probably to be found in the fact that the trial before the Sanhedrim was ineffective until the decision had been ratified by Pilate, as well as in the circumstance noted by John that the decision of Caiaphas was a foregone conclusion. Caiaphas was an unscrupulous politician who allowed nothing to stand between him and his objects. To the weak councillors who had expressed a fear that it might be difficult to convict a person so innocent as Jesus he said with supreme contempt: "Ye know nothing at all. Do you not see the opportunity we have of showing our zeal for the Roman Government by sacrificing this man who claims to be King of the Jews? Innocent of course He is, and all the better so, for the Romans cannot think He dies for robbery or wrong-doing. He is a Galilean of no consequence, connected with no good family who might revenge His death." This was the scheme of Caiaphas. He saw that the Romans were within a very little of terminating the incessant troubles of this Judæan province by enslaving the whole population and devastating the land; this catastrophe might be staved off a few years by such an exhibition of zeal for Rome as could be made in the public execution of Jesus.

So far as Caiaphas and his party were concerned, then, Jesus was prejudged. His trial was not an examination to discover whether He was guilty or innocent, but a cross-questioning which aimed at betraying Him into some acknowledgment which might give colour to the sentence of death already decreed. Caiaphas or Annas[1] invites Him to give some account of His disciples and of His doctrines. In some cases His disciples carried arms, and among them was one zealot, and there might be others known to the authorities as dangerous or suspected characters. And Annas might expect that in giving some account of His teaching the honesty of Jesus might betray Him into expressions which could easily be construed to His prejudice. But he is disappointed. Jesus replies that it is not for Him, arraigned and bound as a dangerous prisoner, to give evidence against Himself. Thousands had heard Him in all parts of the country. He had delivered those supposed inflammatory addresses not to midnight gatherings and secret societies, but in the most public places He could find—in the Temple, from which no Jew was excluded, and in the synagogues, where official teachers were commonly present. Annas is silenced; and mortified though he is, he has to accept the ruling of his prisoner as indicating the lines on which the trial should proceed. His mortification does not escape the notice of one of those poor creatures who are ever ready to curry favour with the great by cruelty towards the defenceless, or at the

---

[1] See note to chapter xviii.

best of that large class of men who cannot distinguish between official and real dignity; and the first of those insults is given to the hitherto sacred person of Jesus, the first of that long series of blows struck by a dead, conventional religion seeking to quench the truth and the life of what threatens its slumber with awakening.

Had the Roman governor not been present in the city the high priests and their party might have ventured to carry into effect their own sentence. But Pilate had already shown during his six years of office that he was not a man to overlook anything like contempt of his supremacy. Besides, they were not quite sure of the temper of the people; and a rescue, or even an attempted rescue, of their prisoner would be disastrous. Prudence therefore bids them hand Him over to Pilate, who had both legal authority to put Him to death and means to quell any popular disturbance. Besides, the purpose of Caiaphas could better be served by bringing before the governor this claimant to the Messiahship.

Pilate was present in Jerusalem at this time in accordance with the custom of the Roman procurators of Judæa, who came up annually from their usual residence at Cæsarea to the Jewish capital for the double purpose of keeping order while the city was crowded with all kinds of persons who came up to the feast, and of trying cases reserved for his decision. And the Jews no doubt thought it would be easy to persuade a man who, as they knew to their cost, set a very low value on human blood to add one victim more to the robbers or insurgents who might be awaiting execution. Accordingly, as soon as day dawned and they dared to disturb the governor, they put Jesus in chains as a condemned criminal and led Him away, all their leading men following, to the quarters of Pilate, either in the fortress Antonia or in the magnificent palace of Herod. Into this palace, being the abode of a Gentile, they could not enter lest they should contract pollution and incapacitate themselves for eating the Passover,—the culminating instance of religious scrupulosity going hand in hand with cruel and bloodthirsty criminality. Pilate with scornful allowance for their scruples goes out to them, and with the Roman's instinctive respect for the forms of justice demands the charge brought against this prisoner, in whose appearance the quick eye so long trained to read the faces of criminals is at a loss to discover any index to His crime.

This apparent intention on Pilate's part, if not to reopen the case at least to revise their procedure, is resented by the party of Caiaphas, who exclaim, " If He were not a malefactor we would not have delivered Him up unto thee. Take our word for it; He is guilty; do not scruple to put Him to death." But if they were indignant that Pilate should propose to revise their decision, he is not less so that they should presume to make him their mere executioner. All the Roman pride of office, all the Roman contempt and irritation at this strange Jewish people, come out in his answer, "If you will make no charge against Him and refuse to allow me to judge Him, take Him yourselves and do what you can with Him," knowing well that they dared not inflict death without his sanction, and that this taunt would pierce home. The taunt they did feel, although they could not afford to show that they felt it, but contented themselves with laying the charge that He had forbidden the people to give tribute to Cæsar and claimed to be Himself a king.

As Roman law permitted the examination to be conducted within the prætorium, though the judgment must be pronounced outside in public, Pilate re-enters the palace and has Jesus brought in, so that apart from the crowd he may examine Him. At once he puts the direct question, Guilty or not guilty of this political offence with which you stand charged?—"Art Thou the King of the Jews?" But to this direct question Jesus cannot give a direct answer, because the words may have one sense in the lips of Pilate, another in His own. Before He answers He must first know in which sense Pilate uses the words. He asks therefore, "Sayest thou this thing of thyself, or did others tell it thee?" Are you inquiring because you are yourself concerned in this question? or are you merely uttering a question which others have put in your mouth? To which Pilate with some heat and contempt replies, "Am I a Jew? How can you expect me to take any personal interest in the matter? Thine own nation and the chief priests have delivered Thee unto me."

Pilate, that is to say, scouts the idea that he should take any interest in questions about the Messiah of the Jews. And yet was it not possible that, like some of his subordinates, centurions and others, he too should perceive the spiritual grandeur of Jesus and should not be prevented by his heathen upbringing from seeking to belong to this kingdom of God? May not Pilate also be awakened to see that man's true inheritance is the world unseen? may not that expression of fixed melancholy, of hard scorn, of sad, hopeless, proud indifference, give place to the humble eagerness of the inquiring soul? may not the heart of a child come back to that bewildered and world-encrusted soul? Alas! this is too much for Roman pride. He cannot in presence of this bound Jew acknowledge how little life has satisfied him. He finds the difficulty so many find in middle life of frankly showing that they have in their nature deeper desires than the successes of life satisfy. There is many a man who seals up his deeper instincts and does violence to his better nature because, having begun his life on worldly lines, he is too proud now to change, and crushes down, to his own eternal hurt, the stirrings of a better mind within him, and turns from the gentle whisperings that would fain bring eternal hope to his heart.

It is possible that Jesus by His question meant to suggest to Pilate the actual relation in which this present trial stood to His previous trial by Caiaphas. For nothing could more distinctly mark the baseness and malignity of the Jews than their manner of shifting ground when they brought Jesus before Pilate. The Sanhedrim had condemned Him, not for claiming to be King of the Jews, for that was not a capital offence, but for assuming Divine dignity. But that which in their eyes was a crime was none in the judgment of Roman law; it was useless to bring Him before Pilate and accuse Him of blasphemy. They therefore accused Him of assuming to be King of the Jews. Here, then, were the Jews "accusing Jesus before the Roman governor of that which, in the first place, they knew that Jesus denied in the sense in which they urged it, and which, in the next place, had the charge been true, would have been so far from a crime in their eyes that it would have been popular with the whole nation."

But as Pilate might very naturally misunderstand the character of the claim made by the accused, Jesus in a few words gives him clearly to understand that the kingdom He sought to establish could not come into collision with that which Pilate represented : " My kingdom is not of this world." The most convincing proof had been given of the spiritual character of the kingdom in the fact that Jesus did not allow the sword to be used in forwarding His claims. " If My kingdom were of this world, then would My servants fight, that I should not be delivered to the Jews : but now is My kingdom not from hence." This did not quite satisfy Pilate. He thought that still some mystery of danger might lurk behind the words of Jesus. There was nothing more acutely dreaded by the early emperors than secret societies. It might be some such association Jesus intended to form. To allow such a society to gain influence in his province would be a gross oversight on Pilate's part. He therefore seizes upon the apparent admission of Jesus and pushes Him further with the question, " Thou art a king then ? " But the answer of Jesus removes all fear from the mind of His judge. He claims only to be a king of the truth, attracting to Himself all who are drawn by a love of truth. This was enough for Pilate. "Aletheia" was a country beyond his jurisdiction, a Utopia which could not injure the Empire. " Tush ! " he says, " what is Aletheia ? Why speak to me of ideal worlds ? What concern have I with provinces that can yield no tribute and offer no armed resistance ? "

Pilate, convinced of the innocence of Jesus, makes several attempts to save Him. All these attempts failed, because, instead of at once and decidedly proclaiming His innocence and demanding His acquittal, he sought at the same time to propitiate His accusers. One generally expects from a Roman governor some knowledge of men and some fearlessness in his use of that knowledge. Pilate shows neither. His first step in dealing with the accusers of Jesus is a fatal mistake. Instead of at once going to his judgment-seat and pronouncing authoritatively the acquittal of his Prisoner, and clearing his court of all riotously disposed persons, he in one breath declared Jesus innocent and proposed to treat Him as guilty, offering to release Him as a boon to the Jews. A weaker proposal could scarcely have been made. There was nothing, absolutely nothing, to induce the Jews to accept it, but in making it he showed a disposition to treat with them—a disposition they did not fail to make abundant use of in the succeeding scenes of this disgraceful day. This first departure from justice lowered him to their own level and removed the only bulwark he had against their insolence and blood-thirstiness. Had he acted as any upright judge would have acted and at once put his Prisoner beyond reach of their hatred, they would have shrunk like cowed wild beasts; but his first concession put him in their power, and from this point onwards there is exhibited one of the most lamentable spectacles in history,—a man in power tossed like a ball between his convictions and his fears; a Roman not without a certain doggedness and cynical hardness that often pass for strength of character, but held up here to view as a sample of the weakness that results from the vain attempt to satisfy both what is bad and what is good in us.

His second attempt to save Jesus from death was more unjust and as futile as the first. He scourges the Prisoner whose innocence he had himself declared, possibly under the idea that if nothing was confessed by Jesus under this torture it might convince the Jews of His innocence, but more probably under the impression that they might be satisfied when they saw Jesus bleeding and fainting from the scourge. The Roman scourge was a barbarous instrument, its heavy thongs being loaded with metal and inlaid with bone, every cut of which tore away the flesh. But if Pilate fancied that when the Jews saw this lacerated form they would pity and relent, he greatly mistook the men he had to do with. He failed to take into account the common principle that when you have wrongfully injured a man you hate him all the more. Many a man becomes a murderer, not by premeditation, but having struck a first blow and seeing his victim in agony he cannot bear that that eye should live to reproach him and that tongue to upbraid him with his cruelty. So it was here. The people were infuriated by the sight of the innocent, unmurmuring Sufferer whom they had thus mangled. They cannot bear that such an object be left to remind them of their barbarity, and with one fierce yell of fury they cry, "Crucify Him, crucify Him."[1]

A third time Pilate refused to be the instrument of their inhuman and unjust rage, and flung the Prisoner on their hands: "Take Him yourselves, and crucify Him: for I find no crime in Him." But when the Jews answered that by their law He ought to die, because "He made Himself the Son of God," Pilate was again seized with dread, and withdrew his Prisoner for the fourth time into the palace. Already he had remarked in His demeanour a calm superiority which made it seem quite possible that this extraordinary claim might be true. The books he had read at school and the poems he had heard since he grew up had told stories of how the gods had sometimes

---

[1] The cry according to the best reading was simply "Crucify, crucify" or as it might be rendered, "The cross. the cross."

come down and dwelt with men. He had long since discarded such beliefs as mere fictions. Still, there was something in the bearing of this Prisoner before him that awakened the old impression, that possibly this single planet with its visible population was not the whole universe, that there might be some other unseen region out of which Divine beings looked down upon earth with pity, and from which they might come and visit us on some errand of love. With anxiety written on his face and heard in his tone he asks, "Whence art Thou?" How near does this man always seem to be to breaking through the thin veil and entering with illumined vision into the spiritual world, the world of truth and right and God! Would not a word now from Jesus have given him entrance? Would not the repetition of the solemn affirmation of His divinity which He had given to the Sanhedrim have been the one thing wanted in Pilate's case, the one thing to turn the scale in the favour of Jesus? At first sight it might seem so; but so it seemed not to the Lord. He preserves an unbroken silence to the question on which Pilate seems to hang in an earnest suspense. And certainly this silence is by no means easy to account for. Shall we say that He was acting out His own precept, "Give not that which is holy to dogs"? Shall we say that He who knew what was in man saw that though Pilate was for the moment alarmed and in earnest, yet there was beneath that earnestness an ineradicable vacillation? It is very possible that the treatment He had received at Pilate's hand had convinced Him that Pilate would eventually yield to the Jews; and what need, then, of protracting the process? No man who has any dignity and self-respect will make declarations about his character which he sees will do no good: no man is bound to be at the beck of every one to answer accusations they may bring against him; by doing so he will often only involve himself in miserable, petty wranglings, and profit no one. Jesus therefore was not going to make revelations about Himself which He saw would only make Him once again a shuttlecock driven between the two contending parties.

Besides—and this probably is the main reason of the silence—Pilate was now forgetting altogether the relation between himself and his Prisoner. Jesus had been accused before him on a definite charge which he had found to be baseless. He ought therefore to have released Him. This new charge of the Jews was one of which Pilate could not take cognisance; and of this Jesus reminds him by His silence. Jesus might have made influence for Himself by working upon the superstition of Pilate; but this was not to be thought of.

Offended at His silence, Pilate exclaims: "Speakest Thou not unto me? Knowest Thou not that I have power to release Thee, and have power to crucify Thee?" Here was an unwonted kind of prisoner who would not curry favour with His judge. But instead of entreating him to use this power in His favour Jesus replies: "Thou wouldest have no power against Me, except it were given thee from above; therefore he that delivered Me unto thee hath greater sin." Pilate's office was the ordinance of God, and therefore his judgments should express the justice and will of God; and it was this which made the sin of Caiaphas and the Jews so great: they were making use of a Divine ordinance to serve their own God-resisting purposes. Had Pilate been a mere irresponsible executioner their sin would have been sufficiently heinous; but in using an official who is God's representative of law, order, and justice to fulfil their own wicked and unjust designs they recklessly prostitute God's ordinance of justice and involve themselves in a darker criminality.

More impressed than ever by this powerful statement falling from the lips of a man weakened by the scourging, Pilate makes one more effort to save Him. But now the Jews play their last card and play it successfully. "If thou release this man, thou art not Cæsar's friend." To lay himself open to a charge of treason or neglect of the interests of Cæsar was what Pilate could not risk. At once his compassion for the Prisoner, his sense of justice, his apprehensions, his proud unwillingness to let the Jews have their way, are overcome by his fear of being reported to the most suspicious of emperors. He prepared to give his judgment, taking his place on the official seat, which stood on a tesselated pavement, called in Aramaic "Gabbatha," from its elevated position in sight of the crowds standing outside. Here, after venting his spleen in the weak sarcasm "Shall I crucify your King?" he formally hands over his Prisoner to be crucified. This decision was at last come to, as John records, about noon of the day which prepared for and terminated in the Paschal Supper.

Pilate's vacillation receives from John a long and careful treatment. Light is shed upon it, and upon the threat which forced him at last to make up his mind, from the account which Philo gives of his character and administration. "With a view," he says, "to vex the Jews, Pilate hung up some gilt shields in the palace of Herod, which they judged a profanation of the holy city, and therefore petitioned him to remove them. But when he steadfastly refused to do so, for he was a man of very inflexible disposition and very merciless as well as very obstinate, they cried out, 'Beware of causing a tumult, for Tiberius will not sanction this act of yours; and if you say that he will, we ourselves will go to him and supplicate your master.' This threat exasperated Pilate in the highest degree, as he feared that they might really go to the Emperor and impeach him with respect to other acts of his government—his corruption, his acts of insolence, his habit of insulting people, his cruelty, his continual murders of people untried and uncondemned, and his never-ending and gratuitous and most grievous inhumanity. Therefore, being exceedingly angry, and being at all times a man of most ferocious passions, he was in great perplexity, neither venturing to take down what he had once set up nor wishing to do anything which could be acceptable to his subjects, and yet fearing the anger of Tiberius. And those who were in power among the Jews, seeing this and perceiving that he was inclined to change his mind as to what he had done, but that he was not willing to be thought to do so, appealed to the Emperor."[1] This sheds light on the whole conduct of Pilate during this trial—his fear of the Emperor, his hatred of the Jews and desire to annoy them, his vacillation and yet obstinacy; and we see that the mode the Sanhedrim now adopted with Pilate was their usual mode of dealing with him: now, as always, they saw his vacillation, disguised as it was by fierceness of speech, and they knew he must yield to the threat of complaining to Cæsar.

The very thing that Pilate feared, and to avoid which he sacrificed the life of our Lord, came upon him six years

---

[1] Philo, *Ad Caium*, c. 38.

after. Complaints against him were sent to the Emperor; he was deposed from his office, and so stripped of all that made life endurable to him, that, "wearied with misfortunes," he died by his own hand. Perhaps we are tempted to think Pilate's fate severe; we naturally sympathise with him; there are so many traits of character which show well when contrasted with the unprincipled violence of the Jews. We are apt to say he was weak rather than wicked, forgetting that moral weakness is just another name for wickedness, or rather is that which makes a man capable of any wickedness. The man we call wicked has his one or two good points at which we can be sure of him. The weak man we are never sure of. That he has good feelings is nothing, for we do not know what may be brought to overcome these feelings. That he has right convictions is nothing; we may have thought he was convinced to-day, but to-morrow his old fears have prevailed. And who is the weak man who is thus open to every kind of influence? He is the man who is not single-minded. The single-minded, worldly man makes no pretension to holiness, but sees at a glance that that interferes with his real object; the single-minded, godly man has only truth and righteousness for his aim, and does not listen to fears or hopes suggested by the world. But the man who attempts to gratify both his conscience and his evil or weak feelings, the man who fancies he can so manipulate the events of his life as to secure his own selfish ends as well as the great ends of justice and righteousness, will often be in as great a perplexity as Pilate, and will come to as ruinous if not to so appalling an end.

In this would-be equitable Roman governor, exhibiting his weakness to the people and helplessly exclaiming,

"What shall I do with Jesus which is called Christ?"[1] we see the predicament of many who are suddenly confronted with Christ—disconcerted as they are to have such a prisoner thrown on their hands, and wishing that anything had turned up rather than a necessity for answering this question, What shall I do with Jesus? Probably when Jesus was led by the vacillating Pilate out and in, back and forward, examined and re-examined, acquitted, scourged, defended, and abandoned to His enemies, some pity for His judge mingled with other feelings in His mind. This was altogether too great a case for a man like Pilate, fit enough to try men like Barabbas and to keep the turbulent Galileans in order. What unhappy fate, he might afterwards think, had brought this mysterious Prisoner to his judgment-seat, and for ever linked in such unhappy relation his name to the Name that is above every name? Never with more disastrous results did the resistless stream of time bring together and clash together the earthen and the brazen pitcher. Never before had such a prisoner stood at any judge's bar. Roman governors and emperors had been called to doom or to acquit kings and potentates of all degrees and to determine every kind of question, forbidding this or that religion, extirpating old dynasties, altering old landmarks, making history in its largest dimensions; but Pilate was summoned to adjudicate in a case that seemed of no consequence at all, yet really eclipsed in its importance all other cases put together.

Nothing could save Pilate from the responsibility attaching to his connection with Jesus, and nothing can save us from the responsibility of determining

---

[1] Mark xv. 12.

what judgment we are to pronounce on this same Person. It may seem to us an unfortunate predicament we are placed in ; we may resent being called upon to do anything decided in a matter where our convictions so conflict with our desires ; we may inwardly protest against human life being obstructed and disturbed by choices that are so pressing and so difficult and with issues so incalculably serious. But second thoughts assure us that to be confronted with Christ is in truth far from being an unfortunate predicament, and that to be compelled to decisions which determine our whole after-course and allow fullest expression of our own will and spiritual affinities is our true glory. Christ stands patiently awaiting our decision, maintaining His inalienable majesty, but submitting Himself to every test we care to apply, claiming only to be the King of the truth by whom we are admitted into that sole eternal kingdom. It has come to be our turn, as it came to be Pilate's, to decide upon His claims and to act upon our decision—to recognise that we men have to do, not merely with pleasure and place, with earthly rewards and relations, but above all with the truth, with that which gives eternal significance to all these present things, with the truth about human life, with the truth embodied for us in Christ's person and speaking intelligibly to us through His lips, with God manifest in the flesh. Are we to take part with Him when He calls us to glory and to virtue, to the truth and to eternal life, or yielding to some present pressure the world puts upon us attempt some futile compromise and so renounce our birthright?

Could Pilate really persuade himself he made everything right with a basin of water and a theatrical transference of his responsibility to the Jews? Could he persuade himself that by merely giving up the contest he was playing the part of a judge and of a man? Could he persuade himself that the mere words, "I am innocent of the blood of this righteous man: see ye to it," altered his relation to the death of Christ? No doubt he did. There is nothing commoner than for a man to think himself forced when it is his own fear or wickedness that is his only compulsion. Would every man in Pilate's circumstances have felt himself forced to surrender Jesus to the Jews? Would even a Gallio or a Claudius Lysias have done so? But Pilate's past history made him powerless. Had he not feared exposure, he would have marched his cohort across the square and cleared it of the mob and defied the Sanhedrim. It was not because he thought the Jewish law had any true right to demand Christ's death, but merely because the Jews threatened to report him as conniving at rebellion, that he yielded Christ to them; and to seek to lay the blame on those who made it difficult to do the right thing was both unmanly and futile. The Jews were at least willing to take their share of the blame, dreadful in its results as that proved to be.

Fairly to apportion blame where there are two consenting parties to a wickedness is for us, in many cases, impossible; and what we have to do is to beware of shifting blame from ourselves to our circumstances or to other people. However galling it is to find ourselves mixed up with transactions which turn out to be shameful, or to discover that some vacillation or imbecility on our part has made us partakers in sin, it is idle and worse to wash our hands ostentatiously and try to persuade ourselves we have no guilt in the matter. The fact that we have been brought in contact with unjust, cruel, heartless, fraudulent, unscrupulous, worldly, passionate people may explain many of our sins, but it does not excuse them. Other people in our circumstances would not have done what we have done; they would have acted a stronger, manlier, more generous part. And if we have sinned, it only adds to our guilt and encourages our weakness to profess innocence now and transfer to some other party the disgrace that belongs to ourselves. Nothing short of physical compulsion can excuse wrong-doing.

The calmness and dignity with which Jesus passed through this ordeal, alone self-possessed, while all around Him were beside themselves, so impressed Pilate that he not only felt guilty in giving Him up to the Jews, but did not think it impossible that He might be the Son of God. But what is perhaps even more striking in this scene is the directness with which all these evil passions of men—fear, and self-interest, and injustice, and hate—are guided to an end fraught with blessing. Goodness finds in the most adverse circumstances material for its purposes. We are apt in such circumstances to despair and act as if there were never to be a triumph of goodness; but the little seed of good that one individual can contribute even by hopeful and patient submission is that which survives and produces good in perpetuity, while the passion and the hate and the worldliness cease. In so wild a scene what availed it, we might have said, that one Person kept His steadfastness and rose superior to the surrounding wickedness? But the event showed that it did avail. All the rest was scaffolding that fell away out of sight, and this solitary integrity remains as the enduring monument. In our measure we must pass through similar ordeals, times when it seems vain to contend, useless to hope. When all we have done seems to be lost, when our way is hid and no further step is visible, when all the waves and billows of an ungodly world seem to threaten with extinction the little good we have cherished, then must we remember this calm, majestic Prisoner, bound in the midst of a frantic and blood-thirsty mob, yet superior to it because He was living in God.

## XX.
### MARY AT THE CROSS.

"They took Jesus therefore: and He went out, bearing the cross for Himself, unto the place called The place of a skull, which is called in Hebrew Golgotha: where they crucified Him, and with Him two others, on either side one, and Jesus in the midst. And Pilate wrote a title also, and put it on the cross. And there was written, JESUS OF NAZARETH, THE KING OF THE JEWS. This title therefore read many of the Jews: for the place where Jesus was crucified was nigh to the city: and it was written in Hebrew, and in Latin, and in Greek. The chief priests of the Jews therefore said to Pilate, Write not, The King of the Jews; but, that He said, I am King of the Jews. Pilate answered, What I have written I have written. The soldiers therefore, when they had crucified Jesus, took His garments, and made four parts, to every soldier a part; and also the coat: now the coat was without seam, woven from the top throughout. They said therefore one to another, Let us not rend it, but cast lots for it, whose it shall be: that the scripture might be fulfilled, which saith, They parted My garments among them, And upon My vesture did they cast lots. These things therefore the soldiers did. But there were standing by the cross of Jesus His mother, and His mother's sister, Mary the wife of Clopas, and Mary Magdalene. When Jesus therefore saw His mother, and the disciple standing by, whom He loved, He saith unto His mother, Woman, behold thy son! Then saith He to the disciple, Behold, thy mother! And from that hour the disciple took her unto his own home."—JOHN xix. 17-27.

## XX.

### MARY AT THE CROSS.

IF we ask on what charge our Lord was condemned to die, the answer must be complex, not simple. Pilate indeed, in accordance with the usual custom, painted on a board the name and crime of the Prisoner, that all who could understand any of the three current languages might know who this was and why He was crucified. But in the case of Jesus the inscription was merely a ghastly jest on Pilate's part. It was the coarse retaliation of a proud man who found himself helpless in the hands of people he despised and hated. There was some relish to him in the crucifixion of Jesus when by his inscription he had turned it into an insult to the nation. A gleam of savage satisfaction for a moment lit up his gloomy face when he found that his taunt had told, and the chief priests came begging him to change what he had written.

Pilate from the first look he got of his Prisoner understood that he had before him quite another kind of person than the ordinary zealot, or spurious Messiah, or turbulent Galilean. Pilate knew enough of the Jews to feel sure that if Jesus had been plotting rebellion against Rome He would not have been informed against by the chief priests. Possibly he knew enough of what had been going on in his province to understand that it was precisely because Jesus would *not* allow Himself to be made a king in opposition to Rome that the Jews detested and accused Him. Possibly he saw enough of the relations of Jesus to the authorities to despise the abandoned malignity and baseness which could bring an innocent man to his bar and charge Him with what in their eyes was no crime at all and make the charge precisely because He was innocent of it.

Nominally, but only nominally, Jesus was crucified for sedition. If we pass, in search of the real charge, from Pilate's judgment-seat to the Sanhedrim, we get nearer to the truth. The charge on which He was in this court condemned was the charge of blasphemy. He was indeed examined as to His claims to be the Messiah, but it does not appear that they had any law on which He could have been condemned for such claims. They did not expect that the Messiah would be Divine in the proper sense. Had they done so, then any one falsely claiming to be the Messiah would thereby have falsely claimed to be Divine, and would therefore have been guilty of blasphemy. But it was not for claiming to be the Christ that Jesus was condemned; it was when He declared Himself to be the Son of God that the high priest rent His garments and declared Him guilty of blasphemy.

Now, of course it was very possible that many members of the Sanhedrim should sincerely believe that blasphemy had been uttered. The unity of God was the distinctive creed of the Jew, that which had made his nation, and for any human lips to claim equality with the one infinite God was not to be thought of. It must have fallen upon their ears like a thunderclap; they must have fallen back on their seats or started from them in horror when so awful a claim was made by the human figure standing bound before them. There were men among them who would have advocated His claim to be the Messiah, who believed Him to be a man sent from God; but not a voice could be raised in His defence when the claim to be Son of God in a Divine sense passed His lips. His best friends must have doubted and been disappointed, must have supposed He was confused by the events of the night, and could only await the issue in sorrow and wonder.

Was the Sanhedrim, then, to blame for condemning Jesus? They sincerely believed Him to be a blasphemer, and their law attached to the crime of blasphemy the punishment of death. It was in ignorance they did it; and knowing only what they knew, they could not have acted otherwise. Yes, that is true. But they were responsible for their ignorance. Jesus had given abundant opportunity to the nation to understand Him and to consider His claims. He did not burst upon the public with an uncertified demand to be accepted as Divine. He lived among those who were instructed in such matters; and though in some respects He was very different from the Messiah they had looked for, a little openness of mind and a little careful inquiry would have convinced them He was sent from God. And had they acknowledged this, had they allowed themselves to obey their instincts and say, This is a true man, a man who has a message for us—had they not sophisticated their minds with quibbling literalities, they would have owned His superiority and been willing to learn from Him. And had they shown any disposition to learn, Jesus was too wise a teacher to hurry them and overleap needed steps in conviction and experience. He would have been slow to extort from any a confession of His divinity until they had reached the belief of it by the working of their own minds. Enough for Him that they were willing to see the truth about Him and to declare it as they saw it. The great charge He brought against His accusers was that they did violence to their own convictions. The uneasy suspicions they had about His dignity they suppressed; the attraction they at times felt to His goodness they resisted; the duty to inquire patiently into His claims they refused. And thus their darkness deepened, until in their culpable ignorance they committed the greatest of crimes.

From all this, then, two things are apparent. First, that Jesus was condemned on the charge of blasphemy— condemned because He made Himself equal with God. His own words, pronounced upon oath, administered in the most solemn manner, were understood by the Sanhedrim to be an explicit claim to be the Son of God in a sense in which no man could without blasphemy claim to be so. He made no explanation of His words when He saw how they were understood. And yet, were He not truly Divine, there was no one who could have been more shocked than Himself by such a claim. He understood, if any man did, the majesty of God; He knew better than any other the difference between the Holy One and His sinful creatures; His whole life was devoted to the purpose of revealing to men the unseen God. What could have seemed to Him more monstrous, what could more effectually have stultified the work and aim of His life, than that He, being a man, should allow Himself to be taken for God? When Pilate told Him that He was charged with claiming to be a king, He explained to Pilate in what sense He did so, and removed from Pilate's mind the erroneous supposition this claim had given birth to.

Had the Sanhedrim cherished an erroneous idea of what was involved in His claim to be the Son of God, He must also have explained to them in what sense He made it, and have removed from their minds the impression that He was claiming to be properly Divine. He did not make any explanation; He allowed them to suppose He claimed to be the Son of God in a sense which would be blasphemous in a mere man. So that if any one gathers from this that Jesus was Divine in a sense in which it were blasphemy for any other man to claim to be, he gathers a legitimate, even a necessary, inference.

Another reflection which is forced upon the reader of this narrative is, that disaster waits upon stifled inquiry. The Jews honestly convicted Christ as a blasphemer because they had dishonestly denied Him to be a good man. The little spark which would have grown into a blazing light they put their heel upon. Had they at the first candidly considered Him as He went about doing good and making no claims, they would have become attached to Him as His disciples did, and, like them, would have been led on to a fuller knowledge of the meaning of His person and work. It is these beginnings of conviction we are so apt to abuse. It seems so much smaller a crime to kill an infant that has but once drawn breath than to kill a man of lusty life and busy in his prime; but the one, if fairly dealt with, will grow to be the other. And while we think very little of stifling the scarcely breathed whisperings in our own heart and mind, we should consider that it is only such whisperings that can bring us to the loudly proclaimed truth. If we do not follow up suggestions, if we do not push inquiry to discovery, if we do not value the smallest grain of truth as a seed of unknown worth and count it wicked to kill even the smallest truth in our souls, we can scarcely hope at any time to stand in the full light of reality and rejoice in it. To accept Christ as Divine may be at present beyond us; to acknowledge Him as such would simply be to perjure ourselves; but can we not acknowledge Him to be a true man, a good man, a teacher certainly sent from God? If we do know Him to be all that and more, then have we thought this out to its results? Knowing Him to be a unique figure among men, have we perceived what this involves? Admitting Him to be the best of men, do we love Him, imitate Him, ponder His words, long for His company? Let us not treat Him as if He were non-existent because He is not as yet to us all that He is to some. Let us beware of dismissing *all* conviction about Him because there are some convictions spoken of by other people which we do not feel. It is better to deny Christ than to deny our own convictions; for to do so is to extinguish the only light we have, and to expose ourselves to all disaster. The man who has put out his own eyes cannot plead blindness in extenuation of his not seeing the lights and running the richly laden ship on the rocks.

Guided by the perfect taste which reverence gives, John says very little about the actual crucifixion. He shows us indeed the soldiers sitting down beside the little heap of clothes they had stripped off our Lord, parcelling them out, perhaps already assuming them as their own wear. For the clothes by which our Lord had been known these soldiers would now carry into unknown haunts of drunkenness and sin, emblems of our ruthless, thoughtless desecration of our Lord's name with which we outwardly clothe ourselves and yet carry into scenes the most uncongenial. John, writing long after the event, seems to have no heart to record the poor taunts with which the crowd sought to increase the suffering of the Crucified, and force home upon His spirit a sense of the desolation and ignominy of the cross. Gradually the crowd wearies and scatters, and only here and there a little whispering group remains. The day waxes to its greatest heat; the soldiers lie or stand silent; the centurion sits motionless on his motionless, statue-like horse; the stillness of death falls upon the scene, only broken at intervals by a groan from one or other of the crosses. Suddenly through this silence there sound the words, "Woman, behold thy son: son, behold thy mother," —words which remind us that all this dreadful scene which makes the heart of the stranger bleed has been witnessed by the mother of the Crucified. As the crowd had broken up from around the crosses, the little group of women whom John had brought to the spot edged their way nearer and nearer till they were quite close to Him they loved, though their lips apparently were sealed by their helplessness to minister consolation.

These hours of suffering, as the sword was slowly driven through Mary's soul, according to Simeon's word, who shall measure? Hers was not a hysterical, noisy sorrow, but quiet and silent. There was nothing wild, nothing extravagant, in it. There was no sign of feminine weakness, no outcry, no fainting, no wild gesture of uncontrollable anguish, nothing to show that she was the exceptional mourner and that there was no sorrow like unto her sorrow. Her reverence for the Lord saved her from disturbing His last moments. She stood and saw the end. She saw His head lifted in anguish and falling on His breast in weakness, and she could not gently take it in her hands and wipe the sweat of death from His brow. She saw His pierced hands and feet become numbed and livid, and might not chafe them. She saw Him gasp with pain as cramp seized part after part of His outstretched body, and she could not change His posture nor give liberty to so much as one of His hands. And she had to suffer this in profound desolation of spirit. Her life seemed to be buried at the cross. To the mourning there often seems nothing left but to die with the dying. One heart has been the light of life, and now that light is quenched. What significance, what motive, can life have any more?[1] We valued no past where that heart was not; we had no future which was not concentrated upon it or in which it had no part. But the absorption of common love must have been far surpassed in Mary's case. None had been blessed with such a love as hers. And now none estimated as she did the spotless innocence of the Victim; none could know as she knew the depth of His goodness, the unfathomable and unconquerable love He had for all; and none could estimate as she the ingratitude of those whom He had healed and fed and taught and comforted with such unselfish devotedness. She knew that there was none like Him, and that if any could have brought blessing to this earth it was He, and there she saw Him nailed to the cross, the end actually reached. We know not if in that hour she thought of the trial of Abraham; we know not whether she allowed herself to think at all, whether she did not merely suffer as a mother losing her son; but certainly it must

---

[1] See Faber's *Bethlehem*.

have been with intensest eagerness she heard herself once more addressed by Him.

Mary was commended to John as the closest friend of Jesus. These two would be in fullest sympathy, both being devoted to Him. It was perhaps an indication to those who were present, and through them to all, that nothing is so true a bond between human hearts as sympathy with Christ. We may admire nature, and yet have many points of antipathy to those who also admire nature. We may like the sea, and yet feel no drawing to some persons who also like the sea. We may be fond of mathematics, and yet find that this brings us into a very partial and limited sympathy with mathematicians. Nay, we may even admire and love the same person as others do, and yet disagree about other matters. But if Christ is chosen and loved as He ought to be, that love is a determining affection which rules all else within us, and brings us into abiding sympathy with all who are similarly governed and moulded by that love. That love indicates a certain past experience and guarantees a special type of character. It is the characteristic of the subjects of the kingdom of God.

This care for His mother in His last moments is of a piece with all the conduct of Jesus. Throughout His life there is an entire absence of anything pompous or excited. Everything is simple. The greatest acts in human history He does on the highway, in the cottage, among a group of beggars in an entry. The words which have thrilled the hearts and mended the lives of myriads were spoken casually as He walked with a few friends. Rarely did He even gather a crowd. There was no advertising, no admission by ticket, no elaborate arrangements for a set speech at a set hour.

Those who know human nature will know what to think of this unstudied ease and simplicity, and will appreciate it. The same characteristic appears here. He speaks as if He were not an object of contemplation; there is an entire absence of self-consciousness, of ostentatious suggestion that He is now making atonement for the sins of the world. He speaks to His mother and cares for her as He might have done had they been in the home at Nazareth together. One despairs of ever learning such a lesson, or indeed of seeing others learn it. How like an ant-hill is the world of men! What a fever and excitement! what a fuss and fret! what an ado! what a sending of messengers, and calling of meetings, and raising of troops, and magnifying of little things! what an absence of calmness and simplicity! But this at least we *may* learn—that no duties, however important, can excuse us for not caring for our relatives. They are deceived people who spend all their charity and sweetness out of doors, who have a reputation for godliness, and are to be seen in the forefront of this or that Christian work, but who are sullen or imperious or quick-tempered or indifferent at home. If while saving a world Jesus had leisure to care for His mother, there are no duties so important as to prevent a man from being considerate and dutiful at home.

Those who witnessed the hurried events of the morning when Christ was crucified might be pardoned if their minds were filled with what their eyes saw, and if little but the outward objects were discernible to them. We are in different circumstances, and may be expected to look more deeply into what was happening. To see only the mean scheming and wicked passions of men, to see nothing but the pathetic suffering of an innocent and misjudged person, to take our interpretation of these rapid and disorderly events from the casual spectators without striving to discover God's meaning in them, would indeed be a flagrant instance of what has been called "reading God in a prose translation," rendering His clearest and most touching utterance to this world in the language of callous Jews or barbarous Roman soldiers. Let us open our ear to God's own meaning in these events, and we hear Him uttering to us all His Divine love, and in the most forcible and touching tones. These are the events in which His deepest purposes and tenderest love find utterance. How He is striving to win His way to us to convince us of the reality of sin and of salvation! To be mere spectators of these things is to convict ourselves of being superficial or strangely callous. Scarcely any criminal is executed but we all have our opinion on the justice or injustice of his condemnation. We may well be expected to form our judgment in *this* case, and to take action upon it. If Jesus was unjustly condemned, then we as well as His contemporaries have to do with His claims. If these claims were true, we have something more to do than merely to say so.

# XXI.

## THE CRUCIFIXION.

"The soldiers therefore, when they had crucified Jesus, took His garments, and made four parts, to every soldier a part; and also the coat: now the coat was without seam, woven from the top throughout. They said therefore one to another, Let us not rend it, but cast lots for it, whose it shall be: that the scripture might be fulfilled, which saith, They parted My garments among them, And upon My vesture did they cast lots. These things therefore the soldiers did. . . . After this Jesus, knowing that all things are now finished, that the scripture might be accomplished, saith, I thirst. There was set there a vessel full of vinegar: so they put a sponge full of the vinegar upon hyssop, and brought it to His mouth. When Jesus therefore had received the vinegar, He said, It is finished: and He bowed His head, and gave up His spirit. The Jews therefore, because it was the Preparation, that the bodies should not remain on the cross upon the Sabbath (for the day of that Sabbath was a high day), asked of Pilate that their legs might be broken, and that they might be taken away. The soldiers therefore came, and brake the legs of the first, and of the other which was crucified with Him: but when they came to Jesus, and saw that He was dead already, they brake not His legs: howbeit one of the soldiers with a spear pierced His side, and straightway there came out blood and water. And he that hath seen hath borne witness, and his witness is true: and he knoweth that he saith true, that ye also may believe. For these things came to pass, that the scripture might be fulfilled, A bone of Him shall not be broken. And again another scripture saith, They shall look on Him whom they pierced."—JOHN xix. 23, 24, 28-37.

# XXI.

## THE CRUCIFIXION.

POSSIBLY the account which John gives of the Crucifixion is somewhat spoiled to some readers by his frequent reference to apparently insignificant coincidences with Old Testament prophecy. It is, however, to be remembered that John was himself a Jew, and was writing for a public which laid great stress on such literal fulfilments of prophecy. The wording of the narrative might lead us to suppose that John believed Jesus to be intentionally fulfilling prophecy. Where he says, "After this, Jesus knowing that all things were now accomplished, that the scripture might be fulfilled, saith, I thirst," it might be fancied that John supposed that Jesus said "I thirst" in order that Scripture might be fulfilled. This is, of course, to misconceive the Evangelist's meaning. Such a fulfilment would have been fictitious, not real. But John believes that in each smallest act and word of our Lord the will of God was finding expression, a will which had long since been uttered in the form of Old Testament prophecy. In these hours of dismay, when Jesus was arrested, tried, and crucified before the eyes of His disciples, they tried to believe that this was God's will; and long afterwards, when they had found time to think, and when they had to deal with men who felt the difficulty of believing in a crucified Saviour, they pointed to the fact that even in small particulars the sufferings of the Messiah had been anticipated and were to be expected.

The first instance of this which John cites is the manner in which the soldiers dealt with His clothes. After fixing Jesus to the cross and raising it, the four men who were detailed to this service sat down to watch. Such was the custom, lest friends should remove the crucified before death supervened. Having settled themselves for this watch, they proceeded to divide the clothes of Jesus among them. This also was customary among the Romans, as it has been everywhere usual that the executioners should have as their perquisite some of the articles worn by the condemned. The soldiers parted the garments of Jesus among them, each of the four taking what he needed or fancied—turban, shoes, girdle, or under-coat; while for the large seamless plaid that was worn over all they cast lots, being unwilling to tear it. All this fulfilled an old prediction to the letter. The reason why it had been spoken of was that it formed a weighty element in the suffering of the crucified. Few things can make a dying man feel more desolate than to overhear those who sit round his bed already disposing of his effects, counting him a dead man who can no longer use the apparatus of the living, and congratulating themselves on the profit they make by his death. How furious have old men sometimes been made by any betrayal of eagerness on the part of their heirs! Even to calculate on a man's death and make arrangements for filling his place is justly esteemed indecorous and unfeeling. To ask a sick man for anything he has been accustomed to use, and must use again if he recovers health, is an act which only an indelicate nature could be guilty of. It was a cruel addition, then, to our Lord's suffering to see these men heartlessly dividing among them all He had to leave. It forced on His mind the consciousness of their utter indifference to His feelings. His clothes were of some little value to them : He Himself of no value. Nothing could have made Him feel more separated from the world of the living—from their hopes, their ways, their life—as if already He were dead and buried.

This distribution of His clothes was also calculated to make Him intensely sensible of the reality and finality of death. Jesus knew He was to rise again ; but let us not forget that Jesus was human, liable to the same natural fears, and moved by the same circumstances as ourselves. He knew He was to rise again ; but how much easier had it been to believe in that future life had all the world been expecting Him to rise! But here were men showing that they very well knew He would never again need these clothes of His.

A comparison of this narrative with the other Gospels brings out that the words "I thirst" must have been uttered immediately after the fearful cry "My God, My God, why hast Thou forsaken Me?" For when the soldier was mercifully pressing the sponge steeped in vinegar to His parched lips, some of the bystanders called out, "Let be : let us see whether Elias will come to save Him," referring to the words of Jesus, which they had not rightly understood. And this expression of bodily suffering is proof that the severity of the spiritual struggle was over. So long as that deep darkness covered His spirit He was unconscious of His body; but with the agonised cry to His Father the darkness had passed away; the very uttering of His desolation had disburdened His spirit, and at once the body asserts itself. As in the wilderness at the opening of His career He had been for many days so agitated and absorbed in mind that He did not once think of food, but no sooner was the spiritual strife ended than the keen sensation of hunger was the first thing to demand His attention, so here His sense of thirst is the sign that His spirit was now at rest.

The last act of the Crucifixion, in which John sees the fulfilment of Old Testament prophecy, is the omission in the case of Jesus of the common mode of terminating the life of the crucified by breaking the legs with an iron bar. Jesus being already dead, this was considered unnecessary; but as possibly He might only have swooned, and as the bodies were immediately taken down, one of the soldiers makes sure of His death by a lance thrust. Medical men and scholars have largely discussed the causes which might produce the outflow of blood and water which John affirms followed this spear thrust, and various causes have been assigned. But it is a point which has apparently only physiological interest. John indeed follows up his statement of what he saw with an unusually strong asseveration that what he says is true. "He that saw it bare record, and his record is true: and he knoweth that he saith true, that ye might believe." But this strong asseveration is introduced, not for the sake of persuading us to believe that water as well as blood flowed from the lance wound, but for the sake of certifying the actual death of Jesus. The soldiers who had charge of the execution discharged their duty. They made sure that the Crucified was actually dead. And John's reason for insisting on this and appending to his statement so unusual a confirmation is sufficiently obvious. He was about to relate the Resurrection, and he knows that a true resurrection must be preceded by a real death. If he has no means of establishing the actual death, he has no means of establishing the Resurrection. And therefore for the first and only time in his narrative he departs from simple narration, and most solemnly asseverates that he is speaking the truth and was an eyewitness of the things he relates.

The emphatic language John uses regarding the certainty of Christ's death is, then, only an index to the importance he attached to the Resurrection. He was aware that whatever virtue lay in the life and death of Christ, this virtue became available for men through the Resurrection. Had Jesus not risen again all the hopes His friends had cherished regarding Him would have been buried in His tomb Had He not risen His words would have been falsified and doubt thrown upon all His teaching. Had He not risen His claims would have been unintelligible and His whole appearance and life a mystery, suggesting a greatness not borne out—different from other men, yet subject to the same defeat. Had He not risen the very significance of His life would have been obscured; and if for a time a.few friends cherished His memory in private, His name would have fallen back to an obscure, possibly a dishonoured, place.

It is not at once obvious what we are to make of the physical sufferings of Christ. Certainly it is very easy to make too much of them. For, in the first place, they were very brief and confined to one part of His life. He was exempt from the prolonged weakness and misery which many persons endure throughout life.

Born, as we may reasonably suppose, with a healthy and vigorous constitution, carefully reared by the best of mothers, finding a livelihood in His native village and in His father's business, His lot was very different from the frightful doom of thousands who are born with diseased and distorted body, in squalid and wicked surroundings, and who never see through the misery that encompasses them to any happy or hopeful life. And even after He left the shelter and modest comforts of the Nazareth home His life was spent in healthy conditions, and often in scenes of much beauty and interest. Free to move about through the country as He pleased, passing through vineyards and olive-groves and cornfields, talking pleasantly with His little company of attached friends or addressing large audiences, He lived an open-air life of a kind in which of necessity there must have been a great deal of physical pleasure and healthful enjoyment. At times He had not where to lay His head; but this is mentioned rather as a symptom of His want of friends than as implying any serious physical suffering in a climate like that of Palestine. And the suffering at the close of His life, though extreme, was brief, and was not to be compared in its cruelty to what many of His followers have endured for His sake.

Two things, however, the physical sufferings of Christ do secure: they call attention to His devotedness, and they illustrate His willing sacrifice of self. They call attention to His devotedness and provoke a natural sympathy and tenderness of spirit in the beholder, qualities which are much needed in our consideration of Christ. Had He passed through life entirely exempt from suffering, in high position, with every want eagerly ministered to, untouched by any woe, and at last passing away by a painless decease, we should find it much harder to respond to His appeal or even to understand His work. Nothing so quickly rivets our attention and stirs our sympathy as physical pain. We feel disposed to listen to the demands of one who is suffering, and if we have a lurking suspicion that we are somehow responsible for that suffering and are benefited by it, then we are softened by a mingled pity, admiration, and shame, which is one of the fittest attitudes a human spirit can assume.

Besides, it is through the visible suffering we can read the willingness of Christ's self-surrender. It was always more difficult for Him to suffer than for us. We have no option: He might have rescued Himself at any moment. We, in suffering, have but to subdue our disposition to murmur and our sense of pain: He had to subdue what was much more obstinate—His consciousness that He might if He pleased abjure the life that involved pain. The strain upon His love for us was not once for all over when He became man. He Himself intimates, and His power of working miracles proves, that at each point of His career He might have saved Himself from suffering, but would not.

When we ask ourselves what we are to make of these sufferings of Christ, we naturally seek aid from the Evangelist and ask what he made of them. But on reading his narrative we are surprised to find so little comment or reflection interrupting the simple relation of facts. At first sight the narrative seems to flow uninterruptedly on, and to resemble the story which might be told of the closing scenes of an ordinary life terminating tragically. The references to Old Testament prophecy alone give us the clue to John's thoughts about the significance of this death. These references show us that he considered that in this public execution, conducted wholly by Roman soldiers, who could not read a word of Hebrew and did not know the name of the God of the Jews, there was being fulfilled the purpose of God towards which all previous history had been tending. That purpose of God in the history of man was accomplished when Jesus breathed His last upon the cross. The cry "It is finished" was not the mere gasp of a worn-out life; it was not the cry of satisfaction with which a career of pain and sorrow is terminated: it was the deliberate utterance of a clear consciousness on the part of God's appointed Revealer that now all had been done that could be done to make God known to men and to identify Him with men. God's purpose had ever been one and indivisible. Declared to men in various ways, a hint here, a broad light there, now by a gleam of insight in the mind of a prophet, now by a deed of heroism in king or leader, through rude symbolic contrivances and through the tenderest of human affections and the highest human thoughts God had been making men ever more and more sensible that His one purpose was to come closer and closer into fellowship with them and to draw them into a perfect harmony with Him. Forgiveness and deliverance from sin were provided for them, knowledge of God's law and will that they might learn to know and to serve Him—all these were secured when Jesus cried, "It is finished."

Why, then, does John just at this point of the life of Jesus see so many evidences of the fulfilment of all prophecy? Need we ask? Is not suffering that which is the standing problem of life? Is it not grief and trouble and sorrow which press home upon our minds most convincingly the reality of sin? Is it not death which is common to all men of every age, race, station, or experience ? And must not One who identifies Himself with men identify Himself in this if in anything ? It is the cross of Jesus that stands before the mind of John as the completion of that process of incarnation, of entrance into human experience, which fills his Gospel; it is here he sees the completion and finishing of that identification of God with man he has been exhibiting throughout. The union of God with man is perfected when God submits Himself to the last darkest experience of man. To some it seems impossible such a thing should be; it seems either unreal, unthought-out verbiage, or blasphemy. To John, after he had seen and pondered the words and the life of Jesus, all his ideas of the Father were altered. He learned that God is love, and that to infinite love, while there remains one thing to give, one step of nearness to the loved to be taken, love has not its perfect expression. It came upon him as a revelation that God was really in the world. Are we to refuse to God any true participation in the strife between good and evil ? Is God to be kept out of all reality ? Is He merely to look on, to see how His creatures will manage, how this and that man will bear himself heroically, but Himself a mere name, a lay figure crowned but otiose, doing nothing to merit His crown, doing nothing to warrant the worship of untold worlds, commanding others to peril themselves and put all to the proof, but Himself well out of range of all risk, of all conflict, of all tragedy? How can we hope to love a God we remove to a throne remote and exalted, from which He looks down on human life, and cannot look on it as we do from the inside! Is God to be only a dramatist, who arranges thrilling situations for others to pass through, and assigns to each the part he is to play, but Himself has no real interests at stake and no actual entrance into the world of feeling, of hope, of trial?

And if a Divine Person were in the course of things to come into this human world, to enter into our actual experiences, and feel and bear the actual strain that we bear, it is obvious He must come incognito—not distinguished by such marks as would bring the world to His feet, and make an ordinary human life and ordinary human trials impossible to Him. When sovereigns wish to ascertain for themselves how their subjects live, they do not proclaim their approach and send in advance an army of protection, provision, and display; they do not demand to be met by the authorities of each town, and to be received by artificial, stereotyped addresses, and to be led from one striking sight to another and from one comfortable palace to another: but they leave their robes of state behind them, they send no messenger in advance, and they mix as one of the crowd with the crowd, exposed to whatever abuse may be going, and living for the time on the same terms as the rank and file. This has been done often in sport, sometimes as matter of policy or of interest, but never as the serious method of understanding and lifting the general habits and life of the people. Christ came among us, not as a kind of Divine adventure to break the tedium of eternal glory, nor merely to make personal observations on His own account, but as the requisite and only means available for bringing the fulness of Divine help into practical contact with mankind. But as all filth and squalor are hidden away in the slums from the senses of the king, so that if he is to penetrate into the burrows of the criminal classes and see the wretchedness of the poor, he must do it incognito, so if Christ sought to bring Divine mercy and might within reach of the vilest, He must visit their haunts and make Himself acquainted with their habits.

It is also obvious that such a Person would concern Himself not with art or literature, not with inventions and discoveries, not even with politics and government and social problems, but with that which underlies all these and for which all these exist—with human character and human conduct, with man's relation to God. It is with the very root of human life He concerns Himself.

The sufferings of Christ, then, were mainly inward, and were the necessary result of His perfect sympathy with men. That which has made the cross the most significant of earthly symbols, and which has invested it with so wonderful a power to subdue and purify the heart, is not the fact that it involved the keenest physical pain, but that it exhibits Christ's perfect and complete identification with sinful men. It is this that humbles us and brings us to a right mind towards God and towards sin, that here we see the innocent Son of God involved in suffering and undergoing a shameful death through our sin. It was His sympathy with men which brought Him into this world, and it was the same sympathy which laid Him open to suffering throughout His life. The mother suffers more in the illness of a child than in her own; the shame of wrong-doing is often more keenly felt by a parent or friend than by the perpetrator himself. If Paul's enthusiasm and devoted life for men made him truly say, " Who is weak, and I am not weak?" who shall measure the burden Christ bore from day to day in the midst of a sinning and suffering world ? With a burning zeal for God, He was plunged into an arctic region where thick-ribbed ice of indifference met His warmth; consumed with devotion to God's purposes, He saw everywhere around Him ignorance, carelessness, self-seeking, total misunderstanding of what the world is for; linked to men with a love which irrepressibly urged Him to seek the highest good for all, He was on all hands thwarted; dying to see men holy and pure and godly, He everywhere found them weak, sinful, gross. It was this which made Him a man of sorrows and acquainted with grief—loving God and man with a love which was the chief element in His being, He could not get man reconciled to God. The mere sorrows of men doubtless affected Him more than they affect the most tenderhearted of men; but these sorrows—poverty, failure, sickness—would pass away and would even work for good, and so might well be borne. But when He saw men disregarding that which would save them from lasting sorrow; when He saw them giving themselves to trivialities with all their might, and doing nothing to recover their right relation to God, the spring of all good; when He saw them day by day defeating the purpose He lived to accomplish, and undoing the one only work He thought worth doing,—who can measure the burden of shame and grief He had to bear?

But it is not the suffering that does us good and brings us to God, but the love which underlies the suffering. The suffering convinces us that it is love which prompts Christ in all His life and death,—a love we may confidently trust to, since it is staggered at no difficulty or sacrifice; a love which aims at lifting and helping us; a love that embraces us, not seeking to accomplish only one thing for us, but necessarily, because it is love for us, seeking our good in all things. The power of earthly love, of the devotedness of mother, wife, or friend, we know;—we know what length such love will go: shall we then deny to God the happiness of sacrifice, the joy of love? Let it not enter our thoughts that He who is more closely related to us than any, and who will far less disclaim this relationship than any, does not love us in practical ways, and cannot fit us by His loving care for all that His holiness requires.

# XXII.

## *THE RESURRECTION.*

"Now on the first day of the week cometh Mary Magdalene early, while it was yet dark, unto the tomb, and seeth the stone taken away from the tomb. She runneth therefore, and cometh to Simon Peter, and to the other disciple, whom Jesus loved, and saith unto them, They have taken away the Lord out of the tomb, and we know not where they have laid Him. Peter therefore went forth, and the other disciple, and they went toward the tomb. And they ran both together: and the other disciple outran Peter, and came first to the tomb; and stooping and looking in, he seeth the linen cloths lying; yet entered he not in. Simon Peter therefore also cometh, following him, and entered into the tomb; and he beholdeth the linen cloths lying, and the napkin, that was upon His head, not lying with the linen cloths, but rolled up in a place by itself. Then entered in therefore the other disciple also, which came first to the tomb, and he saw, and believed. For as yet they knew not the scripture, that He must rise again from the dead. So the disciples went away again unto their own home. But Mary was standing without at the tomb weeping: so, as she wept, she stooped and looked into the tomb; and she beholdeth two angels in white sitting, one at the head, and one at the feet, where the body of Jesus had lain. And they say unto her, Woman, why weepest thou? She saith unto them, Because they have taken away my Lord, and I know not where they have laid Him. When she had thus said, she turned herself back, and beholdeth Jesus standing, and knew not that it was Jesus. Jesus saith unto her, Woman, why weepest thou? whom seekest thou? She, supposing Him to be the gardener, saith unto Him, Sir, if thou hast borne Him hence, tell me where thou hast laid Him, and I will take Him away. Jesus saith unto her, Mary. She turned herself, and saith unto Him in Hebrew, Rabboni; which is to say, Master. Jesus saith to her, Touch Me not; for I am not yet ascended unto the Father: but go unto My brethren, and say to them, I ascend unto My Father and your Father, and My God and your God. Mary Magdalene cometh and telleth the disciples, I have seen the Lord; and how that He had said these things unto her."—JOHN xx. 1-18.

## XXII.

### THE RESURRECTION.

JOHN gives no narrative of the Resurrection itself. He gives us what is much more valuable—a brief account of the manner in which he himself was convinced that a resurrection had taken place. His shy nature, his modest reluctance to put himself forward or use the first person in his narrative, does not prevent him from seeing that the testimony of one who, like himself, was an eyewitness of the facts is invaluable; and nothing but additional interest and reality is added to his testimony by the varied periphrases with which he veils his identity, as "the disciple whom Jesus loved," "that other disciple," and so forth.

When Mary brought the startling intelligence that the tomb was empty, Peter and John instantly made for the spot at the top of their speed. The older man was left behind by John, but natural reverence kept him from entering the rocky chamber. He looked in, however, and to his surprise saw enough to convince him that the body had not been removed for interment elsewhere or to be cast out with the bodies of criminals. For there were the linen cloths in which He had been wrapped, carefully taken off and left behind. The impression made by this circumstance was confirmed when Peter came up, and they both entered and examined the tomb and made their inferences together. For then they saw still clearer evidence of deliberation; the napkin which had been tied round the head of the dead body was there in the tomb, and it was folded and laid in a place by itself, suggesting the leisurely manner of a person changing his clothes, and convincing them that the body had not been removed to be laid elsewhere. At once John was convinced that a resurrection had taken place; his Lord's words took a new meaning in this empty tomb. Standing and gazing at the folded cloths, the truth flashed into his mind: Jesus has Himself risen and disencumbered Himself from these wrappings, and has departed. It was enough for John: he visited no other tomb; he questioned no one; he made no inquiries of his friends in the high priest's household,—he went to his own house, filled with astonishment, with a thousand thoughts chasing one another through his mind, scarcely listening to Peter's voluble tongue, but convinced that Jesus lived.

This simple narrative will be to many minds more convincing than an accumulation of elaborate arguments. The style is that of an eyewitness. Each movement and every particular is before his eye: Mary bursting, breathless, and gasping out the startling news; the hasty springing up of the two men, and their rapid racing along the streets and out through the city gates to the garden; John standing panting at the rock-hewn sepulchre, his stooping down and peering into the dark chamber; Peter toiling up behind, but not hesitating a moment, and entering and gazing at this and that till the dumb articles tell their story; and the two men leave the sepulchre together, awed and convinced. And the eyewitness who thus graphically relates what he knew of that great morning adds with the simplicity of a truthful nature, "he saw and believed"—believed then for the first time; for as yet they had not seen the significance of certain scriptures which now seemed plainly enough to point to this.

To some minds this simple narrative will, I say, carry home the conviction of the truth of the Resurrection more than any elaborate argumentation. There is an assuring matter-of-factness about it. Sceptics tell us that visions are common, and that excited people are easily deceived. But we have no word of visions here. John does not say he saw the Lord: he tells us merely of two fishermen running; of solid, commonplace articles such as grave-clothes; and of observations that could not possibly be mistaken, such as that the tomb was empty and that they two were in it. For my part I feel constrained to believe a narrative like this, when it tells me the grave was empty. No doubt their conclusion, that Jesus had Himself emptied the tomb, was not a certain but only a probable inference, and, had nothing more occurred, even John himself might not have continued so confident; but it is important to notice how John was convinced, not at all by visions or voices or embodied expectations of his own, but in the most matter-of-fact way and by the very same kind of observation that we use and rely upon in common life. And, moreover, more did occur; there followed just such results as were in keeping with so momentous an event.

One of these immediately occurred. Mary, exhausted with her rapid carrying of the news to Peter and John, was not able to keep pace with them as they ran to the tomb, and before she arrived they were gone. Probably she missed them in the streets as she came out of the city; at any rate, finding the tomb still empty and none present to explain the reason of it, she stands there desolate and pours out her distress in tears. That grave being empty, the whole earth is empty to her: the dead Christ was more to her than a living world. She could not go as Peter and John had gone, for she had no thought of resurrection. The rigid form, the unanswering lips and eye, the body passive in the hands of others, had fixed on her heart, as it commonly does, the one impression of death. She felt that all was over, and now she had not even the poor consolation of paying some slight additional attention. She can but stand and lay her head upon the stone and let her tears flow from a broken heart. And yet again in the midst of her grief she cannot believe it true that He is lost to her; she returns, as love will do, to the search, suspects her own eyesight, seeks again where she had sought before, and cannot reconcile herself to a loss so total and overwhelming. So absorbing is her grief that the vision of angels does not astonish her; her heart, filled with grief, has no room for wonder. Their kindly words cannot comfort her; it is another voice she longs for. She had but the one thought, "They have taken away my Lord,"—*my* Lord, as if none felt the bereavement as she. She supposes, too, that all must know about the loss and understand what she is seeking, so that when she sees the gardener she says, "Sir, if thou hast borne *Him* hence." What need to say who? Can any one be thinking of any other but of Him who engrosses her thought?

In all this we have the picture of a real and profound grief, and therefore of a real and profound love. We see in Mary the kind of affection which a knowledge of Jesus was fitted to kindle. And to Mary our Lord remembered His promise: "He that loveth Me shall be loved of My Father, and I will love him and will manifest Myself to him." None is so unable as He to leave any who love Him without any response to their expressions of affection. He could not coldly look on while this woman was eagerly seeking Him; and it is as impossible that He should hide Himself now from any who seek Him with as true a heart. Sometimes it would seem as if real thirst for God were not at once allayed, as if many were allowed to spend the best part of their days in seeking; but this does not invalidate the promise, "He that seeketh, findeth." For as Christ is again and again removed from the view of men, and as He is allowed to become a remote and shadowy figure, He can be restored to a living and visible influence in the world only by this man and that man becoming sensible of the great loss we sustain by His absence, and working his own way to a clear apprehension of His continued life. No experience which an honest man has in his search for the truth is worthless; it is the solid foundation of his own permanent belief and connection with the truth, and it is useful to other men.

Mary standing without at the sepulchre weeping is a concrete representation of a not uncommon state of mind. She stands wondering why she was ever so foolish, so heartless, as to leave the tomb at all—why she had allowed it to be possible to become separated from the Lord. She looks despairingly at the empty grave-clothes which so lately had held all that was dear to her in the world. She might, she thinks, had she been present, have prevented the tomb from being emptied, but now it is empty she cannot fill it again. It is thus that those who have been careless about maintaining communion with Christ reproach themselves when they find He is gone. The ordinances, the prayers, the quiet hours of contemplation, that once were filled with Him are now, like the linen clothes and the napkin, empty, cold, pale forms, remembrances of His presence that make His absence all the more painful. When we ask where we can find Him, only the hard, mocking echo of the empty tomb replies. And yet this self-reproach is itself a seeking to which He will respond. To mourn His absence is to desire and to invite His presence; and to invite His presence is to secure it.[1]

The Evangelist Mark saw more in the Lord's appearance to Mary than a response to her seeking love. He reminds his readers that this was the woman out of whom the Lord had cast seven devils, meaning apparently to suggest that those who have most need of encouragement from Him are surest to get it. He had not appeared to Peter and John, though these men were to build up His Church and be responsible for His cause. To the man whom He loved, who had stood by Him at His trial and in His death, who had received His mother and was now to be in His place to her, He made no sign, but allowed him to examine the empty tomb and retire. But to this woman He discloses Himself at once. The love which sprang from a sense of what she owed Him kept her at the tomb and threw her in His way. Her sense of dependence was the magnetic point on earth which attracted and disclosed His presence. Observe the situation. Earth lay uncertain; some manifestation is needed to guide men at this critical time; blank disappointment or pointless waiting broods everywhere. At what point

---

[1] See Pusey's sermon on this subject.

shall the presence of Christ break through and quicken expectation and faith? Shall He go to the high priest's palace or to Pilate's prætorium and triumph over their dismay? Shall He go and lay busy plans with this and that group of followers? On the contrary, He appears to a poor woman who can do nothing to celebrate His triumph and might only discredit it, if she proclaimed herself His friend and herald. But thus continuous is the character of Jesus through death and resurrection. The meekness, the true perception of the actual sorrows and wants of men, the sense for spiritual need, the utter disregard of worldly powers and glory, characterise Him now as before. The sense of need is what always effectually appeals to Him. The soul that truly recognises the value and longs for the fellowship and possession of Christ's purity, devotion to God, superiority to worldly aims and interests, always wins His regard. When a man prays for these things not with his lips but with his life's effort and his heart's true craving, his prayer is answered. To seek Christ is to feel as Mary felt, to see with practical constraining clearness as she saw, that He is the most precious of all possessions, that to be like Him is the greatest of all attainments; it is to see His character with clearness, and to be persuaded that, if the world gives us opportunity of becoming like Him and actually makes us like Him, it has done for us all that is vital and permanently important.

As Mary answered the angels she heard a step behind or saw the tomb darkened by a shadow, and on turning discerns dimly through her tears a figure which naturally enough she supposes to be the gardener—not because Jesus had assumed the clothes or lifted the tools of the gardener, but because he was the likeliest person to be going about the garden at that early hour. As the heart overburdened with grief is often unconscious of the presence of Christ and refuses to be comforted because it cannot see Him for its sorrow, so Mary through the veil of her tears can see only a human form, and turns away again, unconscious that He for whom she seeks is with her. As she turns, one word wipes the tears from her eyes and penetrates her heart with sudden joy. The utterance of her name was enough to tell her it was some one who knew her that was there; but there was a responsive thrill and an awaking of old memories and a vibration of her nature under the tone of that voice, which told her whose alone it could be. The voice seemed a second time to command a calm within her and turn her whole soul to Himself only. Once before, that voice had banished from her nature the foul spirits that had taken possession of her; she had "awaked from hell beneath the smile of Christ," and now again the same voice brought her out of darkness into light. From being the most disconsolate, Mary became at a word the happiest creature in the world.

Mary's happiness is easily understood. No explanation is needed of the peace and bliss she experienced when she heard herself owned as the friend of the risen Lord, and called by her name in the familiar tone by Him who stood now superior to all risk, assault, and evil. This perfect joy is the reward of all in the measure of their faith. Christ rose, not that He might bring ecstasy to Mary alone, but that He might fill all things with His presence and His fulness, and that our joy also might be full. Has He not called us also by name? Has He not given us at times a consciousness that He understands our nature and what will satisfy it, that He claims an intimacy no other can claim, that His utterance of our name has a significance which no other lips can give it? Do we find it difficult to enter into true intercourse with Him; do we envy Mary her few minutes in the garden? As truly as by the audible utterance of our name does Christ now invite us to the perfect joy there is in His friendship; so truly as if He stood with us alone, as with Mary in the garden, and as if none but ourselves were present; as if our name alone filled His lips, our wants alone occupied His heart. Let us not miss true personal intercourse with Christ. Let nothing cheat us of this supreme joy and life of the soul. Let us not slothfully or shyly say, " I can never be on such terms of intimacy with Christ,— I who am so unlike Him; so full of desires He cannot gratify; so frivolous, superficial, unreal, while He is so real, so earnest; so unloving while He is so loving; so reluctant to endure hardness, with views of life and aims so opposed to His; so unable to keep a pure and elevated purpose steadfastly in my mind." Mary was once trodden under foot of evil, a wreck in whom none but Christ saw any place for hope. It is what is in *Him* that is powerful. He has won His supremacy by love, by refusing to enjoy His private rights without our sharing them; and He maintains His supremacy by love, teaching all to love Him, subduing to devotedness the hardest heart—not by a remote exhibition of cold, unemotional perfection, but by the persistence and depth of His warm and individual love.

Mary had no time to reason and doubt. With one quick exclamation of ecstatic recognition and joy she sprang towards Him. The one word "my Master,"[1]

---

[1] " Rabboni" had more of reverence in it than would be conveyed by "my Teacher," and it is legitimate here to use "Master" in its wider sense.

uttered all her heart. It is related of George Herbert that when he was inducted into the cure of Bemerton he said to a friend: "I beseech God that my humble and charitable life may so win upon others as to bring glory to my Jesus, whom I have this day taken to be my Master and my Governor, and I am so proud of His service that I will always call Him Jesus, my Master." His biographer adds: "He seems to rejoice in that word Jesus, and says that the adding these words 'my Master' to it and the often repetition of them seemed to perfume his mind." With Mary the title was one of indefinite respect; she found in Jesus one she could always reverence and trust. The firm, loving hand that admits no soft evasion of duty; the steadfast step that with equanimity ever goes straight forward; the strong heart that has always room for the distresses of others; the union with God which made Him a medium to earth of God's superiority and availing compassion,—these things had made the words "my Master" His proper designation in her lips. And our spirit cannot be purified and elevated but by worthy love and deserved reverence, by living in presence of that which commands our love and lifts up our nature to what is above it. It is by letting our heart and mind be filled by what is above us that we grow in abiding stature and become in our turn helpful to what is at a still lower stage than we are.

But as Mary sprang forward, and in a transport of affection made as though she would embrace the Lord, she is met by these quick words: "Touch Me not, for I am not yet ascended to My Father." Various conjectural reasons for this prohibition have been supposed,—as, that it was indecorous, an objection which Christ did not make when at a dinner-table a woman kissed his feet, scandalising the guests and provoking the suspicions of the host; or, that she wished to assure herself by touch of the reality of the appearance, an assurance which He did not object to the disciples making, but rather encouraged them to make, as He would also have encouraged Mary had she needed any such test, which she did not; or, that this vehement embrace would disturb the process of glorification which was proceeding in His body! It is idle to conjecture reasons, seeing that He Himself gives the reason, "for I am not yet ascended," implying that such "touching" would no longer be prohibited when He was ascended. Mary seems to have thought that already the "little while" of His absence was past, and that now He was to be always with them upon earth, helping them in the same familiar ways and training them by His visible presence and spoken words. This was a misconception. He must first ascend to the Father, and those who love Him on earth must learn to live without the physical appearance, the actual seeing, touching, hearing, of the well-known Master. There must be no more kissing of His feet, but homage of a sterner, deeper sort; there must be no more sitting at table with Him, and filling the mind with His words, until they sit down with Him in the Father's presence. Meanwhile His friends must walk by faith, not by sight—by their inward light and spiritual likings; they must learn the truer fidelity that serves an absent Lord; they must acquire the independent and inherent love of righteousness which can freely grow only when relieved from the overmastering pressure of a visible presence, encouraging us by sensible expressions of favour, guaranteeing us against defeat and danger. Thus only can the human spirit freely grow, showing its native bent, its true tastes and convictions; thus only can its capacities for self-development and for choosing and fulfilling its own destiny be matured.

And if these words of Jesus seemed at first chilling and repellent, they were followed by words of unmistakable affection: "Go to my brothers, and say unto them, I ascend unto My Father and your Father, and to My God and your God." This is the message of the risen Lord to men. He has become the link between us and all that is highest and best. We know that He has overcome all evil and left it behind; we know that He is worthy of the highest place, that by His righteousness and love He merits the highest place. We know that if such an one as He cannot go boldly to the highest heaven and claim God as His God and Father, there is no such thing as moral worth, and all effort, conscience, hope, responsibility, are vain and futile. We know that Christ must ascend to the highest, and yet we know also that He will not enter where we cannot follow. We know that His love binds Him to us as strongly as His rights carry Him to God. We can as little believe that He will abandon us and leave us out of His eternal enjoyment, as we can believe that God would refuse to own Him as Son. And it is this which Christ puts in the forefront of His message as risen and ascending: "I ascend unto My Father and your Father." The joy that awaits Me with God awaits you also; the power I go to exercise is the power of your Father. This affinity for heaven which you see in Me is coupled with affinity for you. The holiness, the power, the victory, I have achieved and now enjoy are yours; I am your Brother: what I claim, I claim for you.

## XXIII.
*THOMAS TEST.*

"When therefore it was evening, on that day, the first day of the week, and when the doors were shut where the disciples were, for fear of the Jews, Jesus came and stood in the midst, and saith unto them, Peace be unto you. And when He had said this, He showed unto them His hands and His side. The disciples therefore were glad, when they saw the Lord. Jesus therefore said to them again, Peace be unto you : as the Father hath sent Me, even so send I you. And when He had said this, He breathed on them, and saith unto them, Receive ye the Holy Ghost : whosesoever sins ye forgive, they are forgiven unto them ; whosesoever sins ye retain, they are retained. But Thomas, one of the twelve, called Didymus, was not with them when Jesus came. The other disciples therefore said unto him, We have seen the Lord. But he said unto them, Except I shall see in His hands the print of the nails, and put my finger into the print of the nails, and put my hand into His side, I will not believe. And after eight days again His disciples were within, and Thomas with them. Jesus cometh, the doors being shut, and stood in the midst, and said, Peace be unto you. Then saith He to Thomas, Reach hither thy finger, and see My hands ; and reach hither thy hand, and put it into My side : and be not faithless, but believing. Thomas answered and said unto Him, My Lord and my God. Jesus saith unto him, Because thou hast seen Me, thou hast believed : blessed are they that have not seen, and yet have believed."
—JOHN xx. 19-29.

## XXIII.

### *THOMAS' TEST.*

ON the evening of the day whose dawning had been signalised by the Resurrection, the disciples, and, according to Luke, some others, were together. They expected that the event which had restored hope in their own hearts would certainly excite the authorities and probably lead to the arrest of some of their number. They had therefore carefully closed the doors, that some time for parley and possibly for escape might be interposed. But to their astonishment and delight, while they were sitting thus with closed doors, the well-known figure of their Lord appeared in their midst, and His familiar greeting, "Peace be with you," sounded in their ears. Further to identify Himself and remove all doubt or dread He showed them His hands and His side; and, as St. Luke tells us, even ate before them. There is here a strange mingling of identity and difference between the body He now wears and that which had been crucified. Its appearance is the same in some respects, but its properties are different. Immediate recognition did not always follow His manifestation. There was something baffling in His appearance, suggesting a well-known face, and yet not quite the same. The marks on the body, or some characteristic action or movement or utterance, were needed to complete the identification. The properties of the body also were not reducible to any known type. He could eat, speak, walk, yet He could dispense with eating and could apparently pass through physical obstacles. His body was a glorified, spiritual body, not subject to the laws which govern the physical part of man in this life. These characteristics are worth noticing, not only as giving us some inkling of the type of body which awaits ourselves, but in connection with the identification of the risen Lord. Had the appearance been the mere fancy of the disciples, how should they have required any identification?

Having saluted them and removed their consternation, He fulfils the object of His appearance by giving them their commission, their equipment, and their authority as His Apostles: "As the Father hath sent Me, even so send I you"—to fulfil still the same purpose, to complete the work begun, to stand to Him in the same intimate relation as He had occupied to the Father. To impart to them at once all that they required for the fulfilment of this commission He bestows upon them the Holy Spirit, breathing on them, to convey to them the impression that He was actually there and then communicating to them that which constituted the very breath of His own life. This is His first act as Lord of all power in heaven and on earth, and it is an act which inevitably conveys to them the assurance that His life and theirs is one life. Impulse and power to proclaim Him as risen they did not yet experience. They must be allowed time to settle to some composure of mind and to some clear thoughts after all the disturbing events of these last days. They must also have the confirmatory testimony to the Resurrection, which could only be furnished after repeated appearances of the Lord to themselves and to others.

The gift of the Spirit, therefore, as a spirit of powerful witness-bearing, was reserved for six weeks.

With this perfect equipment our Lord added the words: "Whosoever sins ye forgive, they are forgiven unto them; whosoever sins ye retain, they are retained." These words have been the occasion of endless controversy.[1] They certainly convey the ideas that the Apostles were appointed to mediate between Christ and their fellow-men, that the chief function they should be required to discharge in this mediation was the forgiving and retention of sins, and that they were furnished with the Holy Spirit to guide them in this mediation. Apparently this must mean that the Apostles were to be the agents through whom Christ was to proclaim the terms of admission to His kingdom. They received authority to say in what cases sins were to be forgiven and in what to be retained. To infer from this that the Apostles have successors, that these successors are constituted by an external ordinance or nomination, that they have power to exclude or admit individuals seeking entrance into the kingdom of God, is to leave logic and reason a long way behind, and to erect a kind of government in the Church of Christ which will never be submitted to by those who live in the liberty wherewith His truth has made them free. The presence of the Holy Spirit, and no bare external appointment, is that which gives authority to those who guide the Church of Christ. It is because they are inwardly one with Christ, not because they happen to be able to claim a doubtful outward connection with Him, that they have that authority which Christ's people own.

---

[1] See Steitz' article *Schlüsselgewalt* in *Herzog*.

But when our Lord thus appeared on the day of His resurrection to His disciples one of their number was absent. This might not have been noticed had not the absentee been of a peculiar temper, and had not this peculiarity given rise to another visit of the Lord and to a very significant restoration of belief in the mind of a sceptical disciple. The absent disciple was commonly known as Thomas or Didymus, the Twin. On various occasions he appears somewhat prominently in the gospel-story, and his conduct and conversation on those occasions show him to have been a man very liable to take a desponding view of the future, apt to see the darker side of everything, but at the same time not wanting in courage, and of a strong and affectionate loyalty to Jesus. On one occasion, when our Lord intimated to the disciples His intention of returning within the dangerous frontier of Judæa, the others expostulated, but Thomas said, " Let us also go, that we may die with Him "—an utterance in which his devoted loyalty to his Master, his dogged courage, and his despondent temperament are all apparent. And when, some time afterwards, Jesus was warning His disciples that He must shortly leave them and go to the Father, Thomas sees in the departure of his Master the extinction of all hope; life and the way to life seem to him treacherous phrases, he has eyes only for the gloom of death: " Lord, we know not whither Thou goest ; and how can we know the way ? "

The absence of such a man from the first meeting of the disciples was to be expected.[1] If the bare possibility of his Lord's death had plunged this loving and gloomy heart in despondency, what dark despair must

---

[1] In this chapter there are reminiscences of Trench.

have preyed upon it when that death was actually accomplished! How the figure of his dead Master had burnt itself into his soul is seen from the manner in which his mind dwells on the print of the nails, the wound in the side. It is by these only, and not by well-known features of face or peculiarities of form, he will recognise and identify his Lord. His heart was with the lifeless body on the cross, and he could not bear to see the friends of Jesus or speak with those who had shared his hopes, but buried his disappointment and desolation in solitude and silence. His absence can scarcely be branded as culpable. None of the others expected resurrection any more than himself, but his hopelessness acted on a specially sensitive and despondent nature. Thus it was that, like many melancholy persons, he missed the opportunity of seeing what would effectually have scattered his darkness.

But though he might not be to blame for absenting himself, he was to blame for refusing to accept the testimony of his friends when they assured him they had seen Jesus risen. There is a tone of doggedness that grates upon us in the words, " Except I shall see in His hands the print of the nails, *and put my finger* into the print of the nails, and thrust my hand into His side, I will not believe." Some deference was due to the testimony of men whom he knew to be truthful and as little liable to delusion as himself. We cannot blame him for not being convinced on the spot; a man cannot compel himself to believe anything which does not itself compel belief. But the obstinate tone sounds as if he was beginning to nurse his unbelief, than which there is no more pernicious exercise of the human spirit. He demands, too, what may never be possible—the evidence of his own senses. He claims that he shall be on the same footing as the rest. Why is he to believe on less evidence than they? It has cost him pain enough to give up his hope: is he then to give up his hopelessness as cheaply as all this? He is supremely miserable; his Lord dead and life left to him—a life which already during these few days had grown far too long, a weary, intolerable burden. Is he in a moment and on their mere word to rise from his misery? A man of Thomas' temperament hugs his wretchedness. You seem to do him an injury if you open the shutters of his heart and let in the sunshine.

Obviously, therefore, the first inference we naturally draw from this state of mind is that it is weak and wrong to lay hold of one difficulty and insist that except this be removed we will not believe. Let this difficulty about the constitution of Christ's person, or this about the impossibility of proving a miracle, or this about the inspiration of Scripture be removed, and I will accept Christianity; let God grant me *this* petition, and I will believe that He is the hearer of prayer; let me see this inconsistency or that explained, and I will believe He governs the course of things in this world. The understanding begins to take a pride in demanding evidence more absolute and strict than has satisfied others, and seems to display acuteness and fairness in holding to one difficulty. The test which Thomas proposed to himself seemed an accurate and legitimate one; but that he should have proposed it shows that he was neglecting the evidence already afforded him, the testimony of a number of men whose truthfulness he had for years made proof of. True, it was a miracle they required him to believe; but would his own senses be better authentication of a miracle than the unanimous and explicit declaration of a company of veracious men? He could have no doubt that they believed they had seen the Lord. If they could be deceived, ten of them, or many more, why should his senses prove more infallible? Was he to reject their testimony on the ground that their senses had deceived them, and accept the testimony of his own senses? Was the ultimate test in his own case to be that very evidence which in the case of others he maintained was insufficient?

But if this tells seriously against Thomas, we must not leave out of account what tells in his favour. It is true he was obstinate and unreasonable and a shade vain in his refusal to accept the testimony of the disciples, but it is also true that he was with the little Christian community on the second Lord's Day. This puts it beyond a doubt that he was not so unbelieving as he seemed. That he did not now avoid the society of those happy, hopeful men shows that he was far from unwilling to become, if possible, a sharer in their hope and joy. Perhaps already he was repenting having pledged himself to unbelief, as many another has repented. Certainly he was not afraid of being convinced that his Lord had arisen; on the contrary, he sought to be convinced of this and put himself in the way of conviction. He had doubted because he wished to believe, doubted because it was the full, entire, eternal confidence of his soul that he was seeking a resting-place for. He knew the tremendous importance to him of this question—knew that it was literally everything to him if Christ was risen and was now alive and to be found by His people, and therefore he was slow to believe. Therefore also he kept in the company of believers; it was on their side he wished to get out of the terrible mire and darkness in which he was involved.

It is this which distinguishes Thomas and all right-minded doubters from thorough-going and depraved unbelievers. The one wishes to believe, would give the world to be free from doubt, will go mourning all his days, will pine in body and sicken of life because he cannot believe: "he *waits* for light, but behold obscurity, for brightness, but he walks in darkness." The other, the culpable unbeliever, thrives on doubt; he likes it, enjoys it, sports it, lives by it; goes about telling people his difficulties, as some morbid people have a fancy for showing you their sores or detailing their symptoms, as if everything which makes them different from other men, even though it be disease, were a thing to be proud of. Convince such a man of the truth and he is angry with you; you seem to have done him a wrong, as the mendicant impostor who has been gaining his livelihood by a bad leg or a useless eye is enraged when a skilled person restores to him the use of his limb or shows him that he can use it if he will. You may know a dishonest doubter by the fluency with which he states his difficulties or by the affectation of melancholy which is sometimes assumed. You may always know him by his reluctance to be convinced, by his irritation when he is forced to surrender some pet bulwark of unbelief. When you find a man reading one side of the question, courting difficulties, eagerly seizing on new objections, and provoked instead of thankful when any doubt is removed, you may be sure that this is not a scepticism of the understanding so much as an evil *heart* of unbelief.

The hesitancy and backwardness, the incredulity and niggardliness of faith, of Thomas have done as much to confirm the minds of succeeding believers as the forward and impulsive confidence of Peter. Then, as now, this critical intellect, when combined with a sound heart, wrought two great boons for the Church. The doubts which such men entertain continually provoke fresh evidence, as here this second appearance of Christ to the Eleven seems due to the doubt of Thomas. So far as one can gather it was solely to remove this doubt our Lord appeared. And, besides, a second boon which attends honest and godly doubt is the attachment to the Church of men who have passed through severe mental conflict, and therefore hold the faith they have reached with an intelligence and a tenacity unknown to other men.

These two things were simply brought about in Thomas' instance. The disciples were again assembled on the following Sunday, probably in the same place, consecrated for ever in their memories as the place where their risen Lord had appeared. It is doubtful whether they were more expectant of a fresh appearance of their Lord this day than they had been any day throughout the week, but certainly every reader feels that it is not without significance that after a blank and uneventful week the first day should again be singled out to have this honour put upon it. Some sanction is felt to be given to those meetings of His followers which ever since have been assembled on the first day of the week; and the experience of thousands can testify that this day seems still the favourite with our Lord for manifesting Himself to His people, and for renewing the joy which a week's work has somewhat dimmed. Silently and suddenly as before, without warning, without opening of doors, Jesus stood in their midst. But there was no terror now—exclamation, only of delight and adoration. And perhaps it was not in human nature to resist casting a look of triumphant interrogation at Thomas, a look of inquiry to see what he would make of this. Surprise, unutterable surprise, undiminished by all he had been led to expect, must have been written on Thomas' wide-gazing eyes and riveted look. But this surprise was displaced by shame, this eager gaze cast down, when he found that his Lord had heard his obstinate ultimatum and had been witness of his sullen unbelief. As Jesus repeats almost in the same words the hard, rude, bare, material test which he had proposed, and as He holds forth His hands for his inspection, shame and joy struggle for the mastery in his spirit, and give utterance to the humble but glowing confession, "My Lord and my God.' His own test is superseded; he makes no movement to put it in force; he is satisfied of the identity of his Lord. It is the same penetrating knowledge of man's inmost thoughts, the same loving treatment of the erring, the same subduing presence.

And thus it frequently happens that a man who has vowed that he will not believe except this or that be made plain finds, when he does believe, that something short of his own requirements has convinced him. He finds that though he was once so express in his demands for proof, and so clear and accurate in his declarations of the precise amount of evidence required, at the last he believes and could scarcely tell you why, could not at least show his belief as the fine and clean result of a logical process. Thomas had maintained that the rest were too easily satisfied, but at the last he is himself satisfied with precisely the same proof as they. And it is somewhat striking that in so many cases unbelief gives way to belief, not by the removal of intellectual difficulties, not by such demonstration as was granted to Thomas, but by an undefinable conquest of the soul by Christ. The glory, holiness, love of His person, subdue the soul to Him.

The faith of Thomas is full of significance. First, it is helpful to our own faith to hear so decisive and so full a confession coming from the lips of such a man. John himself felt it to be so decisive that after recording it he virtually closes the Gospel which he had undertaken to write in order to persuade men that Jesus is the Son of God. After this confession of Thomas he feels that no more can be said. He stops not for want of matter; "many other signs truly did Jesus in the presence of His disciples" which are not written in this Gospel. These seemed sufficient. The man who is not moved by this will not be moved by any further proof. Proof is not what such a doubter needs. Whatever we think of the other Apostles, it is plain that Thomas at least was not credulous. If Peter's generous ardour carried him to a confession unwarranted by the facts, if John saw in Jesus the reflection of his own contemplative and loving nature, what are we to say of the faith of Thomas? He had no determination to see only what he desired, no readiness to accept baseless evidence and irresponsible testimony. He knew the critical nature of the situation, the unique importance of the matter presented to his faith. With him there was no frivolous or thoughtless underrating of difficulties. He did not absolutely deny the possibility of Christ's resurrection, but he went very near doing so, and showed that practically he considered it either impossible or unlikely in the extreme. But in the end he believes. And the ease with which he passes from doubt to faith proves his honesty and sound-heartedness. As soon as evidence which to him is convincing is produced, he proclaims his faith.

His confession, too, is fuller than that of the other disciples. The week of painful questioning had brought clearly before his mind the whole significance of the Resurrection, so that he does not hesitate to own Jesus as his God. When a man of profound spiritual feeling and of good understanding has doubts and hesitations from the very intensity and subtlety of his scrutiny of what appears to him of transcendent importance; when he sees difficulties unseen by men who are too little interested in the matter to recognise them even though they stare them in the face,—when such a man, with the care and anxiety that befit the subject, considers for himself the claims of Christ, and as the result yields himself to the Lord, he sees more in Christ than other men do, and is likely to be steadier in his allegiance than if he had slurred over apparent obstacles instead of removing them, and stifled objections in place of answering them. It was not the mere seeing of Christ risen which prompted the full confession of Thomas. But slowly during that week of suspense he had been taking in the full significance of the Resurrection, coming at the close of such a life as he knew the Lord had lived. The very idea that such a thing was believed by the rest forced his mind back upon the exceptional character of Jesus, His wonderful works, the intimations He had given of His connection with God. The sight of Him risen came as the keystone of the arch, which being wanting all had fallen to the ground, but being inserted clenched the whole, and could now bear any weight. The truths about His person which Thomas had begun to explain away return upon his mind with resistless force, and each in clear, certain verity. He saw now that his Lord had performed all His word, had proved Himself supreme over all that affected men. He saw Him after passing through unknown conflict with principalities and powers come to resume fellowship with sinful men, standing with all things under His feet, yet giving His hand to the weak disciple to make him partake in His triumph.

This was a rare and memorable hour for Thomas, one of those moments that mark a man's spirit permanently. He is carried entirely out of himself, and sees nothing but his Lord. The whole energy of his spirit goes out to Him undoubtingly, unhesitatingly, unrestrained. Everything is before him in the person of Christ; nothing causes the least diversion or distraction. For once his spirit has found perfect peace. There is nothing in the unseen world that can dismay him, nothing in the future on which he can spend a thought; his soul rests in the Person before him. He does not draw back, questioning whether the Lord will now receive him; he fears no rebuke; he does not scrutinise his spiritual condition, nor ask whether his faith is sufficiently spiritual. He cannot either go back upon his past conduct, or analyse his present feelings, or spend one thought of any kind upon himself. The scrupulous, sceptical man is all devoutness and worship; the thousand objections are swept from his mind; and all by the mere presence of Christ. He is rapt in this one object; mind and soul are filled with the regained Lord; he forgets himself; the passion of joy with which he regains in a transfigured form his lost Leader absorbs him quite: "he had lost a possible king of the Jews; he finds his Lord and his God." There can be no question here about himself, his prospects, his interests. He can but utter his surprise, his joy, and his worship in the cry, "My Lord and my God."

On such a man even the Lord's benediction were useless. This is the highest, happiest, rarest state of the human soul. When a man has been carried out of himself by the clear vision of Christ's worth; when his mind and heart are filled with the supreme excellence of Christ; when in His presence he feels he can but worship, bowing in his soul before actually achieved human perfection rooted in and expressing the true Divine glory of love ineffable; when face to face, soul to soul, with the highest and most affecting known goodness, conscious that he now in this very moment stands within touch of the Supreme, that he has found and need never more lose perfect love, perfect goodness, perfect power,—when a man is transported by such a recognition of Christ, this is the true ecstasy, this is man's ultimate blessedness.

And this blessedness is competent not only to those who saw with the bodily eye, but much more to those who have not seen and yet have believed. Why do we rob ourselves of it, and live as if it were not so— as if such certitude and the joy that accompanies it had passed from earth and were no more possible? We cannot apply Thomas' test, but we can test his test; or, like him, we can forego it, and rest on wider, deeper evidence. Was he right in so eagerly confessing his belief? And are we right to hesitate, to doubt, to despond? Should we have counted it strange if, when the Lord addressed Thomas, he had sullenly shrunk back among the rest, or merely given a verbal assent to Christ's identity, showing no sign of joy? And are we to accept the signs He gives us of His presence as if it made little difference to us and did not lift us into heaven? Have we so little sense of spiritual things that we cannot believe in the life of Him round whom the whole fortunes of our race revolve? Do we not know the power of Christ's resurrection as Thomas could not possibly know it? Do we not see as he could not see the boundless spiritual efficacy and results of that risen life? Do we not see the full bearing of that great manifestation of God's nearness more clearly? Do we not feel how impossible it was that such an one as Christ should be holden of death, that the supremacy in human affairs which He achieved by absolute love and absolute holiness should be proved inferior to a physical law, and should be interrupted in its efficacious exercise by a physical fact? If Thomas was constrained to acknowledge Christ as his Lord and his God, much more may we do so. By the nature of the case our conviction, implying as it does some apprehension of spiritual things, must be more slowly wrought. Even if at last the full conviction that human life is a joy because Christ is with us in it, leading us to eternal partnership with Himself,—even if this conviction flash suddenly through the spirit, the material for it must have been long accumulating. Even if at last we awake to a sense of the present glory of Christ with the suddenness of Thomas, yet in any case this must be the result of purified spiritual affinities and leanings. But on this very account is the conviction more indissolubly intertwined with all that we truly are, forming an essential and necessary part of our inward growth, and leading each of us to respond with a cordial amen to the benediction of our Lord, " Blessed are they that have not seen and yet have believed."

# XXIV.

*APPEARANCE AT SEA OF GALILEE.*

" After these things Jesus manifested Himself again to the disciples at the Sea of Tiberias; and He manifested Himself on this wise. There were together Simon Peter, and Thomas called Didymus, and Nathanael of Cana in Galilee, and the sons of Zebedee, and two other of His disciples. Simon Peter saith unto them, I go a-fishing. They say unto him, We also come with thee. They went forth, and entered into the boat; and that night they took nothing. But when day was now breaking, Jesus stood on the beach : howbeit the disciples knew not that it was Jesus. Jesus therefore saith unto them, Children, have ye aught to eat? They answered Him, No. And He said unto them, Cast the net on the right side of the boat, and ye shall find. They cast therefore, and now they were not able to draw it for the multitude of fishes. That disciple therefore whom Jesus loved saith unto Peter, It is the Lord. So when Simon Peter heard that it was the Lord, he girt his coat about him (for he was naked), and cast himself into the sea. But the other disciples came in the little boat (for they were not far from the land, but about two hundred cubits off), dragging the net full of fishes. So when they got out upon the land, they see a fire of coals there, and fish laid thereon, and bread. Jesus saith unto them, Bring of the fish which ye have now taken. Simon Peter therefore went up, and drew the net to land, full of great fishes, a hundred and fifty and three : and for all there were so many, the net was not rent. Jesus saith unto them, Come and break your fast. And none of the disciples durst inquire of Him, Who art Thou? knowing that it was the Lord. Jesus cometh, and taketh the bread, and giveth them, and the fish likewise. This is now the third time that Jesus was manifested to the disciples, after that He was risen from the dead."— JOHN xxi. 1-14.

# XXIV.

### *APPEARANCE AT SEA OF GALILEE.*

THE removal of the doubts of Thomas restored the Eleven to unity of faith, and fitted them to be witnesses of the Lord's resurrection. And the Gospel might naturally have closed at this point, as indeed the last verses of the twentieth chapter suggest that the writer himself felt that his task was done. But as throughout his Gospel he had followed the plan of adducing such of Christ's miracles as seemed to throw a strong light on His spiritual power, he could not well close without mentioning the last miracle of all, and which seemed to have only a didactic purpose. Besides, there was another reason for John adding this chapter. He was writing at the very close of the century. So long had he survived the unparalleled events he narrates that an impression had gone abroad that he would never die. It was even rumoured that our Lord had foretold that the beloved disciple should tarry on earth till He Himself should return. John takes the opportunity of relating what the Lord had really said, as well as of recounting the all-important event out of which the misreported conversation had arisen.

When the disciples had spent the Passover week at Jerusalem, they naturally returned to their homes in Galilee. The house of the old fisherman Zebedee was probably their rendezvous. We need not listen to their talk as they relate what had passed in Jerusalem, in order to see that they are sensible of the peculiarity of their situation and are in a state of suspense.

They are back among the familiar scenes, the boats are lying on the beach, their old companions are sitting about mending their nets as they themselves had been doing a year or two before when summoned by Jesus to follow Him on the moment. But though old associations are thus laying hold of them again, there is evidence that new influences are also at work; for with the fishermen are found Nathanael and others who were there, not for the sake of old associations, but of the new and common interest they had in Christ. The seven men have kept together; they participate in an experience of which their fellow-townsmen know nothing; but they must live. Hints have been thrown out that seven strong men must not depend on other arms than their own for a livelihood. And as they stand together that evening and watch boat after boat push off, the women wishing their husbands and sons good-speed, the men cheerily responding and busily getting their tackle in trim, with a look of pity at the group of disciples, Peter can stand it no longer, but makes for his own or some unoccupied boat with the words, "I go a-fishing." The rest were only needing such an invitation. The whole charm and zest of the old life rushes back upon them, each takes his own accustomed place in the boat, each hand finds itself once more at home at the long-suspended task, and with an ease that surprises themselves they fall back into the old routine.

And as we watch their six oars flashing in the setting sun, and Peter steering them to the familiar fishing ground, we cannot but reflect in how precarious a position the whole future of the world is. That boat carries the earthly hope of the Church; and as we weigh the feelings of the men that are in it, what we see chiefly is, how easily the whole of Christianity might here have broken short off, and never have been heard of, supposing it to have depended for its propagation solely on the disciples. Here they were, not knowing what had become of Jesus, without any plan for preserving His name among men, open to any impulse or influence, unable to resist the smell of the fishing boats and the freshness of the evening breeze, and submitting themselves to be guided by such influences as these, content apparently to fall back into their old ways and obscure village life, as if the last three years were a dream, or were like a voyage to foreign parts, which they might think of afterwards, but were not to repeat. All the facts they were to use for the conversion of the world were already in their possession; the death of Christ and His resurrection were not a fortnight old; but as yet they had no inward impulse to proclaim the truth; there was no Holy Ghost powerfully impelling and possessing them; they were not endued with power from on high. One thing only they seemed to be decided and agreed about—that they must live; and therefore they go a-fishing.

But apparently they were not destined to find even this so easy as they expected. There was One watching that boat, following it through the night as they tried place after place, and He was resolved that they should not be filled with false ideas about the satisfactoriness of their old calling. All night they toiled, but caught nothing. Every old device was tried; the fancies of each particular kind of fish were humoured, but in vain. Each time the net was drawn up, every hand knew before it appeared that it was empty. Weary with the fruitless toil, and when the best part of the night was gone, they made for a secluded part of the shore, not wishing to land from their first attempt empty in presence of the other fishermen. But when about one hundred yards from the shore a voice hails them with the words, "Children"—or, as we would say, "Lads"—"have you taken any fish?" It has been supposed that our Lord asked this question in the character of a trader who had been watching for the return of the boats that he might buy, or that it was with the natural interest every one takes in the success of a person that is fishing, so that we can scarcely pass without asking what take they have had. The question was asked for the purpose of arresting the boat at a sufficient distance from the shore to make another cast of the net possible. It has this effect; the rowers turned round to see who is calling them, and at the same time tell Him they have no fish. The Stranger then says, "Cast the net on the right side of the ship, and ye shall find"; and they do so, not thinking of a miracle, but supposing that before any man would give them such express instructions he must have had some good reason for believing there were fish there. But when they found that the net was at once absolutely loaded with fish, so that they could not draw it into the boat, John looks again at the Stranger, and whispers to Peter, "It is the Lord." This was no sooner heard by Peter than he snatched up and threw over him his upper garment, and throwing himself into the water swam or waded ashore.

In every trifling act character betrays itself. It is John who is first to recognise Jesus; it is Peter who casts himself into the sea, just as he had done once before on that same lake, and as he had been first to enter the sepulchre on the morning of the Resurrection. John recognises the Lord, not because he had better eyesight than the rest, nor because he had a better position in the boat, nor because while the rest were busied with the net he was occupied with the figure on the beach, but because his spirit had a quicker and profounder apprehension of spiritual things, and because in this sudden turn of their fortune he recognised the same hand which had filled their nets once before and had fed thousands with one or two little fishes.

The reason of Peter's impetuousness on this occasion may partly have been that their fishing vessel was now as near the land as they could get it, and that he was unwilling to wait till they should get the small boat unfastened. The rest, we read, came ashore, not in the large vessel in which they had spent the night, but in the little boat they carried with them, the reason being added, "for they were not far from land"—that is to say, not far enough to use the larger vessel any longer. Peter, therefore, ran no risk of drowning. But his action reveals the eagerness of love. No sooner has he only heard from another that his Lord is near, than the fish for which he had been watching and waiting all night are forgotten, and for him, the master of the vessel, the net and all its contents might have sunk to the bottom of the lake. What this action of Peter suggested to the Lord is apparent from the question which a few minutes later He put to him: "Lovest thou Me more than these?"

Neither would Peter have sustained any serious loss even though his nets had been carried away, for when he reaches the shore he finds that the Lord was to be their host, not their guest. A fire is ready lit, fish laid on it and bread baking. He who could so fill their nets could also provide for His own wants. But there was to be no needless multiplication of miracles; the fish already on the fire was not to be multiplied in their hands when plenty were lying in the net. He directs them, therefore, to bring of the fish they had caught. They go to the net, and mechanically, in their old fashion, count the fish they had taken, one hundred and fifty and three; and John, with a fisher's memory can tell you, sixty years after, the precise number. From these miraculously provided fish they break their long fast.

The significance of this incident has perhaps been somewhat lost by looking at it too exclusively as symbolical. No doubt it was so; but it carried in the first place a most important lesson in its bare, literal facts. We have already noticed the precarious position in which the Church at this time was. And it will be useful to us in many ways to endeavour to rid our mind of all fancies about the beginning of the Christian Church, and look at the simple, unvarnished facts here presented to our view. And the plain and significant circumstance which first invites our attention is, that the nucleus of the Church, the men on whom the faith of Christ depended for its propagation, were fishermen.

This was not merely the picturesque drapery assumed by men of ability so great and character so commanding that all positions in life were alike to them. Let us recall to memory the group of men we have seen standing at a corner in a fishing village or with whom we have spent a night at sea fishing, and whose talk has been *at the best* old stories of their craft or legends of the water. Such men were the Apostles. They were men who were not at home in cities, who simply could not understand the current philosophies, who did not so much as know the names of the great contemporary writers of the Roman world, who took only so much interest in politics as every Jew in those troublous times was forced to take—men who were at home only on their own lake, in their fishing boat, and who could quite contentedly, even after all they had recently gone through, have returned to their old occupation for life. They were in point of fact now returning to their old life—returning to it partly because they had no impulse to publish what they knew, and partly because, even though they had, they must live, and did not know how they should be supported but by fishing.

And this is the reason of this miracle; this is the reason why our Lord so pointedly convinced them that without Him they could not make a livelihood: that they might fish all the night through and resort to every device their experience could contrive and yet could catch nothing, but that He could give them sustenance as He pleased. If any one thinks that this is a secular, shallow way of looking at the miracle, let him ask what it is that chiefly keeps men from serving God as they think they should, what it is that induces men to live so much for the world and so little for God, what it is that prevents them from following out what conscience whispers is the right course. Is it not mainly the feeling that by doing God's will we ourselves are likely to be not so well off, not so sufficiently provided for. Above all things, therefore, both we and the Apostles need to be convinced that our Lord, who asks us to follow Him, is much better able to provide for us than we ourselves are. They had the same transition to make as every man among ourselves has to make; we and they alike have to pass from the natural feeling that we depend on our own energy and skill for our support to the knowledge that we depend on God. We have to pass from the life of nature and sense to the life of faith. We have to come to know and believe that the fundamental thing is God, that it is He who can support us when nature fails, and *not* that we must betake ourselves to nature at many points where God fails—that we live, not by bread alone, but by every word that proceedeth out of the mouth of God, and are much safer in doing His bidding than in struggling anxiously to make a livelihood.

And if we carefully read our own experience, might we not see, as clearly as the Apostles that morning saw, the utter futility of our own schemes for bettering ourselves in the world? Is it not the simple fact that we also have toiled through every watch of the night, have borne fatigue and deprivation, have abandoned the luxuries of life and given ourselves to endure hardness, have tried contrivance after contrivance to win our cherished project, and all in vain? Our net is empty and light at the rising sun as it was at the setting. Have we not again and again found that when every boat round was being filled we drew nothing but disappointment? Have we not many times come back empty-handed to our starting-place? But no matter how much we have thus lost or missed every man will tell you it is much better so than if he had succeeded, if only his own ill-success has induced him to trust Christ, if only it has taught him really what he used with everybody else verbally to say,—that in that Person dimly discerned through the light that begins to glimmer round our disappointments there is all power in heaven and on earth—power to give us what we have been trying to win, power to give us greater happiness without it.

But this being so, it being the case that our Lord came this second time and called them away from their occupations to follow Him, and showed them how amply He could support them, they could not but remember how He had once before in very similar circumstances summoned them to leave their occupation as fishermen and to become fishers of men. They could not but interpret the present by the former miracle, and read in it a renewed summons to the work of catching men, and a renewed assurance that in that work they should not draw empty nets. Most suitably, then, does this miracle stand alone, the only one wrought after the Resurrection, and most suitably does it stand last, giving the Apostles a symbol which should continually reanimate them to their laborious work. Their work of preaching was well symbolised by *sowing*; they passed rapidly through the field of the world, at every step scattering broadcast the words of everlasting life, not examining minutely the hearts into which these words might fall, not knowing where they might find prepared soil and where they might find inhospitable rock, but assured that after a time whoso followed in their track should see the fruit of their words. Not less significant is the figure of the net; they let down the net of their good tidings, not seeing what persons were really enclosed in it, but trusting that He who had said, "Cast your net on the right side of the ship," knew what souls it would fall over. By this miracle He gave the Apostles to understand that not only when with them in the flesh could He give them success. Even now after His resurrection and when they did not recognise Him on the shore He blessed their labour, that they might even when they did not see Him believe in His nearness and in His power most effectually to give them success.

This is the miracle which has again and again restored the drooping faith and discouraged spirit of all Christ's followers who endeavour to bring men under His influence, or in any way to spread out this influence over a wider surface. Again and again their hope is disappointed and their labour vain; the persons they wish to influence glide out from below the net, and it is drawn empty; new opportunities are watched for, and new opportunities arrive and are used, but with the same result; the patient doggedness of the fisherman long used to turns of ill-success is reproduced in the persevering efforts of parental love or friendly anxiety for the good of others, but often the utmost patience is at last worn out, the nets are piled away, and the gloom of disappointment settles on the mind. Yet this apparently is the very hour which the Lord often chooses to give the long-sought-for success; in the dawn, when already the fish might be supposed to see the net and more vigilantly to elude it, our last and almost careless effort is made, and we achieve a substantial, countable success—a success not doubtful, but which we could accurately detail to others, which makes a mark in the memory like the hundred and fifty and three of these fishers, and which were we to relate to others they must acknowledge that the whole weary night of toil is amply repaid. And it is then a man recognises who it is that has directed his labour—it is then he for the moment forgets even the success in the more gladdening knowledge that such a success could only have been given by One, and that it is the Lord who has been watching his disappointments, and at last turning them into triumph.

The Evangelist adds, "None of the disciples durst ask Him, Who art Thou? knowing that it was the Lord"—a remark which unquestionably implies that there was some ground for the question, Who art Thou? They knew it was the Lord from the miracle He had wrought and from His manner of speaking and acting; but yet there was in His appearance something strange, something which, had it not also inspired them with awe, would have prompted the question, Who art Thou? The question was always on their lips, as they found afterwards by comparing notes with one another, but none of them durst put it. There was this time no certification of His identity further than the aid He had given, no showing of His hands and feet. It was, that is to say, by faith now they must know Him, not by bodily eyesight; if they wished to deny Him, there was room for doing so, room for questioning who He was. This was in the most delicate correspondence with the whole incident. The miracle was wrought as the foundation and encouraging symbol of their whole vocation as fishers of men during His bodily absence; it was wrought in order to encourage them to lean on One whom they could not see, whom they could at best dimly descry on another element from themselves, and whom they could not recognise as their Lord apart from the wonderful aid He gave them; and accordingly even when they come ashore there is something mysterious and strange about His appearance, something that baffles eyesight, something that would no longer have satisfied a Thomas, something therefore which is the fit preparation for a state in which they were to live altogether by faith and not at all by sight. This is the state in which we now live. He who believes will know that his Lord is near him; he who refuses to believe will be able to deny His nearness. It is faith then that we need: we need to know our Lord, to understand His purposes and His mode of fulfilling them, so that we may not need the evidence of eyesight to say where He is working and where He is not. If we are to be His followers, if we are to recognise that He has made a new life for us and all men, if we are to recognise that He has begun and is now carrying forward a great cause in this world, and if we see that, let our lives deny it as they may, there is nothing else worth living for than this cause, and if we are seeking to help it, then let us confirm our faith by this miracle and believe that our Lord, who has all power in heaven and on earth, is but beyond eyesight, has a perfectly distinct view of all we are doing and knows when to give us the success we seek.

This, then, explains why it was that our Lord appeared only to His friends after His resurrection. It might have been expected that on His rising from the dead He would have shown Himself as openly as before He suffered, and would specially have shown Himself to those who had crucified Him; but this was not the case. The Apostles themselves were struck with this circumstance, for in one of his earliest discourses Peter remarks that He showed Himself "not to all the people, but unto witnesses chosen before of God, even to us who did eat and drink with Him after He rose from the dead." And it is obvious from the incident before us and from the fact that when our Lord showed Himself to five hundred disciples at once in Galilee, probably a day or two after this, some even of them doubted—it is obvious from this that no good or permanent effect could have been produced by His appearing to all and sundry. It might have served as a momentary triumph, but even this is doubtful; for plenty would have been found to explain away the miracle or to maintain it was a deception, and that He who appeared was not the same as He who died. Or even supposing the miracle had been admitted, why was this miracle to produce any more profound spiritual effect in hearts unprepared than the former miracles had produced? It was not by any such sudden process men could become Christians and faithful witnesses of Christ's resurrection. "Men are not easily wrought upon to be faithful advocates of any cause." They advocate causes to which they are by nature attached, or else they become alive to the merit of a cause only by gradual conviction and by deeply impressed and often repeated instruction. To such a process the Apostles were submitted: and even after this long instruction their fidelity to Christ was tested by a trial which shook to the foundations their whole character, which threw out one of their number for ever, and which revealed the weaknesses of others.

In other words, they needed to be able to certify Christ's spiritual identity as well as His physical sameness. They were so to know Him and so to sympathize with His character that they might be able after the Resurrection to recognize Him by the continuity of that character and the identity of purpose He maintained. They were by daily intercourse with Him to be gradually led to dependence upon Him, and to the strongest attachment to His person; so that when they became witnesses to Him they might not only be able to say, "Jesus whom you crucified rose again," but might be able to illustrate His character by their own, to represent the beauty of His holiness by simply telling what they had seen Him do and heard Him say, and to give convincing evidence in their own persons and lives that He whom they loved on earth lives and rules now in heaven.

And what we need now and always is, not men who can witness to the fact of resurrection, but who can bear in upon our spirits the impression that there is a risen Lord and a risen life through dependence on Him.

## XXV.

### RESTORATION OF PETER.

"So when they had broken their fast, Jesus saith to Simon Peter, Simon, son of John, lovest thou Me more than these? He saith unto Him, Yea, Lord; Thou knowest that I love Thee. He saith unto him, Feed my lambs. He saith to him again a second time, Simon, son of John, lovest thou Me? He saith unto Him, Yea, Lord; Thou knowest that I love Thee. He saith unto him, Tend My sheep. He saith unto him the third time, Simon, son of John, lovest thou Me? Peter was grieved because He said unto him the third time, Lovest thou Me? And he said unto Him, Lord, Thou knowest all things; Thou knowest that I love Thee. Jesus saith unto him, Feed my sheep."—JOHN xxi. 15-17.

## XXV.

### *RESTORATION OF PETER.*

TO the interpretation of this dialogue between the Lord and Peter we must bring a remembrance of the immediately preceding incident. The evening before had found several of those who had followed Jesus standing among the boats that lay by the sea of Galilee. Boat after boat put out from shore; and as the familiar sights and smells and sounds awakened slumbering instincts and stirred old associations, Peter with characteristic restlessness and independence turned away to where his own old boat lay, saying, "I go a-fishing." The rest only needed the example. And as we watch each man taking his old place at the oar or getting ready the nets, we recognise how slight a hold the Apostolic call had taken of these men, and how ready they were to fall back to their old life. They lack sufficient inward impulse to go and proclaim Christ to men; they have no plans; the one inevitable thing is that they must earn a livelihood. And had they that night succeeded as of old in their fishing, the charm of the old life might have been too strong for them. But, like many other men, their failure in accomplishing their own purpose prepared them to discern and to fulfil the Divine purpose, and from catching fish worth so much a pound they became the most influential factors in this world's history. For the Lord had need of them, and again called them to labour for Him, showing them how easily He could maintain them in life and how full their nets would be when cast under His direction.

When the Lord made Himself known by His miraculous action while yet the disciples were too far off to see His features, Peter on the moment forgot the fish he had toiled for all night, and though master of the vessel left the net to sink or go to pieces for all he cared, and sprang into the water to greet his Lord. Jesus Himself was the first to see the significance of the act. This vehemence of welcome was most grateful to Him. It witnessed to an affection which was at this crisis the most valuable element in the world. And that it was shown not by solemn protestations made in public or as part of a religious service, but in so apparently secular and trivial an incident, makes it all the more valuable. Jesus hailed with the deepest satisfaction Peter's impetuous abandonment of his fishing gear and impatient springing to greet Him, because as plainly as possible it showed that after all Christ was incomparably more to him than the old life. And therefore when the first excitement had cooled down Jesus gives Peter an opportunity of putting this in words by asking him, "Simon, son of Jonas, lovest thou Me more than these?" Am I to interpret this action of yours as really meaning what it seems to mean—that I am more to you than boat, nets, old ways, old associations? Your letting go the net at the critical moment, and so risking the loss of all, seemed to say that you love Me more than your sole means of gaining a livelihood. Well, is it so? Am I to draw this conclusion? Am I to understand that with a mind made up you do love Me more than these things? If so, the way is again clear for Me to commit to your care what I love and prize upon earth—to say again, " Feed My sheep."

Thus mildly does the Lord rebuke Peter by suggesting that in his recent conduct there were appearances which must prevent these present expressions of his love from being accepted as perfectly genuine and trustworthy. Thus gracefully does He give Peter opportunity to renew the profession of attachment he had so shamefully denied by three times over swearing that he not only did not love Jesus, but knew nothing whatever about the man. And if Peter at first resented the severity of the scrutiny, he must afterwards have perceived that no greater kindness could have been done him than thus to press him to clear and resolved confession. Peter had probably sometimes compared himself to Judas, and thought that the difference between his denial and Judas' betrayal was slight. But the Lord distinguished. He saw that Peter's sin was unpremeditated, a sin of surprise, while his heart was essentially sound.

We also must distinguish between the forgetfulness of Christ, to which we are carried by the blinding and confusing throng of this world's ways and fashions and temptations, and a betrayal of Christ that has in it something deliberate. We admit that we have acted *as if* we had no desire to serve Christ and to bring our whole life within His kingdom; but it is one thing to deny Christ through thoughtlessness, throug' inadvertence, through sudden passion or insidious, unperceived temptation—another thing consciously and habitually to betake ourselves to ways which He condemns, and to let the whole form, appearance, and meaning of our life plainly declare that our regard for

Him is very slight when compared with our regard for success in our calling or anything that nearly touches our personal interests. Jesus lets Peter breakfast first, He lets him settle, before He puts His question, because it matters little what we say or do in a moment of excitement. The question is, what is our deliberate choice and preference—not what is our judgment, for of that there can be little question; but when we are self-possessed and cool, when the whole man within us is in equilibrium, not violently pulled one way or other, when we feel, as sometimes we do, that we are seeing ourselves as we actually are, do we then recognise that Christ is more to us than any gain, success, or pleasure the world can offer?

There are many who when the alternative is laid before them in cold blood choose without hesitation to abide with Christ at all costs. Were we at this moment as conscious as Peter was when this question fell from the lips of the living Person before him, whose eyes were looking for his reply, that we now must give our answer, many of us, God helping us, would say with Peter, "Thou knowest that I love Thee." We could not say that our old associations are easily broken, that it costs us nothing to hang up the nets with which so skilfully we have gathered in the world's substance to us, or to take a last look of the boat which has so faithfully and merrily carried us over many a threatening wave and made our hearts glad within us. But our hearts are not set on these things; they do not command us as Thou dost: and we can abandon whatever hinders us from following and serving Thee. Happy the man who with Peter feels that the question is an easily answered one, who can say, "I may often have blundered, I may often have shown myself greedy of gain and glory, but Thou knowest that I love Thee."

In this restoration of Peter our Lord, then, tests not the conduct, but the heart. He recognises that while the conduct is the legitimate and normal test of a man's feeling, yet there are times at which it is fair and useful to examine the heart itself apart from present manifestations of its condition; and that the solace which a poor soul gets after great sin, in refusing to attempt to show the consistency of his conduct with love to Christ, and in clinging simply to the consciousness that with all his sin there is most certainly a surviving love to Christ, is a solace sanctioned by Christ, and which He would have it enjoy. This is encouraging, because a Christian is often conscious that, if he is to be judged solely by his conduct, he must be condemned. He is conscious of blemishes in his life that seem quite to contradict the idea that he is animated by a regard for Christ. He knows that men who see his infirmities and outbreaks may be justified in supposing him a self-deceived or pretentious hypocrite, and yet in his own soul he is conscious of love to Christ. He can as little doubt this as he can doubt that he has shamefully denied this in his conduct. He would rather be judged by omniscience than by a judgment that can scrutinise only his outward conduct. He appeals in his own heart from those who know in part to Him who knows all things. He knows perfectly well that if men are to be expected to believe that he is a Christian he must prove this by his conduct; nay, he understands that love must find for itself a constant and consistent expression in conduct; but it remains an indubitable satisfaction to be conscious that, despite all his conduct has said to the contrary, he does in his soul love the Lord.

The determination of Christ to clear away all misunderstanding and all doubtfulness about the relation His professed followers hold to Him is strikingly exhibited in His subjecting Peter to a second and third interrogation. He invites Peter to search deeply into his spirit and to ascertain the very truth. It is the most momentous of all questions; and our Lord positively refuses to take a superficial, careless, matter-of-course answer. He will thus question, and thrice question, and probe to the quick all His followers. He seeks to scatter all doubt about our relation to Him, and to make our living connection with Him clear to our own consciousness, and to place our whole life on this solid basis of a clear, mutual understanding between Him and us. Our happiness depends upon our meeting His question with care and sincerity. Only the highest degree of human friendship will permit this persistent questioning, this beating of us back and back on our own feelings, deeper and deeper into the very heart of our affections, as if still it were doubtful whether we had not given an answer out of mere politeness or profession or sentiment. The highest degree of human friendship demands certainty, a basis on which it can build, a love it can entirely trust. Christ had made good His right thus to question His followers and to require a love that was sure of itself, because on His part He was conscious of such a love and had given proof that His affection was no mere sentimental, unfruitful compassion, but a commanding, consuming, irrepressible, unconquerable love—a love that left Him no choice, but compelled Him to devote Himself to men and do them all the good in His power.

Peter's self-knowledge is aided by the form the

question now takes. He is no longer asked to compare the hold Christ has upon him with his interest in other things; but he is asked simply and absolutely whether love is the right name for that which connects him with his Lord. "*Lovest thou Me?*" Separating yourself and Me from all others, looking straight and simply at Me only, is "love" the right name for that which connects us? Is it love, and not mere impulse? Is it love, and not sentiment or fancy? Is it love, and not sense of duty or of what is becoming? Is it love, and not mere mistake? For no mistake is more disastrous than that which takes something else for love.

Now, to apprehend the significance of this question is to apprehend what Christianity is. Our Lord was on the point of leaving the world; and He left its future, the future of the sheep He loved so well and had spent His all upon, in the keeping of Peter and the rest, and the one security He demanded of them was the confession of love for Himself. He did not draw up a creed or a series of articles binding them to this and that duty, to special methods of governing the Church or to special truths they were to teach it; He did not summon them into the house of Peter or of Zebedee, and bid them affix their signatures or marks to such a document. He rested the whole future of the work He had begun at such cost on their love for Him. This security alone He took from them. This was the sufficient guarantee of their fidelity and of their wisdom. It is not great mental ability that is wanted for the furtherance of Christ's aims in the world. It is love of what is best, devotion to goodness. No question is made about their knowledge; they are not asked what views they have about the death of Christ; they are not required to analyse their feelings and say whence their love has sprung—whether from a due sense of their indebtedness to Him for delivering them from sin and its consequence, or from the grace and beauty of His character, or from His tender and patient consideration of them. There is no omission of anything vital owing to His being hurried in these morning hours. Three times over the question comes, and the third is as the first, a question solely and exclusively as to their love. Three times over the question comes, and three times over, when love is unhesitatingly confessed, comes the Apostolic commission, "Feed My sheep." Love is enough—enough not only to save the Apostles themselves, but enough to save the world.

The significance of this cannot be exaggerated. What is Christianity? It is God's way of getting hold of us, of attaching us to what is good, of making us holy, perfect men. And the method He uses is the presentation of goodness in a personal form. He makes goodness supremely attractive by exhibiting to us its reality and its beauty and its permanent and multiplying power in Jesus Christ. Absolutely simple and absolutely natural is God's method. The building up of systems of theology, the elaborate organisation of churches, the various, expensive, and complicated methods of men, how artificial do they seem when set alongside of the simplicity and naturalness of God's method! Men are to be made perfect. Show them, then, that human perfection is perfect love for them, and can they fail to love it and themselves become perfect? That is all. The mission of Christ and the salvation of men through Him are as natural and as simple as the mother's caress of her child. Christ came to earth because He loved men and could not help coming. Being on earth, He expresses what is in Him—His love, His goodness. By His loving all men and satisfying all their needs, men came to feel that this was the Perfect One, and humbly gave themselves to Him. As simply as love works in all human affairs and relationships, so simply does it work here.

And God's method is as effectual as it is simple. Men do learn to love Christ. And this love secures everything. As a bond between two persons, nothing but love is to be depended upon. Love alone carries us out of ourselves and makes other interests than our own dear to us.

But Christ requires us to love Him and invites us to consider whether we do now love Him, because this love is an index to all that is in us of a moral kind. There is so much implied in our love of Him, and so much inextricably intertwined with it, that its presence or absence speaks volumes regarding our whole inward condition. It is quite true that nothing is more difficult to understand than the causes of love. It seems to ally itself with equal readiness with pity and with admiration. It is attracted sometimes by similarity of disposition, sometimes by contrast. It is now stirred by gratitude and again by the conferring of favours. Some persons whom we feel we ought to love we do not draw to. Others who seem comparatively unattractive strongly draw us. But there are always some persons in every society who are universally beloved; and these are persons who are not only good, but whose goodness is presented in an attractive form —who have some personal charm, in appearance or manner or disposition. If some churlish person does not own the ascendency, you know that the churlishness goes deep into the character.

But this poorly illustrates the ascendency of Christ

and what our denial of it implies. His goodness is perfect and it is complete. Not to love Him is not to love goodness; it is to be out of sympathy with what attracts pure and loving spirits. For whatever be the apparent or obscure causes of love, this is certain—that we love that which best fits and stimulates our whole nature. Love lies deeper than the will; we cannot love because we wish to do so, any more than we can taste honey bitter because we wish to do so. We cannot love a person because we know that their influence is needful to forward our interests. But if love lies deeper than the will, what power have we to love what at present does not draw us? We have no power to do so immediately; but we can use the means given us for altering, purifying, and elevating our nature. We can believe in Christ's power to regenerate us, we can faithfully follow and serve Him, and thus we shall learn one day to love Him.

But the presence or absence in us of the love of Christ is an index not only to our present state, but a prophecy of all that is to be. The love of Christ was that which enabled and impelled the Apostles to live great and energetic lives. It was this simple affection which made a life of aggression and reformation possible to them. This gave them the right ideas and the sufficient impulse. And it is this affection which is open to us all and which equally now as at first impels to all good. Let the love of Christ possess any soul and that soul cannot avoid being a blessing to the world around. Christ scarcely needed to say to Peter, " Feed My sheep; be helpful to those for whom I died," because in time Peter must have seen that this was his calling. Love gives us sympathy and intelligence. Our conscience is enlightened by sympathy with the person we love;

through their desires, which we wish to gratify, we see higher aims than our own, aims which gradually become our own. And wherever the love of Christ exists, there sooner or later will the purposes of Christ be understood, His aims be accepted, His fervent desire and energetic endeavour for the highest spiritual condition of the race become energetic in us and carry us forward to all good. Indeed, Jesus warns Peter of the uncontrollable power of this affection he expressed. "When you were younger," He says, "you girded yourself and walked where you would; but when you are old another shall gird you, and carry you on to martyrdom." For he who is possessed by the love of Christ is as little his own master and can as little shrink from what that love carries him to as the man that is carried to execution by a Roman guard. Self-possession terminates when the soul can truly say, "Thou knowest that I love Thee." There is henceforth no choosing of ways of our own; our highest and best self is evoked in all its power, and asserts itself by complete abnegation of self and eager identification of self with Christ. This new affection commands the whole life and the whole nature. No more can the man spend himself in self-chosen activities, in girding himself for great deeds of individual glorification, or in walking in ways that promise pleasure or profit to self; he willingly stretches forth his hands, and is carried to much that flesh and blood shrink from, but which is all made inevitable, welcome, and blessed to him through the joy of that love that has appointed it.

But are we not thus pronouncing our own condemnation? This is, it is easy to see, the true and natural education of the human spirit—to love Christ, and so learn to see with His eyes and become enamoured of His aims and grow up to His likeness. But where in us is this absorbing, educating, impelling, irresistible power? To recognise the beauty and the certainty of God's method is not the difficulty; the difficulty is to use it, to find in ourselves that which carries us into the presence of Christ, saying, "Thou knowest all things; thou knowest that I love Thee." Admiration we have; reverence we have; faith we have; but there is more than these needed. None of these will impel us to life-long obedience. Love alone can carry us away from sinful and selfish ways. But this testing question, "Lovest thou Me?" was not the first but the last put to Peter by our Lord. It was only put after they had passed through many searching experiences together. And if we feel that for us to adopt as our own Peter's assured answer would only be to deceive ourselves and trifle with the most serious of matters, we are to consider that Christ seeks to win our love also, and that the ecstasy of confessing our love with assurance is reserved even for us. It is possible we may already have more love than we think. It is no uncommon thing to love a person and not know it until some unusual emergency or conjuncture of circumstances reveals us to ourselves. But if we are neither conscious of love nor can detect any marks of it in our life, if we know ourselves to be indifferent to others, deeply selfish, unable to love what is high and self-sacrificing, let us candidly admit the full significance of this, and even while plainly seeing what we are, let us not relinquish the great hope of being at length able to give our heart to what is best and of being bound by an ever-increasing love to the Lord.

# XXVI.
## CONCLUSION.

" Verily, verily, I say unto thee, When thou wast young, thou girdedst thyself, and walkedst whither thou wouldest : but when thou shalt be old, thou shalt stretch forth thy hands, and another shall gird thee, and carry thee whither thou wouldest not.  Now this he spake signifying by what manner of death he should glorify God.  And when He had spoken this, He saith unto him, Follow Me.  Peter, turning about, seeth the disciple whom Jesus loved following ; which also leaned back on His breast at the supper, and said, Lord, who is he that betrayed Thee?  Peter therefore seeing Him saith to Jesus, Lord, and what shall this man do?  Jesus saith unto him, If I will that he tarry till I come, what is that to thee? follow thou Me.  This saying therefore went forth among the brethren, that that disciple should not die : yet Jesus said not unto him, that he should not die ; but, If I will that he tarry till I come, what is that to thee?  This is the disciple which beareth witness of these things, and wrote these things : and we know that his witness is true.  And there are also many other things which Jesus did, the which if they should be written every one, I suppose that even the world itself would not contain the books that should be written."— JOHN xxi. 18-25.

## XXVI.

### CONCLUSION.

PETER, springing up in the boat, and snatching his fisher's coat, and girding it round him, and dashing into the water, seemed to Jesus a picture of impetuous, inexperienced, fearless love. And as He looked upon it another picture began to shine through it from behind and gradually take its place—the picture of what was to be some years later when that impetuous spirit had been tamed and chastened, when age had damped the ardour though it had not cooled the love of youth, and when Peter should be bound and led out to crucifixion for his Lord's sake. As Peter wades and splashes eagerly to the shore the eye of Jesus rests on him with pity, as the eye of a parent who has passed through many of the world's darkest places rests on the child who is speaking of all he is to do and to enjoy in life. Fresh from His own agony, our Lord knows how different a temper is needed for prolonged endurance. But little disposed to throw cold water on genuine, however miscalculating enthusiasm, having it for His constant function to fan not to quench the smoking flax, He does not disclose to Peter all His forebodings, but merely hints, as the disciple comes dripping out of the water, that there are severer trials of love awaiting him than those which mere activity and warmth of feeling can overcome. "When thou wast young, thou girdedst thyself and walkedst whither thou wouldest : but when thou shalt be old, thou shalt stretch forth thy hands, and another shall gird thee, and carry thee whither thou wouldest not."

To a man of Peter's impulsive and independent temperament no future could seem less desirable than that in which he should be unable to choose for himself and do as he pleased. Yet this was the future to which the love he was now expressing committed him. This love, which at present was a delightful stimulus to his activities, diffusing joy through all his being, would gain such mastery over him that he would be impelled by it to a course of life full of arduous undertaking and entailing much suffering. The free, spontaneous, self-considering life to which Peter had been accustomed ; the spirit of independence and right of choosing his own employments which had so clearly shown itself the evening before in his words, "I go a-fishing"; the inability to own hindrances and recognise obstacles which so distinctly betrayed itself in his leaping into the water,—this confident freedom of action was soon to be a thing of the past. This ardour was not useless; it was the genuine heat which, when plunged in the chilling disappointments of life, would make veritable steel of Peter's resolution. But such trial of Peter's love did await it ; and it awaits all love. The young may be arrested by suffering, or they may be led away from the directions they had chosen for themselves ; but the chances of suffering increase with years, and what is possible in youth becomes probable and almost certain in the lapse of a lifetime. So long as our Christian life utters itself in ways we choose for ourselves and in which much active energy can be spent and much influence exerted, there is so much in this that is pleasing to self that the amount of love to Christ required for such a life may seem very small. Any little disappointment or difficulty we meet with acts only as a tonic, like the chill of the waters of the lake at dawn. But when the ardent spirit is bound in the fetters of a disabled, sickly body; when a man has to lay himself quietly down and stretch forth his hands on the cross of a complete failure that nails him down from ever again doing what he would, or of a loss that makes his life seem a living death; when the irresistible course of events leads him past and away from the hopefulness and joy of life; when he sees that his life is turning out weak and ineffectual, even as the lives of others,—then he finds he has a more difficult part to play than when he had to choose his own form of activity and vigorously put forth the energy that was in him. To suffer without repining, to be laid aside from the stir and interest of the busy world, to submit when our life is taken out of our own hands and is being moulded by influences that pain and grieve us— this is found to test the spirit more than active duty.

The contrast drawn by our Lord between the youth and age of Peter is couched in language so general that it throws light on the usual course of human life and the broad characteristics of human experience. In youth attachment to Christ will naturally show itself in such gratuitous and yet most pardonable and even touching exhibitions of love as Peter here made. There is a girding of oneself to duty and to all manner of attainment. There is no hesitation, no shivering on the brink, no weighing of difficulties; but an impulsive and almost headstrong commital of oneself to duties unthought of by others, an honest surprise at the laxity of the Church, much brave speaking, and much brave acting too. Some of us, indeed, taking a hint from our own experience, may affirm that a good deal we hear about youth being warmer in Christ's service than maturity is not true, and that it had been a very poor prospect for ourselves if it had been true; and that with greater truth it may be said that youthful attachment to Christ is often delusive, selfish, foolish, and sadly in need of amendment. This may be so.

But however this may be, there can be no doubt that in youth we are free to choose. Life lies before us like the unhewn block of marble, and we may fashion it as we please. Circumstances may seem to necessitate our departing from one line of life and choosing another; but, notwithstanding, all the possibilities are before us. We may make ours a high and noble career; life is not as yet spoiled for us, or determined, while we are young. The youth is free to walk whither he will; he is not yet irrecoverably pledged to any particular calling; he is not yet doomed to carry to the grave the marks of certain habits, but may gird on himself whatever habit may fit him best and leave him freest for Christ's service.

Peter heard the words "Follow Me," and rose and went after Jesus; John did the same without any special call. There are those who need definite impulses, others who are guided in life by their own constant love. John would always absorbedly follow. Peter had yet to learn to follow, to own a leader. He had to learn to seek the guidance of his Lord's will, to wait upon that will and to interpret it—never an easy thing to do, and least of all easy to a man like Peter, fond of managing, of taking the lead, too hasty to let his thoughts settle and his spirit fixedly consider the mind of Christ.

It is obvious that when Jesus uttered the words "Follow Me," He moved away from the spot where they had all been standing together. And yet, coming as they did after so very solemn a colloquy, these words must have carried to Peter's mind a further significance than merely an intimation that the Lord wished His company then. Both in the mind of the Lord and of Peter there seems still to have been a vivid remembrance of Peter's denial; and as the Lord has given him opportunity of confessing his love, and has hinted what this love will lead him to, He appropriately reminds him that any penalties he might suffer for his love were all in the path which led straight to where Christ Himself for ever is. The superiority to earthly distresses which Christ now enjoyed would one day be his. But while he is beginning to take in these thoughts Peter turns and sees John following; and, with that promptness to interfere which characterised him, he asked Jesus what was to become of this disciple. This question betrayed a want of steadiness and seriousness in contemplating his own duty, and met therefore with rebuke: "If I will that he tarry till I come, what is that to thee? follow thou Me." Peter was prone to intermeddle with matters beyond his sphere, and to manage other people's affairs for them. Such a disposition always betrays a lack of devotion to our own calling. To brood over the easier lot of our friend, to envy him his capacity and success, to grudge him his advantages and happiness, is to betray an injurious weakness in ourselves. To be unduly anxious about the future of any part of Christ's Church, as if He had omitted to arrange for that future, to act as if we were essential to the well-being of some part of Christ's Church, is to intermeddle like Peter. To show astonishment or entire incredulity or misunderstanding if a course in life quite different from ours is found to be quite as useful to Christ's people and to the world as ours; to show that we have not yet apprehended how many men, how many minds, how many methods, it takes to make a world, is to incur the rebuke of Peter. Christ alone is broad as humanity and has sympathy for all. He alone can find a place in His Church for every variety of man.

Coming to the close of this Gospel, we cannot but most seriously ask ourselves whether in our case it has accomplished its object. We have admired its wonderful compactness and literary symmetry. It is a pleasure to study a writing so perfectly planned and wrought out with such unfailing beauty and finish. No one can read this Gospel without being the better for it, for the mind cannot pass through so many significant scenes without being instructed, nor be present at so many pathetic passages without being softened and purified. But after all the admiration we have spent upon the form and the sympathy we have felt with the substance of this most wonderful of literary productions, there remains the question: Has it accomplished its object? John has none of the artifice of the modern teacher who veils his didactic purpose from the reader. He plainly avows his object in writing: "These signs are written that ye might believe that Jesus is the Christ, the Son of God, and that believing ye might have life through His name." After half a century's experience and consideration, he selects from the abundant material afforded him in the life of Jesus those incidents and conversations which had most powerfully impressed himself and which seemed most significant to others, and these he presents as sufficient evidence of the divinity of his Lord. The mere fact that he does so is itself very strong evidence of his truth. Here is a Jew, trained to believe that no sin is so heinous as blasphemy, as the worshipping more gods than one or making any equal with God—a man to whom the most attractive of God's attributes was His truth, who felt that the highest human joy was to be in fellowship with Him in whom is no darkness at all, who knows the truth, who is the truth, who leads and enables men to walk in the light as He is in the light. What has this hater of idolatry and of lying found as the result of a holy, truth-seeking life? He has found that Jesus, with whom he lived on terms of the most intimate friendship, whose words he listened to, the working of whose feelings he had scanned, whose works he had witnessed, was the Son of God. I say the mere fact that such a man as John seeks to persuade us of the divinity of Christ goes far to prove that Christ was Divine. This was the impression His life left on the man who knew Him best, and who was, judging from his own life and Gospel, better able to judge than any man who has since lived. It is sometimes even objected to this Gospel that you cannot distinguish between the sayings of the Evangelist and the sayings of his Master. Is there any other writer who would be in the smallest danger of having his words confounded with Christ's? Is not this the strongest proof that John was in perfect sympathy with Jesus, and was thus fitted to understand Him? And it is this man, who seems alone capable of being compared with Jesus, that explicitly sets Him immeasurably above himself, and devotes his life to the promulgation of this belief.

John, however, does not expect that men will believe

this most stupendous of truths on his mere word. He sets himself therefore to reproduce the life of Jesus, and to retain in the world's memory those salient features which gave it its character. He does not argue nor draw inferences. He believes that what impressed him will impress others. One by one he cites his witnesses. In the simplest language he tells us what Christ said and what He did, and lets us hear what this man and that man said of Him. He tells us how the Baptist, himself pure to asceticism, so true and holy as to command the submission of all classes in the community, assured the people that he, though greater and felt to be greater than any of their old prophets, was not of the same world as Jesus. This man who stands on the pinnacle of human heroism and attainment, reverenced by his nation, feared by princes for the sheer purity of his character, uses every contrivance of language to make the people understand that Jesus is infinitely above him, incomparable. He himself, he said, was of the earth: Jesus was from above and above all; He was from heaven, and could speak of things He had seen; He was the Son.

The Evangelist tells us how the incredulous but guileless Nathanael was convinced of the supremacy of Jesus, and how the hesitating Nicodemus was constrained to acknowledge Him a teacher sent by God. And so he cites witness after witness, never garbling their testimony, not making all bear the one uniform testimony which he himself bears; nay, showing with as exact a truthfulness how unbelief grew, as how faith rose from one degree to another, until the climax is reached in Thomas's explicit confession, "My Lord and my God!" No doubt some of the confessions which John records were not acknowledgments of the full and proper divinity of Christ. The term "Son of God" cannot, wherever used, be supposed to mean that Christ is God. We, though human, are all of us sons of God—in one sense by our natural birth, in another by our regeneration. But there are instances in which the interpreter is compelled to see in the term a fuller significance, and to accept it as attributing divinity to Christ. When, for example, John says, "No man hath seen God at any time: the *only-begotten Son*, which is in the bosom of the Father, He hath declared Him," it is evident that he thinks of Christ as standing in a unique relation to God, which separates Him from the ordinary relation in which men stand to God. And that the disciples themselves passed from a more superficial use of the term to a use which had a deeper significance is apparent in the instance of Peter. When Peter in answer to the inquiry of Jesus replied, "Thou art the Christ, the Son of the living God," Jesus replied, "Flesh and blood hath not revealed this unto thee"; but this was making far too much of Peter's confession if he only meant to acknowledge Him to be the Messiah. In point of fact, flesh and blood did reveal the Messiahship of Jesus to Peter, for it was his own brother Andrew who told Peter that he had found the Messiah, and brought him to Jesus. Plainly therefore Jesus meant that Peter had now made a further step in his knowledge and in his faith, and had learned to recognise Jesus as not only Messiah, but as Son of God in the proper sense.

In this Gospel, then, we have various forms of evidence. We have the testimonies of men who had seen and heard and known Jesus, and who, though Jews, and therefore intensely prejudiced against such a conception, enthusiastically owned that Christ was in the proper sense Divine. We have John's own testimony, who writes his Gospel for the purpose of winning men to faith in Christ's Sonship, who calls Christ Lord, applying to Him the title of Jehovah, and who in so many words declares that "the Word was God" —the Word who became flesh in Jesus Christ. And what is perhaps even more to the purpose, we have affirmations of the same truth made by Jesus Himself: "Before Abraham was I am"; "I and the Father are one"; "The glory which I had with Thee before the world was"; "He that hath seen Me hath seen the Father." Who that listens to these sayings can marvel that the horrified Jews considered that He was making Himself equal with God and took up stones to stone Him for blasphemy? Who does not feel that when Jesus allowed this accusation to be brought against Him at the last, and when He allowed Himself to be condemned to death on the charge, He must have put the same meaning on His words that they put? Otherwise, if He did not mean to make Himself equal with the Father, would He not have been the very first to unmask and protest against so misleading a use of language? Had He not known Himself to be Divine, no member of the Sanhedrim could have been so shocked as He to listen to such language or to use it.

But in reading this Gospel one cannot but remark that John lays great stress on the miracles which Christ wrought. In fact, in announcing his object in writing it is especially to the miracles he alludes when he says, "These signs are written that ye might believe." In recent years there has been a reaction against the use of miracles as evidence of Christ's claim to be sent by God. This reaction was the necessary consequence of a defective view of the nature, meaning, and use of miracles. For a long period they were considered as merely wonders wrought in order to prove the power and authority of the Person who wrought them. This view of miracles was so exclusively dwelt upon and urged, that eventually a reaction came; and now this view is discredited. This is invariably the process by which steps in knowledge are gained. The pendulum swings first to the one extreme, and the height to which it has swung in that direction measures the momentum with which it swings to the opposite side. A one-sided view of the truth, after being urged for a while, is found out and its weakness is exposed, and forthwith it is abandoned as if it were false; whereas it is only false because it claimed to be the whole truth. Unless it be carried with us, then, the opposite extreme to which we now pass will in time be found out in the same way and its deficiencies be exposed.

In regard to miracles the two truths which must be held are: first, that they were wrought to make known the character and the purposes of God; and, secondly, that they serve as evidence that Jesus was the revealer of the Father. They not only authenticate the revelation; they themselves reveal God. They not only direct attention to the Teacher; they are themselves the lessons He teaches.

During the Irish famine agents were sent from England to the distressed districts. Some were sent to make inquiries, and had credentials explaining who they were and on what mission; they carried documents identifying and authenticating them. Other agents went with money and waggon-loads of flour, which were their own authentication. The charitable gifts told their own story; and while they accomplished the object the charitable senders of the mission had in view, they made it easy of belief that they came from the charitable in England. So the miracles of Christ were not bare credentials accomplishing nothing else than this—that they certified that Christ was sent from God; they were at the same time, and in the first place, actual expressions of God's love, revealing God to men as their Father.

Our Lord always refused to show any bare authentication. He refused to leap off a pinnacle of the Temple, which could serve no other purpose than to prove He had power to work miracles. He resolutely and uniformly declined to work mere wonders. When the people clamoured for a miracle, and cried, "How long dost Thou make us doubt?" when they pressed Him to the uttermost to perform some marvellous work solely and merely for the sake of proving His Messiahship or His mission, He regularly declined. On no occasion did He admit that such authentication of Himself was a sufficient cause for a miracle. The main object, then, of the miracles plainly was not evidential. They were not wrought chiefly, still less solely, for the purpose of convincing the onlookers that Jesus wielded superhuman power.

What, then, was their object? Why did Jesus so constantly work them? He wrought them because of His sympathy with suffering men,—never for Himself, always for others; never to accomplish political designs or to aggrandise the rich, but to heal the sick, to relieve the mourning; never to excite wonder, but to accomplish some practical good. He wrought them because in His heart He bore a Divine compassion for men and felt for us in all that distresses and destroys. His heart was burdened by the great, universal griefs and weaknesses of men: "Himself took our infirmities and bare our sicknesses." But this was the very revelation He came to make. He came to reveal God's love and God's holiness, and every miracle He wrought was an impressive lesson to men in the knowledge of God. Men learn by what they see far more readily than by what they hear, and all that Christ taught by word of mouth might have gone for little had it not been sealed on men's minds by these consistent acts of love. To tell men that God loves them may or may not impress them, may or may not be believed; but when Jesus declared that He was sent by God, and preached His gospel by giving sight to the blind, legs to the lame, health to the hopeless, that was a form of preaching likely to be effectual. And when these miracles were sustained by a consistent holiness in Him who worked them; when it was felt that there was nothing ostentatious, nothing self-seeking, nothing that appealed to mere vulgar wonder in them, but that they were dictated solely by love,—when it was found that they were thus a true expression of the character of Him who worked them, and that that character was one in which human judgment at least could find no stain, is it surprising that He should have been recognised as God's true representative?

Supposing, then, that Christ came to earth to teach men the fatherhood and fatherliness of God—could He have more effectually taught it than by these miracles of healing? Supposing He wished to lodge in the minds of men the conviction that man, body and soul, was cared for by God; that the diseased, the helpless, the wretched were valued by Him,—were not these works of healing the most effectual means of making this revelation? Have not these works of healing in point of fact proved the most efficient lessons in those great truths which form the very substance of Christianity? The miracles are themselves, then, the revelation, and carry to the minds of men more directly than any words or arguments the conception of a loving God, who does not abhor the affliction of the afflicted, but feels with His creatures and seeks their welfare.

And, as John is careful throughout his Gospel to show, they suggest even more than they directly teach. John uniformly calls them "signs," and on more than one occasion explains what they were signs of. He that loved men so keenly and so truly could not be satisfied with the bodily relief He gave to a few. The power He wielded over disease and over nature seemed to hint at a power supreme in all departments. If He gave sight to the blind, was He not also the light of the world? If He fed the hungry, was He not Himself the bread which came down from heaven?

The miracles, then, are evidences that Christ is the revealer of the Father, because they do reveal the Father. As the rays of the sun are evidences of the sun's existence and heat, so are the miracles evidences that God was in Christ. As the natural and unstudied actions of a man are the best evidences of his character; as almsgiving that is not meant to disclose a charitable spirit, but for the relief of the poor, is evidence of charity; as irrepressible wit, and not clever sayings studied for effect, is the best evidence of wit—so these miracles, though not wrought for the sake of proving Christ's union with the Father, but for the sake of men, do most effectually prove that He was one with the Father. Their evidence is all the stronger because it was not their primary object.

But for us the question remains, What has this Gospel

and its careful picture of Christ's character and work done for us? Are we to close the Gospel and shut away from us this great revelation of Divine love as a thing in which we claim no personal share? This exhibition of all that is tender and pure, touching and hopeful, in human life—are we to look at it and pass on as if we had been admiring a picture and not looking into the very heart of all that is eternally real? This accessibility of God, this sympathy with our human lot, this undertaking of our burdens, this bidding us be of good cheer—is it all to pass by us as needless for us? The presence that shines from these pages, the voice that sounds so differently from all other voices—are we to turn from these? Is all that God can do to attract us to be in vain? Is the vision of God's holiness and love to be without effect? In the midst of all other history, in the tumult of this world's ambitions and contendings, through the fog of men's fancies and theories, shines this clear, guiding light: are we to go on as if we had never seen it? Here we are brought into contact with the truth, with what is real and abiding in human affairs; here we come into contact with God, and can for a little look at things as He sees them: are we, then, to write ourselves fools and blind by turning away as if we needed no such light—by saying, "We see, and need not be taught?"

www.ingramcontent.com/pod-product-compliance
Lightning Source LLC
Chambersburg PA
CBHW051728300426
44115CB00007B/513